Growing Up in the Wartime Army:
A GI in the 1940s

Growing Up in the Wartime Army:
A GI in the 1940s

Cliff Hope

Sunflower University Press®

1531 Yuma (Box 1009), Manhattan, Kansas 66502-4228

ISBN 0-89745-113-9

Edited by
Abigail T. Siddall

Layout by
Lori L. Daniel

To my parents, Clifford R. Hope and Pauline Sanders Hope,

and to the men of the 16th Field Artillery
Observation Battalion who did not return

Joseph Turansky
Gordon Priebe
J. Michael
Gordon Thompson
Tennis Humphrey

Foreword

Probably from the era of prehistoric mankind, veterans of military service have felt obliged to recount their combat adventures to anyone who would listen. As a veteran of the Korean Conflict, though I saw no action closer than Tokyo, I, too, felt compelled to regale my listeners with stories from what was the greatest adventure of my life.

Later, during my more than 35 years as a professional "public" historian, I read more war diaries and reminiscences, both published and in manuscript form, than I can today recall. With but few exceptions, the writer pictured him or herself as a model soldier who endured great hardships and performed outstanding combat duty. A secondary theme in many of these was a continuing tirade of hatred against the enemy or self-pity for having to serve while others stayed safely home.

It seemed to make little difference whether the reminiscences were of Civil War, Indian Wars, Spanish American War, World Wars, Korean Conflict, or Vietnam. Naturally, the syntax and overall patriotic tone (or lack thereof) varied with the war and the tenor of the times, but soldiers were soldiers and tended to view their service, no matter how insignificant, as an adventure worth telling others about.

My service as a historian was performed entirely at the Kansas State Historical Society, first as Curator of Manuscripts and then as Executive Director. When I assumed the latter position in April 1977, I became acquainted with a gentleman who has since become one of my closest friends and a man I grew to respect and admire. Cliff Hope was vice president of the society when I became executive director, and six months later he became president and my immediate boss. As such, he became my valued advisor and a good friend.

Cliff is an attorney in Garden City, a relatively small town in southwest Kansas, where he lives a low-key life in the house in which he was born.

After some years, Cliff began to talk about his desire to go through his wartime diary, correspondence, and documents, and perhaps write a manuscript of life in the European Theater of Operations as he saw it through a young man's eyes. In those early days I don't think he ever had any intention of having the manuscript published; he merely wanted to bring his feelings together for his own benefit and that of his immediate family.

My wife and I encouraged him to go ahead, because we knew how much my own lackluster military service meant to me. In fact, Cliff's desire was so infectious that I soon found myself going through my own letters sent home from Japan in 1951. When Cliff visited Topeka, he would bring maps, photographs, documents, and parts of his own writing to share with us. The story he began to unfold was even more intriguing than we had imagined, and we urged him to get on with the work.

In the manuscript we found the fascinating and utterly truthful story of a young man, with a rather rebellious spirit, concerned about the future of mankind. As the pages passed under our scrutiny, we read about Cliff's devotion to his father, the Congressman; his fond response to his worried mother, though far from her direct influence; his teenage, fickle, and fruitless pursuit of a variety of girls; his intense dislike of the World War II officer-enlisted man relationship; his tyrannical sergeant; and his dreams for a postwar world organization that would monitor global peace. Cliff was not hesitant to disclose his own failures, ineptitudes, boyish infatuations, and other flaws which most of us try to hide when writing about ourselves.

The charm of Cliff's truthful recollection of his wartime experiences was brought home to me all the more, since at the same time I was reading a similar manuscript prepared by another Kansan but written in the Rambo style of blood, guts, and self-glorification. I am not surprised that Cliff chose the style he did to recount his experiences. He is not the kind of man who toots his own horn or overemphasizes his own accomplishments.

The story which follows is much changed, naturally, from that first version my wife and I read a few years ago. With the expert help of his journalist wife, Dolores, Cliff has strengthened the manuscript, made it more concise, and developed its meter. The story remains the same, however, and is still the most truthful personal description of military service I have ever read.

> Joseph W. Snell
> Director Emeritus, Kansas State Historical Society
> July 1988

Acknowledgments

I am especially grateful to my army buddy and former battalion clerk, Edwin L. Kahner, Jr., for his initial help in providing documentary material and for his constant encouragement. But for our two-man reunion in 1980, it is doubtful I ever would have commenced this memoir. My thanks also to Bob Van Houten, Alton (Red) Tyler, Jeff Peltz, Bob (Duck) Mason, Tom Garos, Seymour Solomon, and others of the 16th Field Artillery Observation Battalion for the information, photos, and kind words they provided.

For correction and constructive criticism of the original manuscript, I wish to thank my daughter, Dr. Holly T. Hope, and Maxine Benson, former Director of Publications for the Kansas State Historical Society. I thank Martha Rowley for her typing of an initial portion of the manuscript and Ruth Snell for typing both the initial and the first revision of the manuscript. I am also grateful to Ruth for her great enthusiasm and constant encouragement. I especially thank Joseph W. Snell, then Executive Director of the Kansas State Historical Society, for his help in numerous ways and for his never-failing encouragement. Dr. Donald R. McCoy, Distinguished Professor of History at the University of Kansas, offered many helpful criticisms of both the initial and revised manuscripts, and Adell Harold of the Finney County Public Library staff provided valuable assistance in obtaining many hard-to-locate books through the interlibrary loan system. My thanks go also to Robin Higham, Carol Williams, and Abigail Siddall of Sunflower University Press, for their assistance in selecting photographs and maps and in final editing.

Finally, I thank my wife, Dolores, for her editing, typing, patience, and many helpful suggestions as a professional journalist during the more than seven years this memoir has been in the making.

Contents

List of Maps

Before the Beginning

In June 1980 my World War II army buddy, Ed Kahner, and I met for a one-on-one reunion. We had not seen one another since 1948. In preparation for that visit I re-read the overseas diary I had written from August 1944 through December 1945. Except for reading brief passages about our outfit's rapid retreat during the Battle of the Bulge to my family in some December lapses into reminiscence, I had thought little about the diary in 35 years. It lay in the bottom drawer of the family desk together with numerous Baby Brownie war photographs, virtually undisturbed since the early 1950s.

Reading the diary word by word and having a warm, nostalgic visit with Ed plunged me into memories of Western Europe in 1944-1945. For the first time in decades I remembered, however vaguely, a cardboard filebox in the attic. It contained war memorabilia — letters, maps, documents, and no telling what else. Upon returning to my home in Garden City, Kansas, after seeing Ed, I didn't rush back to my law office as I ordinarily would have. Instead, I took a day off and dug into that box in the attic and, through it, back into the war which changed me from boy to man.

I was not disappointed in the contents of the box. It contained some 250 letters; most of them were to me from my parents and sister, a lesser number were from me to them, and then some — even fewer in number — were from girlfriends and friends who were girls. There were also many maps, assorted documents, scraps of paper, and a notebook filled with my plans to save the postwar world. The latter included a "great thoughts" diary kept from May 1939 through November 1943.

Thus began this memoir.

To supplement my personal records, I visited the Suitland, Maryland, National Archives Center to obtain copies of the records of my outfit, the 16th Field Artillery Observation Battalion. I also studied pertinent volumes of *The United States Army in World War II*, commonly called "The Green Series" (most of the maps in this book were reproduced from those volumes), and other histories of the war from D-Day through V-E Day. The personal records refreshed my memory of certain events and helped me recall other events not specifically recorded. Without them and without the letters my parents and I had saved, I could have written only a hodgepodge of disconnected events and thoughts.

It takes a certain lack of humility for an amateur historian, even one with a great amount of source material, to assume that anything of historical or social value can be added to the thousands of volumes already written about World War II. This is especially true in my case, for my duties in the army were routine, insignificant, and unspectacular. Moreover, during that period I was an immature, selfish, introspective worry-wart, somewhat physically lazy and often short-tempered. My mother told me when I was a teenager, "Cliff, you have inherited the worst qualities of both your parents." I had a lot of growing up to do. I bitched incessantly about my outfit, lipped off to officers and noncoms and did a lot of dumb and foolish things. For all this, I received plenty of extra duty and was lucky to have escaped without more severe punishment. At the same time, I possessed unlimited personal ambition. In the short term, I dreamed of a brilliant military career. Planning ahead, I dreamed of becoming a great statesman in the postwar world. If I had a redeeming quality, it was a sense of humor which, after a certain amount of ranting and raving, usually helped me put things in perspective.

Fully aware of my adolescent attitude and my less-than-admirable attributes as a soldier, I nonetheless feel I have something to say about the war in which I managed not only to survive but also to grow up. I do believe that there were many thousands of others in the war who were not too unlike me.

Overall, I share Professor Richard H. Kohn's belief that "historians must undertake a new look at military service itself by reconstructing the life and environment of the enlisted man in much greater detail and depth than has ever before been attempted. . . . Scholars will need to know not only the traditional areas of what soldiers thought about war, their comrades and officers, the government, service life, and the world around them, but how they thought and behaved, especially in comparison to others of their time and background outside the military.''

In World War II in the days before electronic wonders, a field artillery observation battalion was charged with locating the position of enemy artillery through flash- and sound-ranging machines, with supportive services in survey and meteorology. Ours was a non-combat outfit in a combat zone. To the best of my knowledge, none of us ever engaged in personal combat. However, from time to time we were shot at and bombed and we shared many of the fears of those who were doing the fighting.

My first intent was to write a battalion, or at least a headquarters battery, history. It was soon apparent that I had neither the information nor the talent for such an undertaking. Moreover, I realized I could not separate a narrative of wartime activities from memories of my parents and younger sister on the home front, of life in the Army of Occupation, of my dreams and plans to reform the army and rebuild the postwar world, and of brief friendships and romances with girls on two continents.

Professor Frank Mathias, who served as an enlisted man in the war in the Pacific, has written a memoir of his experiences entitled *G. I. Jive*. In it he observes, ''Most soldiers live in a box constructed of army traditions, regulations, and their own personalities.'' Then he tells how he was enabled to ''lift the lid'' of his box by two fortunate circumstances: his assignment as an army musician and his service as both a musician and an infantryman with the famous 37th ''Buckeye'' Infantry Division.

In my case there are, I believe, three circumstances which let me lift the lid of my box. The first was entirely an accident of birth. In 1943 and for 16 years before that, my father was a Respresentative in Congress from Kansas' southwest district. A modest man of complete candor, he was unlike the public's perception of many Congressmen today. From 1932 on he was the ranking Republican member of the House Committee on Agriculture. Although he was not a national figure, he became a respected Congressional and agricultural leader. His name was a household word in Kansas. His decisions were not dictated by what was deemed to be ''the smart thing politically.''

While I was overseas, my father wrote me many long, informative letters. Most were written late at night after a long day on the Hill. For a year or more, when he, as a Congressman, could have received unlimited gasoline rations, he rode a bus every day, an hour each way, to and from the Capitol. He patiently and uncritically accepted my everlasting complaints about life in the army. His letters were filled with news of national, world, and political events. These letters, along with those from my mother and sister, were a comfort to me and I, even as callow and confused as I was at the time, acknowledged that.

A word about my mother. Caring little for the social aspects of life as a Congressman's wife, she somehow managed to endure if not enjoy 30 years in Washington. She was quite dependent upon my father, but at the same time she was doggedly determined in certain projects. At her insistence, for example, someone in the family wrote to me every day I was in Europe up to V-E Day. She was a good woman and a good mother who accepted all change with difficulty. Born in 1899, she remained a person of that era. The world as she perceived it in her youth was the way she wanted it to remain forever. Her letters to me during the war were full of advice that I often scorned and frequently ignored. But they left their mark. Her constant nagging (she called it "ding-donging") at me to be a good boy in the army made it impossible for me to enjoy my faltering pursuits of wine, women, and sin. It was almost as if her message, translated into my vernacular, came booming down at me from above: "Thou shalt not mess around with girls!"

A second circumstance which helped me escape the military box was my preoccupation with what I had come to regard, however presumptuously, as my "great thoughts." During my army service, both in the United States and in the European Theater of Operations (ETO), while on guard duty and in spare moments, my mind churned with dreams and thoughts and plans for improving the army and all of the postwar world. After only a few weeks of basic training, it was obvious, even to me, that I would not be running the army or any part of it. This did not deter me from griping and making caustic suggestions and displaying a poor attitude toward soldiering. A better side of me let my thoughts soar beyond time and place to devise and perfect idealistic, but not wholly impractical, plans for a postwar, limited world government and lasting world peace.

The third distinguishing circumstance was girls. Most GIs spent a lot of time thinking and talking about girls, women, dames, babes — the female of the species. But I doubt there were many who equaled the attention I devoted to them. I worried about them, fantasized about them, and wrote about them. In high school, I was girl-shy, studious and strange. Today, the word for what I was then is "nerd." This facet of my adolescence was remedied somewhat by my attendance at a military junior college in the school year 1941-1942. My parents thought the military discipline would be good for me, especially in view of the times. My mother had fond hopes that I would learn good manners, "the little niceties" she called them, in which I was sorely lacking. I did learn some discipline, but nary a nicety. Instead, I learned to drink, cuss, talk dirty, and chase girls. All of this helped soften the initial shock of basic training.

In the army I dreamed of emulating those who boasted endlessly of their sexual adventures, real and fancied. My own attempts at girl-chasing, perhaps due in large measure to my puritanical upbringing, my mother's constant warnings, and my conscience, were patently unsuccessful. I failed miserably and now, in retrospect, I am not that sorry. But even had I been as successful as some of my buddies claimed to be, I could not bring myself to write about it now, even knowing that many war novels and some memoirs have utilized the rape-loot-pillage theme to great advantage.

The longing for feminine company pervaded all of my days in the army. So, without attempting to recall all the skirts that crossed my path, I make reference in this memoir to girls who influenced my life and for whom I had genuine admiration and affection. My diary and references in many letters document that I was infatuated and love-sick part of the time and fickle all of the time.

This brings me to a word about army language, *i.e.*, four-letter and related words. Although the ancient Anglo-Saxon word for copulation was as prevalent in the service 40 years ago as it is among much of the civilian population today, my old inhibitions keep me from using it outright in this memoir. I am now, as I was back in the army, amazed at the extent to which that verb, with "ing" added, was and is used by so many to describe everything imaginable. For instance, "Where's my f---ing Bible?" It is no problem for me to use words such as "bitch" and "crap," as I feel they are singularly expressive. There are no adequate synonyms for them. Griping is common complaining; bitching is pure art.

In so far as possible, I have let my diary, letters, and writings speak for themselves rather than attempting to analyze, at this late date and through hindsight, what I was doing and thinking back then. As is the case in many memoirs, the names of some living persons have been changed to protect their privacy. Although I am indebted to many in the preparation of this memoir, any and all errors are my sole responsibility. As one who later became both a lawyer and a historian of sorts, I feel honor-bound to tell the truth. To the best of my knowledge and belief, all that is related here did happen. Memory has been used to describe only those few events for which there are no written records.

I don't recall that any of our six children ever asked, "What did you do in the war, Daddy?" If they had, I could have answered honestly, "I grew up."

My wife likely would have added, "Well, almost. . . ."

Part One

Restless in the States
1943-1944

Private Hope, aged 19, at Ft. Bragg, N.C., in the spring of 1943. (The author never liked to be photographed wearing glasses.)

Chapter 1

Washington and Fort Bragg

The summer of 1942 found millions of young American men in a quandary: should they wait to be drafted into the mighty war machine that was rapidly cranking up, or should they volunteer and thus, perhaps, be able to have some choice in selecting a unit or branch of service?

So it was with me. At age 18½, I had returned to my parents' "home away from home" in Washington, D.C., after a year of college at Kemper Military School, Booneville, Missouri. At the urging of my parents to "get all the education possible now," I enrolled in the summer session at George Washington University. Its campus, a cluster of assorted buildings and small plots of grass, was a short distance west of the White House. I had no interest at all in my studies — second-year Spanish, United States government, and economics. I only grunted when anyone inquired if I knew Senator Harry Truman's daughter, Margaret, then a student leader at GWU. I didn't know her, never met her, and couldn't have cared less. A few of my more adventurous 18-year-old friends were enlisting that summer but most, like me, were just waiting, waiting, waiting.

Ambitious dreams and "great thoughts" had preoccupied me since age 13. In my diary of great thoughts during that summer and fall of discontent and uncertainty, I lamented the futility of war, of my life, and of life in general. I had a premonition of death, or at least I wrote that I had. "I don't think I'm coming back," I said. Getting into the war seemed to foreshadow everything. "Someday there shall be no more war," I wrote in my diary, adding dramatically, "I've spent most of my life dreaming about what a great man I was going to be. I'll soon have a chance to prove it."

For the most part, memories of those months of waiting are hazy at best. I kept no diary with regular entries until my outfit landed in France in August 1944. I lived at home, had few dates and was generally miserable. By October I decided to end the uncertainty of waiting to be drafted and applied for the Enlisted Reserve Corps (ERC) of the Army. That would at least ensure I would serve in the Army rather than the Navy, Marines, or Army Air Corps. My service options were limited by 20/200 vision. In addition, I had a sentimental affinity for the Army, probably for purely historical reasons. An ancestor, James Hope, was a private in Washington's army, two great-grandfathers served in the Union army, and my father was an infantry second lieutenant in World War I.

My scant recollections of this time include some associated with George Washington University's chlorine-saturated swimming pool, where I did as little as possible in the compulsory swimming lessons, having always had a dislike for swimming. And I remember not eating well. My weight was about 125 pounds, skinny for a height of five-eight-and-a-half. When I took the army physical, the examining doctor slapped my scrawny butt, exclaiming, "I'll bet you really have fun with the girls!" That remark about one who had just barely brushed the lips of a few maidens was pretty ironic, but I responded with what I hoped was a worldly, knowing smile. Out of his sight, I shook my head at how wrong the doctor was.

In early February 1943 I received instructions from a George Washington University dean to report to the reception center at Camp Lee, Petersburg, Virginia, on 23 February. I left from the Union Station with no one I knew. It was a lonesome ride. That night I wrote home from the camp library, reporting that I had gotten a GI haircut within a few hours of my arrival. This, I knew, would allay my mother's worries about the nervous habit I had of constantly twisting a curly forelock. A few days later, I let my folks know we had been shown the "movie on sex hygiene." I also told them I had requested assignment to the field artillery, and I added a few observations: "The reception center here is really just a Boy Scout Camp compared to the army. So far life has been pretty soft. I'm certainly anxious to get out of here though because as far as learning to fight is concerned this place is worthless."

Somewhat to my surprise, and in contradiction to the army's reputation for screwing up most requests, I was assigned to Fort Bragg. As described on the picture postcard I mailed home on 9

March, Bragg was "the largest Field Artillery Post in the world, known as a North Carolina beauty spot. Climate is ideally adapted for training purposes throughout the year." I was assigned to the Field Artillery Replacement Center, abbreviated FARC, in Battery D-10-4. A battery was the equivalent of a company in other army units.

Dutifully, I reported to my parents every detail of my life in basic training, anticipating my mother's worries about my getting enough sleep and enough to eat and if I was eating enough of what I got and if I was warm enough. I usually managed to include a few mildly unsettling remarks like "Of course, the china and silver aren't clean, but nobody worries about that" or "I'll be on KP (kitchen police) at least once for a two-day stretch — about 15 to 18 hours per day."

In basic training until almost the very end of the 13-week period, I was quite enthusiastic. I anticipated being admitted to OCS (Officer Candidate School). At any rate, I dreamed of it constantly. With others who had entered the army as volunteers from the ERC, I tried very hard to be a hot-shot. I spent much time at night in the service club library, studying all available material on map-reading, organization of field artillery units, and the operation of the 105mm howitzer, the weapon upon which we were being trained. I wrote home, "It's a little early to say this and I may later regret it, but right now I think that if I can become an officer I'd rather be in the Army than anyplace else in the world except in politics. And that's saying quite a lot."

My initial enthusiasm for basic training and the army in general was squelched for a time when I came down with a bad sore throat. For several days, with the help and advice of my buddies, I treated it with home remedies in an effort to avoid missing a single precious moment of basic training. But an eight-mile hike did me in. Reluctantly, I reported for sick call. A 103-degree temperature sent me to the "all colds and sore throat ward 56″ of dreaded Hospital No. 2. There I learned that the initials for Medical Department, U.S. Army, MDUSA, really meant "Many Die. You Shall Also."

My frustration in lying among many soldiers I judged were goldbricks (malingerers) in a large room filled wall-to-wall with cots and surrounded by coughing that sounded like continuous cannon fire was alleviated by a surprise visit from John Isaminger, a Washington high school classmate, who also was among the troops at Fort Bragg.

The author with his father at Fort Bragg, spring 1943.

Always quiet and shy in high school, John, at the age of 19 and with no college education, was a second lieutenant! I nearly fell out of bed when I saw him. Later, John was to invite me out to dinner and a movie and visit me frequently, oblivious to the rule forbidding fraternization between officers and enlisted men.

In the meantime I was finally released from the hospital, despite my mother's concerns because my throat had been painted with iodine frequently. To her, I guess, such treatment was questionable if not downright dangerous. I suppose across the country there were legions of mothers taking dim views of the army's treatment of their sons. At any rate, I was up and out and it even felt good to hear the first sergeant's call to formation, "Git out cheer, one time!" Back then, I believed all first sergeants were required to be natives of either North or South Carolina.

In early April I obtained the last available application blank for OCS from our company clerk. My self-confidence was still such that, on 8 April, I bet my fellow trainee, Bill Moore, five thousand dollars that I would be a captain by 8 April 1945. What a dream! On 1 April 1945, at Daisbach, Germany, I was promoted from private first class to corporal!

Another visitor at this time was a Garden City classmate, Lawton Stanley. Lawton was then taking limited service (eight-week) basic training, which included, he told me, "bayonet training for some ungodly reason." I wrote home, "I think the Army has helped Stanley some, but not too much. However, I was glad to see him." I believe he became a chaplain's assistant. Lawton was intelligent but strange and sensitive.

Letters from Irene, which I described as "very nice" when I mentioned them to my parents, brightened my basic training days. Of course, I initiated the correspondence. Her responses to my letters were — even then I suspected it — probably inspired by patriotism. Irene was Irene Nolan from Garden City. I had known her since she skipped two grades and we became classmates in the seventh grade. My father and her mother, Gladys Finnup, had been high school classmates. Irene was, at least in my dreams, my first real girlfriend, but we saw each other only infrequently after the first semester of our sophomore year in high school. After that I attended and graduated from Woodrow Wilson High School in Washington. I idealized Irene, writing about her from time to time in my diary of great thoughts from 1939 through 1941. I filled several pages with ideas and thoughts I planned to tell her and had, indeed, told her in the summer of 1941. Those thoughts, in summary, amounted to what a great man I planned to be. For a time, letters between us were infrequent, but after our outfit went overseas in June 1944 Irene wrote many long letters and sent me a St. Christopher's medal. I really did appreciate her letters and affectionate thoughts even if they were written out of a sense of wartime obligation. She was a girl of good conscience, brought up to do the right things.

Although they never knew it, Irene and her cousin Jeanne Finnup, whom I also was sweet on for a time, had a great influence on my life. They were Roman Catholic girls who took their religion seriously. Because of my admiration and respect for them, at the age of 12 I first began to think of becoming a Catholic. They were thoughts I kept to myself, however. No one on either side of my family was Catholic, and some members were quite hostile to Catholicism. Organized religion at that time, during most of World War II and for some years after, meant little to me. I never consciously let religious beliefs interfere with what I wanted to do. But Irene and Jeanne planted the seed in my mind, and it began to grow, however slowly, during my years in the army.

At camp, basic training on the 105mm howitzers continued. We learned the "cannoneers hop," the duties of each member of the squad. Much of the time we were in the field amid pine trees and red clay in fair weather and foul, firing the howitzers. We also fired old Enfield rifles and new carbines. All of this was new to me. At first I was a miserable shot, but I gradually improved and received the sharpshooter's medal on the carbine in the spring. We also learned the "Cannoneers Song" (not to be confused with the "Field Artillery March"). It went:

> The Cannoneers have dirty ears,
> They're dirty sons-of-bitches,
> They wipe their ass with broken glass,
> And laugh because it itches!

In addition to our formal basic training, there were many details to which we were assigned from time to time — waiting table, policing up the battery area (mainly picking up cigarette butts), hauling trash and garbage, and, of course, KP work in the kitchen for 15 hours or so a day. By dumb luck I managed to miss the most dreaded part of KP — cleaning out the grease traps on the huge stoves. A recitation of what this involved by those unfortunate enough to draw KP on grease-trap-cleaning days struck fear into the hearts of all of us. At the time the only thing more feared was the rumor that anyone being shipped overseas would receive, as the last in the series of medical injections, a special shot in the left testicle with a square needle. Although common sense told me this could not be so, the thought and dread of it lingered there in the back of my head until I boarded the troop ship in New York harbor a year later. In the army I already had learned one lesson well — almost *anything* is possible. Another thing I learned was that one way to avoid being assigned to a detail was to carry a clipboard. The clipboard gave one an appearance of doing something.

Some details could be quite pleasant. One day a small group of us was sent to a remote area of Fort Bragg to patch rifle and carbine targets. We spent the entire day there, without supervision, relaxing and singing "There's a Star-Spangled Banner Waving Somewhere," a song with a Valhalla theme, and other song hits of the time. On that day the fighting war seemed so far away. I felt as if we were small boys having a happy day of play. Often, in the times of trouble that were to come, I looked back to that idyllic interlude. And then there were the goodies, including cakes, which my mother periodically sent me to share with buddies starved for home cooking. She was concerned about the drabness of army chow. I, in turn, worried that the cakes she sent used up too many of the family's food-rationing coupons.

With a pre-war population of 17,000, Fayetteville, North Carolina, endured 100,000 troops on passes from Fort Bragg. The Town Pump, built in the form of an amphitheater, was the largest beer tavern in town. On Saturday nights members of the 82d and 101st Airborne Divisions gathered there to hold forth as kings of the roost. Some of us preferred to visit places not teeming with soldiers on a weekend, so on two successive weekends in May I took the train to Charleston, South Carolina, a city I'd wanted to visit for years. The first trip was with my buddy Al Buckberg, an amiable traveling companion from Washington, D.C. A learned Kentuckian from Louisville, M. H. Smith, made my second trip to Charleston extra interesting. Of all the men in our training unit, he probably was the most likely officer material. Enchanted by the Old South, he had a good time taunting me by calling my hero, Abe Lincoln, "a yellow-

With sister, Martha, 14.

bellied, nigger-lovin' son of a bitch.'' That seems intolerable to me now, but in the segregated army and the society of that time, I accepted it merely as an idiosyncrasy.

A hair-raising train ride to Washington with Buckberg was my last weekend trip before leaving Fort Bragg. Having no idea where we would be sent at the end of basic training, we figured it might be the last chance to visit home for some time. Washington, of course, was far beyond the 60-mile weekend pass limit, but that didn't stop us. We arrived in Washington at 2:30 a.m. Sunday, after 12 hours on the train. After three hours of sleep, I got up early to spend a full day smelling the roses in my father's garden, visiting neighbors, and calling friends. Headed back to Bragg, Buckberg and I missed the 5:10 p.m. and the first section of the 6:40 p.m. train. By the time we had an hour-and-a-half delay in Richmond, we were sweating blood as we envisioned a courtmartial and a sentence to the stockade. "Ten years from now this won't make any difference," I told Al philosophically. That was small comfort and not even very convincing as the packed train slowly made its way to Fayetteville. It was raining hard when we got there. Sneaking in at 5:30 a.m., we signed in at the battery orderly room. An hour later, reveille summoned us to a week in the field.

Along with the usual basic training routine, including the Commando Course and the Infiltration Course (slithering on our backs in the mud under barbed wire to the accompaniment of machine gun fire and occasional dynamite blasts), we were indoctrinated by viewing the seven films in the "Why We Fight" series. The film that impressed me most showed German army clips of the May 1940 breakthrough around the Maginot Line into France through the Ardennes Forest of Belgium and Luxembourg. To this day I remember the commentary: "Into this area, the German army threw 45,000 armored vehicles." It was a premonition of things to come.

It was early April when we first learned of the planned Army Specialized Training Program (ASTP), a massive undertaking to train hundreds of thousands of soldiers in specialized fields and, of course, to keep the nation's colleges open during the war. I was happy enough to get three hours off KP to take the first qualifying test, but in a letter home I expressed the hope that I wouldn't have to accept if I passed. "I think I've seen enough of the Field Artillery by this time to know that I like it and I just don't think my conscience would let me go back to school for a year or so." I was still hoping, of course, to be approved for OCS and "to do a little fighting in the Field Artillery."

Receiving that word upset my mother. She strongly urged me to opt for ASTP. Probably largely in deference to her, by early May my thinking had done a complete flipflop, as was to happen so often in many matters in the next two and a half years. Also, by this time only older men (i.e., older than 19!) were being accepted for OCS. My choices boiled down to accepting ASTP and at least postponing my mother's anxieties, or shipping out as an overseas replacement. I accepted my fate but not without complaint.

"It seems that all my friends are going to have commissions while I'm running around as a buck private," I wrote home. "Being one doesn't bother me half so much as just the *idea* of being one." That pretty well summed up my feelings and my bruised ego at the same time. At this point I began pestering my father for detailed information from the War Department on ASTP. My letters to him were filled with protests and questions about various problems, some of little consequence. Not once in his letters to me did he complain about my complaining. He responded with understanding and made positive suggestions.

On 4 June I and several others were ordered to the ASTP "Star" unit at North Carolina State in Raleigh, and thus we bade farewell, for the first time, to Fort Bragg. The non-ASTPers in our training platoon were shipped to the Shenango, Pennsylvania, Replacement Depot for transfer overseas. "Shenango" had been the dreaded word in the outfit for several weeks. We saw it daily, stamped on the bottom of the mess hall plates: "Shenango China." M. H. Smith, Buckberg, and Moore were admitted to OCS, but the quotas were filled. So Buckberg and Moore transferred to ASTP, and Smith decided to ship out "with the rest of the boys" and then try to transfer. I never saw Smith or the rest of the boys again.

Chapter 2

ASTP Interlude — Marking Time

A stint of several weeks at the North Carolina State "Star" Unit (SCU No. 3411) was the beginning of a seven-month interlude filled with interesting experiences and considerable frustration. It was a time when I felt, and for good reason, that I was making absolutely no contribution to the war effort.

Unable to reach my parents by telephone, I let it all hang out in a long, aggrieved letter to them on 10 June. The part of the war effort I was experiencing was sheer chaos, I wrote. I guessed my unit had been organized for no more than a month. There were five or six hundred men in three dormitories. Everyone was supposed to be restricted to the area, but confusion reigned and we all wandered at will over the campus and throughout Raleigh. I had good words for the food, however — "chicken every night for supper, plenty of milk and bananas, etc." We had 10 minutes of calisthenics every morning but hardly anyone showed up for it. The only calls anyone paid attention to were for mess and mail. There was no bed check at night. One night we had "open post" and everyone was turned loose without a pass. On other nights there were guards on duty, but they paid no attention to anyone slipping in or out. "It's utterly fantastic," I wrote. "Fort Bragg was never like this."

Classification was equally confusing. Interviews were finally scheduled and we had to march ourselves over to them. That was the only thing we ever really had to do. The rest of the time we spent reading or sleeping. The interview wasn't much. It consisted of handing a two-page form listing educational qualifications and a little other information to a corporal who checked it over. That was it. I decided it would be impossible for anyone between the ages of 18 and 22 to flunk out. We were given no tests. I was interested in the language program but I didn't stand a chance. No basic language courses were offered. Anyway, it appeared that only men over 22 with four or five years of languages would be chosen. So, like almost everyone else, I signed up for engineering. Civil engineering, if I got my choice. I figured my chances for going overseas were still excellent.

"At the rate they're selecting engineers around here, it's a damn cinch that all of us can't be used in this country," I wrote home. "There are rumors about us signing up for either two or five years after the war." Something like that seemed reasonable, because it didn't make sense that we would be trained and then released after the duration plus six months. Our theme song, to the tune of "John Brown's Body," was "When the War Is Over, We Will All Be Engineers." All of the engineer candidates were to go to colleges in either Georgia or Maine. "I hope to heck I get Maine (for the summer of course)," I wrote.

Knowing that I had my mother's worry-wart outlook on life, my father replied with comforting words. "Don't get too discouraged about what's going on at the star unit," he wrote. "They recognize at the War Department that it is kind of a letdown for boys to come from active training into the star unit but they say as soon as you get assigned to a school you will have plenty to do." That same week my mother wrote sympathetically, realizing I was restless and dissatisfied. She added her usual admonitons and cautions: "While you're putting in time, don't do anything that Daddy wouldn't do! You know what I mean by that advice." She was referring primarily to girls, and on that score at that time she had nothing to worry about. I had no dates at Fort Bragg and none at North Carolina State. However, my scribbled notes while at NCS did mention the presence of "beautiful girls" on the campus.

To be honest, I did not write my parents about everything I did while waiting and loafing. Only the weekend before I wrote a long, sad saga to them, I hit the high point in my beer-drinking career. In my notes I carefully recorded consumption of 10 bottles of beer with Ginestra, Schmerhorn, and Schneider on Saturday night, and then seven on Sunday night with Ginestra, Buckberg, and Moore, the latter two having arrived from Fort Bragg for a visit. It should be noted that my 17-bottle weekend was a record I never attempted to break.

Much to my surprise, in late June I was ordered to the ASTP 2510th Service Unit at the University of Maryland at College Park, a suburb of Washington, D.C., only a few miles from my parents' home on Brandywine Street, NW. I arrived by way of the Southern Railway with two new friends, Phil Urban and Joe Williams. Thus began two three-month terms in Basic Engineering II and III. My mother, of course, was delighted; I am not certain as to my father's feelings. As for myself, I had mixed emotions about being so close to home. I know it increased my feelings of guilt to be starting a fairly soft life near home while many others, including my basic training buddies, were on their way to combat areas.

During my weeks at North Carolina State, I received news of many friends and relatives. A card from Houston Smith reported he was attending Naval Aviation Radio School in Memphis. Hearing from him reminded me of our early teens in Garden City, when the two of us, together with Sammy Martin, a brilliant kid, devised elaborate plans for conquering the world. Houston and Sammy were Esperanto language enthusiasts. Sammy, at the time, was also enthralled with classical Marxism. We founded the Pan-Monda (All-World) Party, and Sammy attempted to structure it along the then-standard Communist Party chain of command. Pan-Monda never had more than the three of us in its membership. We spent most of our time arguing among ourselves, via long letters, Sammy having moved to Emporia, Kansas, while I was in Washington most of the time. Sammy went on to master a number of languages and became a naval officer and a Japanese language specialist. All three of us were thrown into worlds we had neither planned nor dreamed of.

In mid-June my mother's principal concern, superseding even her everpresent worries about me, was an impending visit from my father's Aunt Coe. A formidable woman, strong-willed and outspoken, Coe intimidated and overwhelmed my mother. She had a way about her. I was infuriated when I learned that Aunt Coe said, "I presume Cliff will have a desk job for the duration of the war." Whatever else was wrong with me, I never even thought of asking for any favorable treatment because my father was a Congressman, and that, of course, was what she was intimating. For his part, my father would have refused to seek any special status for me even if I asked for it. The same letter from my mother mentioned a visit from the son of Kate Hope Corry, a Birmingham, Iowa, cousin of my father. Young Corry was then stationed at the Washington Navy Yard. During the course of the war, my parents entertained a number of lonesome servicemen in their home on weekends — the sons of friends and relatives and of Congressional constituents from Kansas. Being good and kind to others on a one-to-one basis was one of my mother's great virtues.

Before starting ASTP classes I had my first furlough, which I spent with old school friends and new friends from the army. Bob Ludwig was a friend from my days at Woodrow Wilson High School. A scientific genius, he was eventually assigned as a civilian to work on a project at Los Alamos, New Mexico. The project turned out to be the atomic bomb. But at the time of my furlough Bob was a student at George Washington University, where we had been pledges in the Sigma Nu fraternity in the fall of 1942. He arranged a double date for us, he with his friend Betty Lou, and I with her friend Sallie. On 5 July we took an evening cruise down the river on the SS *Potomac*, then walked for several miles to the Sigma Nu house in northwest Washington and back to the old Post Office building on Pennsylvania Avenue, where Sallie caught the Virginia bus to her parents' apartment. Her father, a reserve army major, was stationed in Washington. I arrived home at 4:45 a.m. All of this was meticulously recorded in my notes because Sallie was my first wartime romance: "10 dates with Sallie — never to be forgotten."

Although I was infatuated with Sallie, the feeling was not mutual. She had good reason. Her fiance, an air cadet, had been killed in an air crash in California. He was her lost prince. In my clumsy way I attempted to understand her grief and be sympathetic. At the same time I tried hard to monopolize her and get her to fall for me. For a period of three months or so we saw numerous movies together, attended the New York Avenue Presbyterian Church, and had Sunday dinner with her parents, a delightful couple. Once we met at the Wardman Park Hotel pool, drank Cuba Libras, and argued by the Department of Commerce Building. She kissed me when I gave her my field artillery pin by the old Post Office building. I was miserable if we didn't have a weekend date. This prompted my mother to lecture. In a note in August she wrote, "Don't get so absorbed in Sallie that her seeing or not seeing you makes so much difference in your happiness. You've got lots to live for besides seeing her. You'd better get you another girl, so when you can't see Sallie you can still date & have a good time." Sallie and I drifted apart in October. In my immaturity, I could not know that the last thing she needed then was to be pestered by a lovesick, restless, 19-year-old soldier.

In the meantime, classes had started on 12 July. The courses were analytical geometry, physics, chemistry, English, history, geography, military instruction, and physical education. My notes indicate I flunked "analyt," which I had thought I understood. But I was permitted to take a make-up exam after seeing the dean. With Ds in analytical geometry and physics, and Bs in history and geography, I had a straight C average for the term ending 2 October. I was not proud of that record but hardly surprised. I do remember learning in chemistry that there were and always would be 92 elements. The atomic age had not yet arrived in the classroom. As students, we were organized in cadet companies and I was a cadet first sergeant for a time. We sang on the way to classes and the mess hall. Included were old favorites such as "Wait 'Til the Sun Shines, Nellie." (In my thoughts I substituted "Sallie" for "Nellie.") We lived in adequate rooms in a dormitory we called "Maggie B." The campus was on US Highway 1, the main route to Baltimore. All of the buildings, red brick with white trim, were constructed in colonial style. My most vivid memories of classes are of the non-engineering subjects of American history and English. The history professor, a slender, scrawny man with a raspy voice, gave fascinating lectures. He detested Theodore Roosevelt for his theatrics, and his description of Teddy's charge up San Juan Hill was a classic. Later in my life TR became one of my heroes — but not because of San Juan Hill.

An incident that occurred in English class is one I'll never forget. I've recounted it so often it is a mainstay in the annals of family anecdotes. The class was taught by Professor Warfel, a prim, precise-speaking man with a small, neatly clipped moustache. He fitted the stereotype of an English professor in every detail. For one assignment each of us was to give a demonstrative talk. One student, a former medic, chose to speak on "How to Prevent V.D. (Venereal Disease)." He went to great pains to be graphic and specific in describing how one might administer prophylactic treatment. All, of course, was for the purpose of embarrassing Professor Warfel. Warfel's face was expressionless as he listened attentively.

When the student finished, the professor said evenly, "Mr. Blank, you neglected to mention the most effective method of preventing V.D."

"Why, what's that?" inquired the student, obviously taken aback.

"Keep you peter in your pants," Warfel replied primly. Never again did anyone try to embarrass Professor Warfel.

In the same August letter in which she gave me advice about Sallie, my mother took up several other subjects. "You aren't eating as you should either," she went on, "and I wish you'd cut out smoking — It dulls you mentally & affects you physically and you can't afford to do it. It's a nice 'soother' but you don't need that. You've got to be on your toes every minute. This isn't advice, merely a suggestion & I think you'll agree I'm right. You've simply got to 'stay on the ball' & you can't afford to let girls, smoking, or anything else interfere — Right?" I am certain I was not eating well, not on weekends anyway, because of my stewing about Sallie. I was fooling around with smoking a pipe, but more often than not I was merely chewing on it. I am sure my mother was referring to cigarette smoking, but I truly can't recall ever smoking cigarettes in the army. For years, in fact, I have been telling people the main reason I didn't smoke them was because I resented, and hence defied, the customary order at the beginning of each 10-minute break to "take a smoke."

Just north of the campus on Highway 1 were several taverns frequented by GI students. One, the Knotty Pine, better known as the Naughty Pine, was a favorite watering hole where I spent my share of time. So, regardless of what the facts were concerning my cigarette smoking, I am glad my mother did not mention drinking. She had sincere and firm religious views on that subject, too, and she had expressed them to me repeatedly, starting when I was a small boy. In reading and telling me Bible stories, she carefully pointed out that the water at the wedding at Cana had been changed by our Lord into *sweet*, non-alcoholic wine. She was a firm supporter of the Kansas prohibition law forbidding the sale of all alcoholic beverages except 3.2 beer, which was declared by law to be non-intoxicating. Naturally I never told her about the party held in our Washington home on Labor Day weekend, 1943, while she, my father, and my sister were away attending a Republican conference on Mackinac Island.

In my notes I referred to the weekend event as an "orgy." That was stretching it quite a bit. Three GI classmates and I spent the weekend drinking a goodly amount of booze, but there were no girls present and we left the place well policed. When I made a speech standing on top of the diningroom table, I was careful to remove my shoes and stand on the table pad. Present were Jim Burke, a big Irishman from Michigan, who was, of all my army buddies, my parents' favorite; Thaddeus Napolski from Chicago, who liked to describe himself as "just a dumb Polack," whereas he was quite intelligent; and a GI from Oklahoma who shall remain nameless in this episode. The reason for not naming him may seem strange in this day and age. The fact is, this character charged a longdistance call to my parents' number. It came to $14.98, a tremendous sum at that time. Although my friend promised for months thereafter to repay my parents, he never did. I felt guilty about it, knowing my parents were sticklers for honesty in paying debts. It was some months after V-E Day, after all hope of payment by my friend was gone, that I finally settled up with them.

The Basic III term began in early October. The courses, all of them compulsory, were differential calculus, physics, engineering drawing, English, history, geography, military instruction, and physical education. Only in physics did I receive a D (again). I got an A in history and an overall B minus average. I even got a 94 on one calculus test. Although it was obvious to me I would never be much of an engineer (even if ASTP had not been terminated), I was reasonably confident I could make my way through the social sciences in the event the war ever ended and I was still around.

During the fall term Jim Burke introduced me to Dorothy Ford, from Iowa. She was a friend of his friend Jackie McMann. Jackie and Dorothy, like thousands of other young girls from across the nation, came to Washington to take jobs in the mushrooming bureaucracy, to help the war effort and share in the excitement of wartime Washington. Dorothy was a wonderfully pleasant girl, the kind my mother was always urging me to find. We had several weekend dates, visiting the Washington National Cathedral, the Smithsonian Museum, and the Willard Room in the Willard Hotel and going to the servicemen's dances held at the Hotel Washington. Dorothy and I kept in touch periodically until the end of the war.

During the ASTP days I did not spend much time indulging in grandiose thoughts. There is only one entry, on 18 November 1943, in my "great thoughts" diary. Although ego-filled and quite pompous, it accurately set forth my dreams at that time. I reviewed my mediocre army career but was undaunted by it: "I must never allow personal ambition to gain dominance over the just fulfillment of my ideals, because power for its own sake is criminal," I wrote. "Specifically, I seek to become President of the United States, but only as a means to an end."

Actually, thoughts of becoming President were a comedown from my early teenage aspirations. In addition to the world-conquering plans I had in Kansas with Houston Smith and Sammy Martin, several friends and I in Washington had even more fantastic dreams. We planned to organize a small army of "green shirts," conquer Latvia, expand into Lithuania and Estonia, then conquer the world. Today Latvia, tomorrow the world! By the time I reached high school, these fantasies faded in the face of reality — the violence of the beginning years of World War II. In their place, new plans formed to run for lieutenant governor of Kansas in 1946 (while attending the University of Kansas Law School), for U.S. Representative in 1948, for U.S. Senator in 1954, and for President in 1960. My motto was, "Lincoln, 1860-Hope, 1960." These plans did not take into considerations time spent in the army, the ousting of a popular Congressman (my father) in 1948, and a few other details. At the time, they were only beautiful dreams.

My months of the soft life of ASTP delayed the humbling effect of being an enlisted man in the army. Once I returned to the troops in real army life, I never again made written reference to becoming President. I did, however, continue to dream about many things. On 12 December 1943 I noted in my diary, "Asking to go back to the troops, 'in any event' — Having Pop continually call the Pentagon to get the latest dope on getting out of AST." The second (Basic III) term at Maryland ended 1 January 1944. At about the same time, the "great engineer program" was terminated, although Basic III continued at Maryland for another quarter. It might be said I was terminated from ASTP before I had a chance to resign.

After yet another furlough, my third since entering the army 11 months earlier, I was assigned to the 16th Field Artillery Observation Battalion and reported to Headquarters Battery on 18 January 1944, at Camp Pickett, near Blackstone, Virginia, only a five-hour bus ride from Washington.

Chapter 3

The 16th FOB —
My Own Outfit at Last

When I was transferred to the Sixteenth, I, as was true with most other soldiers, had never even heard of a field artillery observation battalion (FOB). Such battalions were not, as some thought, "the guys who fly those grasshopper planes" nor did they provide artillery forward observers. Their function was to locate the position of enemy artillery by observing the flash and detecting the sound when such artillery was fired. This was accomplished by the use of flash and sound ranging machines. In addition, survey data, which coordinated the positions of our artillery with enemy artillery, was provided to all units in need of it. As a private first class with no special schooling, I had only a general knowledge of survey and knew nothing about flash and sound ranging.

The informal history of the battalion, hastily completed by Jack Jarvis, Robert Adorjan, Bob Gray, and Edwin Kahner as the Sixteenth was being disbanded in June 1945, and the official unit history, completed at the same time and now in the National Archives, give a resume of battalion activities. The former, of course, makes for more interesting reading than the latter.

The Sixteenth was activated at Fort Bragg on 15 June 1942 with a cadre of five officers and 44 enlisted men from the 7th FOB. The unit history (UH) in typical army jargon designates enlisted men transferred to the Sixteenth as "fillers." In July the unit was transferred to hot and dry Fort Leonard Wood, Missouri. It was pretty well filled with 326 inductees from Fort Thomas, Kentucky, and Fort Benjamin Harrison, Indiana, who arrived on 17 October 1942 for basic training. The highlight of Sixteenth training prior to 1944 was the

Louisiana maneuvers in October and November 1943. Some veterans of that ordeal informed us later-arriving ASTP fillers and others that those maneuvers were rougher than anything later encountered in the ETO. In terms of sheer, prolonged physical discomfort, this may well have been true. But there was one substantial difference. In Europe, the Germans used live ammunition!

On 5 January 1944 the battalion moved to Camp Pickett, the new permanent station. Although the UH lists fillers received from hither and yon, there is no record of anyone arriving on 18 January, the date of my arrival. Apparently Dave Shepherd from the Maryland ASTP unit and I were the only ones to ship in on that day. On the same day, however, notation was made of 55 enlisted men being transferred out to firing battalions. That first evening I wrote to let my parents know I had arrived safe and sound and to assure them that ''there's no need of your worrying yet — so don't.''

The battalion, moved about four or five times in the last six months, had been at Pickett for only about two weeks, so the camp was new to everyone. The general feeling was that no one really knew what the score was and no one knew why the battalion was moved to Pickett. There were three batteries — Headquarters, A, and B. I was assigned to Headquarters and Shepherd to A. I figured it must still be more or less of a training unit in that men were constantly coming and going. In Headquarters Battery, it appeared to my untrained eye that there were clerks, wire communications, radio, and survey. Survey seemed to be the best bet. Some men were attending classes in it at the time and I thought that was where I might end up. Most of what I learned I picked up from three men who had graduated from Basic III at Syracuse University; they had been around about a month. I checked out the service club and the theater, which offered wooden benches for seating. I filled a letter to my folks with these random details and expressed my doubts about being able to make it to Washington on a weekend pass. One thing I didn't mention was how the troops described the color of the barracks at Camp Pickett: hen-shit gray. That was especially appropriate on rainy days, but I decided to spare my mother that colorful bit.

Before long I learned of a five-hour special weekend bus service from Pickett to Washington with buses arriving at the Washington Union Station about 10:30 p.m. Saturday and leaving from there for Pickett on Sunday evening, allowing something less than a 24 hour visit. As luck would have it, I pulled no weekend guard or KP while at Camp Pickett. Therefore, I went to Washington every weekend after the first one. That first weekend, Dave Shepherd and I took a bus to Richmond to visit "all the sights of historic interest," I wrote my parents. I also reported we "had a good dinner at the Hotel Richmond," adding, "the whole trip only cost $5 . . .!" Shepherd was my first Ivy League friend. He was a graduate of Phillips Exeter Academy, but I believe he had not attended college before ASTP at Maryland. His father was a colonel in the Eastern Defense Command. In spite of his aristocratic upbringing, Dave, tall and wearing horned-rimmed glasses with thick lenses, was quite friendly and pleasant to everyone.

The only event that sticks in my memory from all of those long bus rides to and from Washington involved an unknown GI seatmate on one trip. Mile after mile, he engaged in a litany of bitching about F.D.R., Congress, and life in general. Compared to his, my complaining was rank amateur. Suddenly, he stopped and, turning to me, asked, "What's your father's occupation in Washington?" I figured the roof would blow off if I said he was a Congressman, so I blurted, "He works with the Department of Agriculture." That was not entirely untrue.

I filled a 24 January letter with news and rumors. The important one was that we probably would be moving to Fort Bragg soon. I also learned the battalion was attached to the XIII Corps and that each corps had one FOB. From the "old" men in it, I found out our battalion was "as disorganized and bad now as it was 17 months ago." I thought a lot about getting a rating (promotion) but most days I doubted that I ever would, partly because everything I had to do made me painfully aware of my lack of mechanical aptitude. I did not take naturally to most of my assigned tasks.

It was a good day when I received mail for the first time. There was a letter from Phil Urban, an ASTP buddy then at Fort Sill, housed in a tent and getting only one pass a month; one from Irene, from Al Buckberg, and from my latest girlfriend, Helen. When I wrote home about Helen, I identified her only as "the girl on R street." Helen and I became acquainted during my last days in ASTP. From a small town in Iowa, she had been attracted to wartime Washington. She was the main reason I knocked myself out getting to Washington every weekend. She was warm and affectionate and I was smitten by her.

And she was as fickle as I! On those Washington weekends, we would have dates from about 11 p.m. to near daylight, returning to her rooming house where the only place to kiss goodnight inside was underneath a stairway in full view on the front door. In those times, going to a girl's room in a rooming house was strictly forbidden. In our semi-innocence, I doubt that either of us even thought about it anyway. During the war and until I was married, I always associated certain current songs with certain girls. The song for Helen was "People Will Say We're in Love."

I began to work as a rodman and taper in survey. The former consisted of holding a red and white "barber pole" for the transit operator. It required no skill at all. Taping, however, took both skill and patience in measuring off distance in 100-foot lengths with a metal tape and dropping a plumb bob to the ground to mark the exact distances measured over rough terrain. At the time I ridiculed both jobs and bitched about the unlikelihood of getting a rating. "I'm just waiting quietly for someting to break," I wrote home. I noted "the general state of confusion in this outfit is typified by the nickname, the 16th 'Aggravation Battalion.' " The fact that other outfits at Pickett were practicing invasion didn't help matters. In the fields to the east of us were many practice "sides of ships" with rope ladders, model invasion barges, and other representations of the real thing in the war over there.

Twenty-two privates were shipped out of Headquarters Battery on 1 February. There were so few privates left I feared I'd probably be alternating between guard and KP every day. I wrote home that corporals were having to walk guard, commenting, "It's developing that this battery is run by a clique of noncoms." At the time, I thought such a situation was unique to the Sixteenth! The lieutenant colonel who had been commanding the battalion left in early February. He was replaced by an officer attached to the battalion from the Coast and Geodetic Survey, Maj. Joseph Lushene, a soft-spoken, non-professional type who was to command the battalion from that time through V-E Day.

When I started duties as a fireman, shoveling coal and tending to the furnaces in several barracks, I reported home, "I have learned another trade for the brave, new post-war world." Receipt of a shipment of tangerines from my mother brightened the week. As were all edibles from home, they were shared with my buddies and gone within a day. Sharing the frequent parcels of goodies from home with some of the oldtimers in the outfit improved their opinion of me, which, given my frequent bitching and sarcastic attitude, needed all the help it could get.

"As yet there's been nothing said of a new Survey School, so I'm probably out of luck," I wrote on 10 February. "Four men who attended classes are going to the survey school at Fort Sill on the 26th. I believe it's a four-week course. One of them is Lu Winsor, a boy from Syracuse." I never did attend a survey school. What little knowledge I picked up was from on-the-job training.

One week when I learned Helen was due back in Washington after a visit home to Iowa, I made plans to meet her train at the Washington Union Station early on a Sunday morning. By this time I was dead serious about her. Needless to say my mother was not at all enthusiastic about any girl who would "stay out all Saturday night." If my father had any thoughts on the subject, he kept them to himself. My infatuation with Helen did not keep me from dreaming of Irene. Shortly after writing home glowingly about Helen, I reminded my mother, "Please don't forget to send the picture (one of me without my glasses, which I wore all the time) to Irene."

The long-expected move back to Fort Bragg was announced by our battery commander on 24 February. I wrote home that we'd go back to Bragg on 2 March and I also mentioned that nearly everyone flunked a test on motors and driving: "They're trying to make drivers (apparently mechanics) out of us, with virtually no previous instruction." The most memorable part of motor maintenance that winter and spring was the command of our motor sergeant, Walter Mueller. He'd yell, "All wight, men, get out and gwease the uniwersal joints." At the time we laughed about his thick German accent and mimicked it. But the next spring, in Germany, Sergeant Mueller, fluent in German, came into his own, and we called him "the Burgomaster" with great respect.

Before leaving Pickett I had a typical army experience. One Monday at about 1:30 a.m. I crawled into bed after a long Washington weekend to be roused less than two hours later to go on guard to relieve a guard who had sprained his ankle. I only had to walk an hour then and four hours again later but I was plenty sleepy when it was over. To top it off, when the first sergeant made out the sick book, he put my name down in place of the name of the guy with the sprained ankle. It was the sergeant's error, but he barked, "Hope, what are you going to have wrong with you?" I chose the common cold and went to the dispensary for pills. In the army, the sick call list was sacred. You couldn't get medical treatment without being on the list and if your name got on the list by mistake, you had to pick an ailment and report for treatment.

Thursday, 2 March, was moving out day, I got up at 3:15 a.m. as usual to take care of the furnances and do some last-minute packing for Fort Bragg. We left at 6 a.m. in a convoy of about 75 or 80 vehicles. It was an impressive sight. About every two hours, we had a break. I don't believe I was ever so cold in my life; my fingers were so stiff I couldn't even button up my pants. We arrived at Fort Bragg by midafternoon and I was immediately put on duty as fireman. The barracks and area were a great improvement over Pickett. We were in the artillery area, left on the main road heading north from Fayette-ville. The barracks were a cream color with red roofs. The service club, a block away, wasn't as good as Pickett's. It was four blocks to the PX and six to the theater.

A surprise inspection by a brigadier general from XIII Corps and a bunch of rumors kept things from getting dull. "The general scared the hell out of all the officers and noncoms," I wrote my parents. "They were running hither and yon trying to avoid him." I couldn't help but hope his visit would result in some changes I was sure were needed. One of the boys from Syracuse, Ed Kahner, not given to spreading rumors, was working in battalion headquarters when he heard the general tell the outfit's commander that we had to be ready to go on maneuvers by 15 April. Kahner heard him mention West Virginia. It looked for sure like we were headed for mountain maneuvers. And none too soon, for it seemed to me the battalion was becoming a labor battalion. I pulled guard, fireman, and KP duty time after time. I was pretty disgruntled. The general said we were supposed to receive 150 men, but no one in headquarters knew anything about it.

Come the weekend, all men not on pass had to unload boxes from Pickett, so Kahner and I managed to get passes and cleared out for a visit to Fayetteville. We had a big dinner at the Prince Charles Hotel. "I literally have to do this to keep my self respect after so many work details," I wrote home. "Otherwise I'd just be gradually ground down to a slave mentality which a lot of guys around here seem to have." It really seemed to be that way. Many of the men talked about it and most of us thought maneuvers would help. No doubt about it, we were restless. I asked my father to keep me posted on any new branches that the army might open up. I didn't mind the thought of shipping out soon after maneuvers, but I sure didn't want to be hanging around in this country testing gun batteries.

My mother responded to my letter of woes, worries, and gripes as only a mother would. She said it was "no less than a crime" that I was in such a poor battalion. She reminded me of how, when I was "a little fellow," I'd rebel when I thought "justice wasn't being done." This, she said, was just another example of that sort of thing. She assured me I had brains and ability to do something other than manual labor. She philosophized, sympathized, and agonized with me. In spite of the "raw deal" I'd been handed, she praised me for taking it with the right attitude and said she was proud of me. It was more important to be "a good soldier with a clean, wholesome attitude toward your job, no matter what it is, than to have forty ratings." To keep the menial jobs from making "a grind" of me, she suggested I compose poetry when I was on guard duty! She encouraged me to keep writing about my feelings to get it all off my chest. It surprised me to get such detailed reaction to my complaints, many of which I forgot as soon as I wrote about them. But it all worked out. My gripes gave her an excuse to give me advice, she admitted.

Her letter went abruptly from the general to the specific. "You ought to get at least another suit of underwear. It's terrible to wear one suit for a week both day and night." In conclusion, she repeated a plea which I did not often heed, "When you are in Fayetteville on Sunday morning, why don't you go to church? I'd try it one Sunday at least. Might fill a need." I don't remember if I got a change of underwear; I'm pretty sure I didn't go to church.

My father did not write often at that time but his letter during my first days at Bragg was worth a lot. He gave a kind of tacit acknowledgment of my diatribe on all that was wrong with everything without disagreeing with me. Instead, he told me not to get too discouraged. He reminded me that when he was my age he was having a tough time making his way through school on "nothing a year," taking any kind of a job he could get. "I didn't like it particularly," he wrote, "but it didn't hurt me a bit." He told me to just be ready for my chance when it came along.

Army life offered a variety of experiences. One day, I put in five hours as a prison chaser (guard). Among my duties was taking a man from the stockade to the hospital and back for his syphilis treatments. Such incidents, along with the rumors that floated around, made welcome breaks in the routine. The latest scoop on maneuvers was that the entire battalion would be going overseas instead of to maneuvers in West Virginia. On 11 March our battery commander told us our overseas priority rating had jumped. He said we'd be subject to a number of inspections of organization and personal equipment, including inspections by XIII Corps headquarters and the inspector general of the army. The next rumor had us going to the Pacific, again skipping maneuvers.

A letter from my mother mentioned that the two sons of one of her acquaintances still had not been drafted. One of them, she made a point of noting, had suddenly become a farmer. "The thought of your going overseas nearly gives me heart failure," she wrote, "but I know we can't fight and win this war if someone doesn't go overseas. I want you to do your share." She enclosed a religious poem, "Separation," by Nina B. Rockefeller. Nearly every letter from her included an inspirational poem or prayer.

We spent a Saturday in early March surveying on the range for firing batteries in preparation for Secretary of War Henry L. Stimson's visit the next day. Coming in for a quick supper, we returned to the range about 15 minutes later. I don't know why we rushed. As usual, I noted critically, the officer in charge didn't know what we were supposed to do, so we built a fire and waited while he roamed around the range in a jeep. About 11 o'clock we left, arriving back at camp about midnight. The days wore on. I spent my time messing around cleaning equipment and hitting guard and KP duty regularly. On survey parties I continued as front rodman and that wasn't too demanding. I wrote home that once I managed to read about 25 pages of *Time* magazine between moves from station to station.

During the winter and spring of 1944 as we prepared to go overseas, "great thoughts" churned around in my head much as they had in my pre-army years. I recorded them whenever I had time on whatever paper was handy at the moment. Late in the spring I completed the short "book" I had been working on for about two years and mailed it to my father, and he had it typed for me. Parts of it have been lost and what is left does not hang together very well.

However, the gist of the book and of my thinking up to that time was recorded on an off-duty Sunday in March. A summary of that rambling writing goes:

"Since I was thirteen years old, I have been developing a plan for permanent organization of the world for the betterment of mankind. At first, those plans took the form of childish dreams of dictatorship, etc. I also believed that the complete job could be done in my lifetime. I do not now believe that, but I still believe it is possible, probable, yes, even inevitable, in the foreseeable centuries ahead. I am a short-term pessimist but a long-term optimist. I believe the peace after this war will be fouled up, but that at least some progress toward permanent world organization will be made. I do not believe this will be the last war, but I do believe that we shall have eventual world peace. That goal I believe is the present primary responsibility of the human race." I concluded with an idea which I had not heard expressed elsewhere at that time: "I believe that the seat of the new world organization, a new League or whatever it may be, should contain a vast, permanent World's Fair — a gigantic exhibit-museum which would graphically illustrate to all worldwide visitors to it the panoramic spectacle of the history and destiny of all the peoples and nations of this earth. Naturally, the brotherhood of man should be its dominant theme. All means of illustration and impression should be used, so that the humblest citizen of this planet could at least begin to fathom the idea of universal brotherhood. Eventually all this could become a true Capital of the World."

Late in March we were notified we were on the "alert" which meant no more transfers from the outfit would be allowed, and going AWOL (absent without leave) would be considered desertion. "The latest dope has it that we'll pull out of here on May 15th, but it's only a rumor," I wrote home. If I was lucky enough to get a furlough, I hoped to go to Garden City or, perhaps, to Indiana to see Irene at St. Mary College in South Bend. Her regular, friendly letters gave me reason to think it would be worthwhile; in any event, I wanted to see her again. It all turned out to be wishful thinking. I didn't get a furlough again until August 1945, long after V-E Day.

However, I left the post every weekend possible. I went with various former ASTP men to Lillington, a village 27 miles away, four times. It was a very small town but we rarely saw more than half a dozen soldiers in it. That alone made it a good place to go to relax and keep our sanity. We Lillington weekenders called ourselves the "Legion of the Damned." Included in the brotherhood were Ed Kahner, Dave Shepherd, Doug Collins, Don Hoppe, and Don Gindele. We spent our time drinking, relaxing, discussing religion and politics, and, of course, bitching about the Sixteenth in particular and the army in general.

Preparing to go overseas meant getting a checkup on everything, including teeth. For me, the dental part turned out to be an all-day affair. At 10 o'clock on a Saturday, we had a full field inspection in the barracks, mainly to check for unserviceable material. At the same time, I was to report to the dental clinic. I hung out in the clinic waiting room until noon, left for chow and came back to wait all afternoon. Then I was told to come back after supper. Finally, at about 7 p.m., I had one small cavity filled. That was something to write home about, along with a suggestion to my father that if he ever wanted to start a Congressional investigation he should begin on the army dental clinics. "There is more inefficiency and goldbricking there than any place I've ever seen," I expounded.

The end of the month brought a not-unexpected "Dear John" letter from Helen. She wrote that she had become engaged to a Marine the previous weekend. When I wrote my folks about it, I grumbled, "I certainly seem to hit the jackpot." Such cynical and hang-dog remarks appeared often in my letters home. They bothered my mother no little. She was really upset when I mentioned I had written the Washington draft board about the sons of my parents' acquaintances. I was sure they were draft-dodgers. At the end of a long letter to the board, I wrote, "I do not believe it is fair that such men be given deferments when men over thirty with children are being drafted everyday from responsible civilian positions. I am sure that the fathers in this outfit feel the same way. In closing, I wish to emphasize that I take complete responsibility for all statements I have made. I have delayed for months in writing this, hoping that the situation would change. My parents have warned me against writing; everything I have said represents my views alone." Of course, the draft board didn't answer. To the best of my knowledge, the status of the sons I wrote about did not change. But I felt a lot better for having blown off steam.

The joys of detached service came with the first week of April. Our survey party, a wire section, and a flash ranging section, were sent to

Camp Butner, near Chapel Hill, North Carolina, to test various gun batteries, including ones from the 35th Division, originally the Kansas-Missouri National Guard. In spite of the tarpaper barracks, the outdoor washrooms and latrines, and the dust that pervaded the area, we loved being away from reveille and other formations. On most days, except for a few hours of work, we led the life of Riley. On a trip to Durham, Dave Shepherd and I visited the two campuses of Duke University. "...Really beautiful," I wrote home. "They appear as the popular conception of a college campus and hence appear almost artificial." We envied the navy men in the V-12 program there. The navy program certainly seemed to have it all over ASTP. We topped off our day in Durham with a pitcher of beer at the Washington Duke Hotel. It was at Camp Butner that we saw prisoners of war for the first time. They were Italians who worked in the service club. They were very conscientious, and it didn't take much to make them happy. On their way to church, they sang Italian songs.

I spent every weeknight at Butner in the library of the service club, where I read serious books and magazines. In a special letter to my mother, I wrote, "I began reading *A Time for Greatness* by Herbert Agar. I finished only the first chapter, but it so impressed me that I wanted to tell you about it. The book analyzes why World War II was inevitable because of a world moral collapse and then seeks to tell what we'll have to do to prevent another. From what I could gather from the 1st chapter, it probably has a tie-in with your religious books — and in any event I think you'd like it."

My writings were not limited to "great thoughts" and letters home. In response to an article in *Harpers'* April 1944 issue, "The Army Quits the Colleges," I spent considerable time preparing a letter in complete agreement with the editor. Dave Shepherd lent his assistance and suggestions. Unlike my other writings, that letter was well written and makes as much sense today as I thought it did when I wrote it. The magazine article severely criticized the AST program. In wholehearted concurrence, I wrote, "The three basic engineering terms were utterly useless to the army and resulted in a great waste of manpower and taxpayer dollars."

I outlined a similar letter to my Kansas hometown paper the Garden City *Daily Telegram*, and prepared a one-page memo to myself entitled "Reasons for a SNAFU Army Career." The note ended with some self-advice — "Get a T.S. slip, Hope, old kid!"

(T.S. was short for tough shit.) And then I laid out a letter to New York Governor Tom Dewey, soon to be the Republican candidate for President, giving him the benefit of my profound thinking! Being a recluse in the library instead of drinking beer every night with most of the survey party did little to endear me to some members. "You should mix with the boys more," one guy said pointedly. He was right, of course. Probably my stubborn nature was responsible for my hanging out in the library so much. It was my way of refusing to conform to the army norm. If most of the men had gone to the library every evening, I suppose I would have gone to the beer hall.

Fifteen letters awaited me back at Fort Bragg. Jim Burke was with an ordnance company in England. Joe Williams, who had remained at the University of Maryland for another quarter, wrote that the great army classification system had scored again: all the men at Maryland from A to O were sent to the 102d Infantry Division at Camp Swift, Texas, and all from Q to Z were sent to Aberdeen, Maryland. By then Williams had been in Aberdeen about two weeks.

Another letter was from Helen. She told me all about her new love and "some other stuff which was just as interesting as hell to me," I wrote home bitterly. Later, realizing how such comments upset her, I wrote my mother, "Don't worry about me becoming too cynical — not yet at least. In regard to Helen — I was just kidding — and besides, the letter I was referring to was a second one she wrote me. I answered the first one in a very magnanimous manner."

I also heard from Dorothy Ford, John Isaminger, and the University of California. (I was constantly writing to universities about correspondence courses.) My sister, Martha, whom I called "Punkie," wrote that she, a ninth-grader, was tutoring another student, and I replied, "If you get good enough, you can help me after the war. You should be just about caught up with me in school by that time."

My father's sister, Mildred Hope of Garden City, wrote me almost every week, taking time from a demanding job as county Red Cross director. Although I said I appreciated her letters, I seldom answered them and saved none of them. Years later she told me how much she hated writing letters. Only then did I fully appreciate her dedication in taking valuable time to write all those newsy letters about Garden City.

A rumor that field artillery OCS was opening up again led me to ask my father to track it down. Don Hoppe, Doug Collins, and I asked our battery commander, Captain Carter, for applications. At that time, with our go-to-hell attitudes, there probably was no one in the battery who would have been considered less likely officer material than the three of us. The battery commander, I complained to my father, "knows nothing about it and probably thinks we're trying to skip out from going overseas." Closer to the truth, he probably was shaking his head about us and smiling to himself as he promised to investigate. Anyway, that was my last thought of OCS until after V-E Day.

In the real world of soldiering, in early April I was one of nine to make private first class in the survey section. The only thing that meant in our outfit, we told ourselves, was four extra bucks per month. Lowly as it was and despite my casualness about it, I was both surprised and pleased over the promotion.

Late in April I received a three-day pass to Washington. When this pass came through I didn't know there'd be a second so I tried to cram everything possible into a Saturday-through-Monday marathon. Although girls were my everlasting interest, I spent much of the time with my parents, attending the Chevy Chase Presbyterian Church, having Sunday dinner with them at the Hotel Statler (now the Statler-Hilton), and going with them for an afternoon visit in the rain to Mt. Vernon. On Monday I went to the Library of Congress and the House and Senate chambers and had lunch with my father in the House restaurant. All were sentimental visits. I might be seeing those historic places for the last time. That thought was ever-present.

But I managed to work in girls. I called Helen for old times' sake, had a Sunday evening date with Dorothy Ford and a long Saturday night date with Barbara at the Rustic Cabin and Casino Royal. I had met Barbara while I was at the University of Maryland but had put her on ice more or less while I pursued Helen. Barbara was young, still in high school. It was a switch. Whereas I was usually the one to succumb to crash crushes, this time it was the girl who did. When I was with her, of course, I told her I loved her and meant it, but those were expressions of what might best be called "temporary sincerity," a condition all too prevalent in wartime. Barbara's hard-drinking parents were rather eccentric, I thought at the time, but in contrast to my straitlaced family, they seemed fascinating and fun-loving. Barbara was affectionate and cuddly but I did not take advantage of her. Her favorite song was "I'll Be Seeing You." The shallowness of my "love" for Barbara was evident in a letter home after that weekend. "I've written Irene asking her more or less what the hell she's going to be doing for the next few years and whether she's still likely to be around when I get back. I certainly wish there was some way I could see her." I found myself using "hell" and other mild cuss words in my letters more and more. I guess it was to show my parents how tough I was getting.

The last weekend in April was our last Lillington weekend. After finishing KP on Saturday, Kahner, Hoppe, Gindele, and I were ready to take off, but we couldn't get a bus until almost 10 p.m. Once there, we held diverse discussions on politics, religion, and the world until 3:30 in the morning. A first lieutenant we met at the bus station insisted on buying our breakfast in return for the bottle of beer we'd set up for him the night before. We took it easy until 2:30 p.m., then had steaks in the Grade A Cafe, the town's only restaurant. The babe waiting on us asked Kahner and me to translate her high school Latin lesson for her. For our help we got a free steak dinner. In a letter home, describing the weekend, I confided, "Don't tell it, but I'm pretty sure now that we're going to England." I asked for the addresses of relatives and friends in England and even asked my father for the name and address of a French family he had stayed with near Fontainebleau in World War I. "You never can tell where I'll be heading."

Preparations for Overseas Movement (POM) prevailed in early May. We were allowed five pounds of personal belongings so I weeded out everything but essentials. "I simply don't want Mrs. Phillips' toilet paper," I wrote my mom, and I further stated I didn't want a pillow a relative sent: "I've never had any use for a pillow in the field yet — but don't tell Georgia (the relative) so." As others were doing, I was mailing many things home. Included was a khaki cap for Bobby Cochrane, the younger brother of one of Punkie's classmates. He asked me for one when I was home once.

I lamented that if I'd waited until May I could've gotten a four-day furlough, with one day of grace. With that I could've seen Irene in South Bend. I still had hopes for the weekend pass from the New York and New Jersey POE (Part of Embarkation) so I hadn't given up seeing her. I convinced myself she really wanted to see me, too. The next week I got lucky. By chasing down Lieutenant Bundy, the officer of the day, I obtained a quickie Saturday-noon-through-Sunday-evening pass and caught the early train to Washington for another long date with Barbara to discover anew how much she meant to me.

Before the end of May I came up with another three-day pass by catching Captain Carter just as he was leaving the orderly room. Russell Hanauer of the wire section offered me a ride, driving to Washington with his wife and a carload of GIs on a Thursday night. That weekend, Barbara, not expecting me to be back so soon, was out of town, so I continued "last time" sentimental journeys to Woodrow Wilson High School, to the Stage Door Canteen in the old Belasco Theater east of Lafayette Square, and to the Willard Room with a high school classmate, Harry Glazer; to Annapolis to see Phil Baylor, a friend from Kemper Military School; to O'Donnell's Grog Shop with Joe Williams; and, on a Sunday afternoon ride with my parents and sister, to Kenwood and the Franciscan Monastery gardens and then supper in our backyard. Hanauer delivered us safely back to Fort Bragg at 3:15 a.m. Monday. Still thinking I'd get a pass from the POE, I didn't know then that my family and I would not be together again for more than 18 months.

Numerous inspections and other POM activities continued. Some GIs really did fit some expressions which were common at the time — I think they were the lyrics in a popular song: "nervous in the service, the rattle of the battle, fed up with the set-up and hysterics in the barracks."

For a wonder the last two weeks at Bragg were mostly pleasant for me. I even stopped bitching for a while. I wrote home, "This afternoon I went swimming in the lake here. The water is a little muddy, but fairly warm. I discovered I can still paddle my way around a little so that with a life preserver I should be able to get along fairly well in case anything happens." Mention of the life preserver added to my mother's growing list of fears. On a Friday night Kahner, Hoppe, Collins, and I killed a bottle of Old Rocking Chair on the steps of Central School in Fayetteville. On the following Saturday night we gave a repeat performance, this time on a woodpile at nearby Lakesdale Mills. But the next night all passes to Fayetteville, even for married men, ceased.

Goofing off, interspersed with duty, continued as we waited. On prison guard duty one day, I took my charge into the woods where he

The Hope family: Cliff, Martha, Pauline, and Clifford at their home on Brandywine Street, Washington, D.C., in May 1944.

was to dig ditches. He dug for about 15 minutes and then we spent the rest of the day reading and sleeping. The ditches were to serve no purpose and we both knew it. After chow that evening I concentrated on sewing PFC stripes on my uniforms for inspection the next day. The tailor shop was closed so Hoppe did most of the work while I succeeded mainly in stabbing my thumb with the needle. There were a number of last-minute promotions — Ed Kahner and Dave Shepherd to T-5s, and Bill Gross to corporal were among them.

Tuesday of our last week at Fort Bragg was D-Day in Normandy. That settled it. There now was no question, even among us who knew nothing officially, as to where we were headed. In the week that followed I wrote five letters home, throwing in last minute thoughts on a variety of subjects. Bill Gross, somewhat older than the ASTP complainers, was one of those subjects. "You remember this fellow Gross I've told you about, don't you Pop? The fellow that used to be with Metropolitan Life Insurance and whose mother has the Stagmire beer fortune? Anyway, almost every day he asks me what you're doing about having the 16th broken up and so, of course, I tell him that you're still working on it." Gross spent every weekend possible on a much higher plane than the rest of us — at the nearby Pinehurst Golf Club.

My father's 51st birthday was on 9 June. I sent a birthday letter two days before, apologizing for forgetting to get him a present in "Fatalsburg" (Fayetteville). Now it was too late, as we were restricted to Fort Bragg. "I just want you to know that I consider you about the finest Dad in the world," I wrote. "Many little things you've said to me have greatly affected me, although there may never have been any visible evidence of it." I asked him to keep giving me advice. I sent my "book" and joked that when he got tired of hearing crackpot schemes all day at the office, he could come home and read another one. I explained the book didn't mean much without the conclusion but I assured him I was working on that.

My father's warm response gave me much to think about and cherish in the months ahead and, indeed, for long afterward. He thanked me for my letter, writing, "Nothing in the world could make me any happier than to get a letter like that from my son." He said he had begun to transfer his ambitions to me and was more interested in what I was doing and how I was getting along than in his own endeavors. He said he was proud of me, my ambitions and attitude toward life, and offered his help. "But most of it," he ended, "depends upon yourself and the lessons you learn yourself and the way you apply them." Once more, he reminded me to do my best and be ready for whatever chance might come along.

On 12 June, we at last had some definite information. I wrote my folks that I couldn't tell them when we were leaving but I could tell them not to write me at Fort Bragg again. When I found that letter years later, there was my mother's printing on the envelope, "Last Letter from Fort Bragg." We spent the day throwing away our surplus clothing, scrubbing barracks, and washing windows. We were to get up at 3:45. So far as I knew, there still was a three-day restriction at the POE but that did not keep me from hoping we'd be there long enough to allow one last pass. Always planning ahead, I had my parents send a khaki shirt and a pair of civilian shoes for my use to the home of Ed Kahner's parents in New York City.

In our barracks the wake-up at 3:45 a.m. was not without ceremony. A center cot was occupied by an older (mid-thirties!) soldier who was highly respected. He was something of a philosopher. Throughout the spring, his voice was the first we heard when awakened by the recorded bugle blowing reveille. "Oh what a life we lead in this f----g army!" was his standard greeting. He wore pajamas while all of the rest of us slept in our underwear, and we gave him a bad time for being different. So on that June morning, as a farewell to barracks life, some of us seized his pajamas and tore them to shreds.

The list of names with the official photo of our battery, taken in early June, shows a roster of 144 men from 33 states and the District of Columbia. Ohio was represented by 22, followed by Kentucky with 16 and Pennsylvania and New York with 14 each. This diverse group of GIs departed for Camp Shanks on the first leg of a journey to the United Kingdom. The departure was late, of course. We hurried to get to the railroad yards and then waited for the train to arrive. An ex-sergeant, returned to civilian life by virtue of ulcers, overcome by memories and cheap liquor, got aboard with us and rode several stations up the line.

"I wish I was goin' with ya! I wish I was goin' with ya!" he whimpered over and over.

In recounting the trip to Shanks on the Aberdeen and Rockfish Railroad and Seaboard Line, the informal battalion history mentioned mess-kit meals and real ice cream, triple-deck bunks in troop sleepers, and crap games on every seat. At every highway crossing the troops hung out the windows waving and shouting. Many men, however, read or sat moody and silent, staring out the windows. Some officers started a mild blackjack game. The train conductor, acting like a poor country cousin, joined the game and won big. It was a slow ride. We went through the outskirts of Washington the next morning. "As we passed the WAVE (female sailors) barracks in Anacostia, we yelled as if we had never seen a white woman before," our battalion historians noted. Those with wives or one-and-only sweethearts were thinking of them. As for myself, I had more American girlfriends than I could handle at that moment and was eagerly looking forward to meeting English, French, and other European girls. But my immediate thought as we passed less than five miles from my parents' home on Brandywine Street was "how near and yet how far."

A rumor that Fort Hamilton in Brooklyn, a short subway ride from Times Square, would be our POE vanished as the train sped along the Jersey shore, past the skyscrapers of Manhattan and the Statue of Liberty, and on north. Our arrival at Camp Shanks, New York, was undramatic and dreary. A penetrating rain made the camouflaged buildings look even drabber. "You're number 6288-WH, aren't

With Martha in Washington, May 1944.

you?'' was the greeting from the transportation officer who met us. Someone answered affirmatively. The response was a barrage of instructions which we forgot as we trudged a block, loaded down

with packs, horseshoe rolls, and carbines. Shanks was a well-oiled
machine going nonstop and at full speed. POE processing included
two fast physicals, and the full field inspection was even faster. So
much for GIs who had sweated for hours over the proper arrangement
and completeness of their gear! We were hit with information on wills
and insurance, censorship, gas chamber tests, and ordnance inspections; orientation films on how to act aboard ship; and a lecture on the
proper use of gasproof clothing.

Despite all this, our immediate concern was getting passes to New
York City. Half the battalion received Saturday night passes; the
other half was supposed to receive passes for Sunday night. On
Sunday we were told there were no more passes. I was among the
unlucky ones, no pass for me. Not considering the additional emotional strain for them, I was sure my parents would be eager to dash
up to Shanks to see me one last time. Ever-faithful Ed Kahner, who
got a Saturday pass, called them and extended my invitation. That
very night my father wrote their regrets. They wouldn't be coming.

Howard Hope, a cousin stationed at Norfolk, was visiting our
home that weekend, so it was late Saturday night when my father
undertook a good and long letter to me. He said he'd read my book
and, while he didn't agree with all of it, found my views to be set out
"in a very logical and interesting way." While expressing his
concern for me, he pointed out that interesting experiences awaited
me. They would prepare me for the big things I wanted to do in life,
he promised. Two people from Washington who did attempt to see
me that weekend were Barbara and her mother. When I was still
hoping for a pass, I got an invitation to them by way of Ed Kahner and
my father. As it turned out, no visitors were allowed at Shanks so
Barbara was not subjected to any more of my capricious terms of
endearment.

Censorship of letters began. My Sunday night letter was returned
for rewriting. I tried again on 20 June, reporting that the food was
"entirely passable" and that I was getting plenty of sleep and had
been to the library, "so there's absolutely nothing for you to worry
about." I was thinking about the Republican National Convention,
which my father would be attending. I asked him to send a complete
report on it as soon as possible and reminded him to make plenty of
noise for me on the convention floor. Nostalgically, I thought of the
GOP convention in 1940, my first. Amazingly, Wendell Wilkie was

nominated on the sixth ballot, and the next day, in a hotel elevator, I overheard, "So it's Clifford Hope for Vice President." I staggered back to my room and lay down. "That was the nearest I've ever come to collapsing," I wrote my dad. The boomlet for Hope was short-lived. It was launched as a contingency plan in the event Senator McNary of Oregon would not accept. Recounting the incident now, I joked, "Let me know if they decide to run you for Vice President again this year." On the day I wrote that letter, Irene, in Indiana, was writing me, sending "love and prayers for a safe journey."

On the morning of 21 June we left Camp Shanks by truck convoy in a drizzling rain, through Nyack to the Hudson River, to board a former excursion steamer which took us to North River pier and the H.M.T. (His Majesty's Transport) *Louis Pasteur*, a former French luxury liner. We had box lunches on the steamer before boarding the *Pasteur* in midafternoon. An army swing band played "Somebody Else Is Taking My Place"; Red Cross girls passed out doughnuts, candy, and smiles; and personnel everywhere checked names and numbers. That day I jotted notes in a "daily entry," a practice I did not resume until mid-August. I noted "D-7 Port — 'the Black hole of Calcutta.' Eating and sleeping in same spot. Watching lights of New York for last time. Sleeping in hammock. Overlapping feet, heads, etc. About 4000 troops on board." H.M.T. *Louis Pasteur* had been captured by the Canadians. As we said at the time, it was a French ship, captured by Canadians, and operated by the British to carry Americans to fight Germans.

I was up early on the morning of 22 June, to look at Governor's Island and watch the New York skyline disappear. Overcrowded and underfed, we definitely were not on a luxury liner pleasure cruise. The latrines weren't designed for the seasick, the "GIs" (diarrhea), or even for routine calls of nature. The outfit's informal history made note that even in the ETO we were not to eat as poorly as we did on the "Rustbucket Maru," our euphemism for the *Pasteur*. GIs who had been at sea before said they'd seen rougher water in a bathtub, while those who weren't used to the ocean thought they were in a typhoon. Some got sick when they stayed below in the stuffy compartments, and others took on that greenish look and raced for the rail when they were out in the fresh air watching the horizon dip and rise.

The daily routine in D-7 Port had us up early and rushing for the latrine and washroom and then on deck until breakfast about an hour later. There was emergency drill and mess kit inspection in mid-morning. At noon we had chow in our compartments. The lines for chow and mess kit washing were long. Afternoons were spent sleeping and reading on deck when it wasn't too cold or too crowded. "Tea" was served at 5:30 p.m.! I became adept at sleeping in a hammock; they were so close together, it was impossible to fall out. The ship's library, by my assessment, had a "God-awful collection of books." We seldom saw any officers except for the one on duty in our compartment. They seemed indifferent to the morale of the troops and everything else. One officer picked up a copy of an old officers' menu and asked, "Is this yours?" I thought I'd croak.

Corporal Bill Gross and I made a practice, whenever possible, of sitting on the door ledge of the magnificent dining room for the officers and watching them with cool, tall drinks. "It's really great to see how good some people have it around here!" Gross said in a loud voice on one occasion. The MPs came along and moved us on. Nowhere in World War II, I was convinced, was there more discrimination between officers and enlisted men than on British-operated troop ships. The ship's newspaper, *Sea Breeze*, was a refreshing publication. A special edition was issued for Sunday, 25 June, with the notation: "This edition of *Sea Breeze* has been edited to comply with censorship regulations and can be mailed home. Tell the folks back home to keep it for you and then someday you can elaborate on all the items and explain to the grandchildren these wonderful happy days."

Early on 29 June, the *Pasteur* anchored off Liverpool, where we waited almost 30 hours to debark. On that day, back in the States, my mother was writing a long letter to me. She closed with, "I couldn't stand the fact that you are where you are and the thought of all that might lie ahead for you if I didn't feel that God is very near you." She said she hoped I'd ask to feel God's presence and talk to him as to a buddy. Every letter from her thereafter urged me to seek God's daily help. I still wasn't thinking of him very much except to pray hard when I thought I needed him to get out of a particular jam. As we prepared to land in England, I might not have been thinking of God as my mother did, but I was thinking of why all of us were there and also about the letter each of us was handed on board ship:

TO MEMBERS OF THE UNITED STATES ARMY
EXPEDITIONARY FORCES:

You are a soldier of the United States Army.

You have embarked for distant places where the war is being fought.

Upon the outcome depends the freedom of your lives: the freedom of the lives of those you love — your fellow citizens — your people.

Never were the enemies of freedom more tyrannical, more arrogant, more brutal.

Yours is a God-fearing, proud, courageous people, which, throughout its history, has put its freedom under God before all other purposes.

We who stay at home have our duties to perform — duties owed in many parts to you. You will be supported by the whole force and power of this Nation. The victory you win will be a victory of all the people — common to them all.

You bear with you the hope, the confidence, the gratitude and the prayers of your family, your fellow-citizens, and your President —

/s/ Franklin D. Roosevelt

Part Two

From Herefordshire to Bohemia — 1944-1945

Chapter 4

Briefly in Britain and Brittany

A pouring rain welcomed us to Liverpool on the last day of June. A band of the Royal Artillery played "Over There," "The Beer Barrel Polka" and other tunes that did little to lighten our spirits as we boarded a toy-like train for Leominster in Herefordshire. Leominster was a picture-postcard town, with fish and chips and pubs named Three Horseshoes, Bowling Green, Blue Boar, and Black Swan, soon to be renamed Dirty Duck. The primary purpose of our stay in Leominister was to draw equipment so we could move to France at the earliest possible moment. The battalion was attached temporarily to the XX Corps of the Third Army under General Patton. Our barracks were situated at the edge of town, with the mess hall, a huge barn-like structure, three blocks away. I remember the mess hall fondly for the small, boiled new potatoes frequently served there. That and other food were a welcome contrast to the "seaweed" meals on the *Louis Pasteur*.

I was enchanted by Leominster and, to the south, Hereford, the county seat of Herefordshire, and most of all by the green, green countryside. It was as I had always imagined England would be. Even though we knew we would probably be landing on the Normandy beaches before long, the war seemed very far away during those two weeks in Herefordshire. I had been an Anglophile as a teenager and had memorized the dates of the reigns of the kings and queens of England from William the Conqueror to the present day. Sometimes I recited the list silently while on guard duty. That was as close as I ever came to my mother's suggestion to compose poetry while standing guard.

A road through Leominster, Herefordshire, England, where the Sixteenth was stationed in July 1944. (Postcard, W.H.S.&S. Ltd., LDN.)

In the Washington, D.C., area I was accustomed to seeing sites that dated back 200 years. The towns in southwest Kansas, my home territory, were founded only after the railroads went through in 1872, barely 70 years before World War II came along. So I was not prepared for the antiquity of sites in Herefordshire. I saw Mortimer's Cross and Kingsland and learned that the church there was built by Edmund Mortimer before 1304, and that Edward, Earl of March, defeated the Lancastrians in the Battle of Mortimer's Cross in 1460 during the War of the Roses, at a site close to the ancient Roman road and just opposite the Flying Horseshoe pub of the current century. Herefordshire, I learned, was the home of Hereford cattle, which had been introduced to western Kansas and were raised extensively by cattlemen and ranchers in the area. I hadn't given the matter a lot of thought, but my assumption was that those sturdy whitefaced cattle originated in Hereford, Texas!

Dreaming in spare moments of Irene and Barbara, simultaneously and separately, I gave no thought to chasing girls while at Leominster. In fact, I behaved more nearly as my mother would have wished than at any other period while in the army. I attended services at the Congregational Church, a small building with an equally small congregation, as compared to the huge Church of England in the town. At that church, some of us met Mr. and Mrs. C. M. Hammond, who invited us to their home, Copper Castle, several times. This gracious couple and their home reminded me of the popular wartime movie, *Mrs. Miniver*. The Hammonds, I judged, were in their sixties. The first invitation to five of us was to Sunday afternoon tea. It was attended also by their granddaughters, aged four and nine, who reminded me of my cousins, Judy and Carol, back in Kansas. The Hammond home was open to soldiers through the six years that Britain was at war. Mrs. Hammond told us how, in June 1940, they had housed survivors of the retreat from Dunkirk, who arrived shoeless and with only the clothes on their backs.

Long after our short stay in Herefordshire, Ed Kahner's mother received a letter from Mrs. Hammond. She wrote, "We often think about the boys. We have entertained so many. Last Xmas we were absolutely full up. Tried to make them feel as happy as we could to make up to them the miss of their own folk at such a time. If you have a moment to spare we should be happy to know if your boy is at home yet. Also if you have a little snap of him for my small granddaughter, she would love to have one. She always tells us that she 'adores Americans.' Is feeling quite lonely now that they have all gone from Leominster. My husband & I send our very kind regards to you. Our grateful thanks for all that the Americans have done for us." As was the case with most wartime friends, I never saw the Hammonds again but I do remember what they did for us.

Mail, getting and sending it, was high on the list of priorities. Some correspondence was by V-mail, a process by which letters on a special form were photographed, reduced in size and sent by air to speed up delivery and save space. Other letters were by regular airmail. Sometimes V-mail was faster and sometimes airmail was.

Again anticipating my mother's questions, I wrote in some detail to let her know that the food was very good — better than in the States — and that the climate, while not good for colds, wasn't bothering me. With the clocks set two hours ahead, darkness didn't fall until nearly 11 p.m. The village and the countryside, I told my father, were just as he had described them from his days in World War I. Indeed, the pubs did have darts and I liked English beer very much. Within a few weeks I had nine letters from my family to answer. On the Fourth of July, my sister, with a classmate and neighbor, Julie Workman, prepared a one-page newspaper just for me. The headline on *The Brandywine Bugle* read "M. HOPE WRITES TO BROTHER."

Leominster, England. (Postcard, W.H.S.&S. Ltd., LDN.)

My letter telling about the voyage to England triggered my father's memories. The war in that respect hadn't changed much from World War I, he noted. My sleeping quarters sounded just like those on ''the good old beef boat, the SS *Uula*'' on which he spent 13 days, ''eleven of them seasick.'' He said, ''I didn't have to sleep below or in a hammock but I was on duty down there two or three nights and I can still smell it.'' It was a jovial letter overall. ''Your mother,'' he went on, ''is sleuthing around the neighborhood among ex Red Cross employees trying to find out exactly where you are. I don't know why she is so anxious to find the exact spot but it may be she's figuring on having Mrs. Roosevelt look you up the first time she comes over.''

He wrote about the political scene, referring, tongue-in-cheek, to the ''big surprise'' announcement that F.D.R. was running again. Aside from that, Washington, with Congress recessed, was a pretty quiet place. There were not more than half-a-dozen Congressmen around. Work on postwar planning was keeping him there. ''The Russians are certianly (*sic*) going great guns, aren't they?'' he wrote. (My father consistently transposed the letters in ''certainly.'' To razz him, the family often pronounced the word to match his spelling: ''cert-i-anly.'') ''We're certianly going to have to step on it to get to Berlin before they do. Of course who gets there first depends to a great extent on the Germans and the way they dispose of their reserves. They can probably let us get there first if they want to and they probably will.''

My plans for a bicycle trip to Wales on a July weekend were canceled by the abrupt ending of our pleasant life in Leominster. At 6:45 a.m. on 14 July the battalion moved by motor convoy to Lopscombe Corners in Wiltshire, near Salisbury and Winchester. The camp there had had a hard life. All of the barracks were half-oval-shaped Nissen huts. The physical facilities appeared worn out and old before their time. It had been a British camp before the war and the American "occupation" of Britain.

Passes were available to Winchester and Salisbury, and evening visits without passes could be made to the villages of Over Wallop, Middle Wallop, Nether Wallop, West Dean, and Winterslow. It was ¯many years later that I learned we were quite close to Stonehenge. At the time, no one mentioned it. We enlisted men ate outside. This would have been tolerable enough had it not been for the bees. The marmalade served with every meal attracted them in droves. They frequently got stuck in it so you had to be careful to avoid chomping on a bee or being stung in the mouth by one. Every evening by the camp gate a middle-aged hooker, whom we dubbed "Ten Shilling Annie," waited. And each day the "honey buckets" (containing the usual outhouse waste matter) were emptied by the honeybucket man, who drove a horsedrawn wagon. He was straight out of a Thomas Hardy novel. We were, after all, in Thomas Hardy country.

One touch of home was getting to see the comic strip "Li'l Abner" each day in *Stars and Stripes.* The strip's adventures of Fearless Fosdick (a caricature of the detective in the comic strip "Dick Tracy") were among the most eagerly awaited news around camp. That, and letters from home. With a backlog of six letters from my parents to respond to, I skipped V-mail and its skimpy space in favor of a fat, six-page airmail missive. In it, I continued the discussion with my father about the trip over. Our boat had never been a cattle boat, but, I assured him, the surging mass of humanity packed on it didn't make it smell like a rose garden. Kahner and I talked about producing a great film epic, the greatest horror film of all time. We would call it *Troopship.*

Being out of the country didn't keep me from being aroused about the upcoming election. My folks got the benefit of my feelings. "It's really an amazing thing that about 90% of the people I've talked to that want Roosevelt to be re-elected admit that they don't want a fourth term and don't like most of the things he's done, but they say he has the 'experience,' whatever the hell that means, and that we can't change horses in midstream, etc. The fact that that idea seems to be so prevalent seems to me to be very dangerous, in that it tends to kill off all potential young leaders, who are the lifeblood of democracy, in favor of the great god 'Experience.' It's really a sign of decadence in the country where so many feel that way and I certainly hope Dewey will make a vigorous campaign upon the theme of youth, efficiency, etc. A fourth term and the return of 10,000,000 veterans who are used to having someone else do their thinking for them would certainly do nothing to arrest this tendency of increasing paternalism.''

Distance made my heart grow even fonder of Irene. I had hoped my parents would see her when they went to Garden City. Rereading her most recent letter, I concluded that it was more than passing friendly. Although I had to admit I didn't know her very well at all, she seemed to represent the ideal girl to me. I was determined to get to know her better after the war. I wrote all this and more in the long letter home. At the end of it, I added an ominous note that could only cause concern for my mother and could certainly have caused trouble for me, ''Would tell you what I've been doing the last few days but it would sound rather petty and profit no one in the telling — although I'll certainly tell you someday.'' Fortunately for me, that letter was ready by Lt. Alton ''Red'' Tyler, the ''GIs' Lieutenant,'' as censor. All overseas GI mail had to be read and approved by an officer. Many officers might have made a federal case of that innocuous little paragraph, but Tyler operated with common sense. He knew I hadn't been up to anything important.

What I was alluding to were a couple of incidents that began for several of us when we were assigned to weaving camouflage nets to cover our vehicles and equipment when we got to France. The nets were spread on the ground, and we were to weave different-colored strips of cloth into them for what seemed like hours on end. The wiseacres among us used the occasion to bitch about and make fun of certain noncoms, officers, and the entire army. We weren't at all circumspect about it and our comments were duly reported to higher authority by loyalists in the ranks.

Shortly afterward I was accused, and with good reason, of leaving an envelope with our battalion address (APO number, etc.) in an empty barracks where I had been writing letters, thereby revealing the name and address of our outfit in plain sight for any spy to pick up. I was certain the accusation was only a pretext. My real crime was the smart remarks I had made while weaving. Be that as it may, I was assigned to various stints of extra duty — cleaning out the latrine (but not the honey buckets!), sweeping the theater, and serving as an officer's orderly. Bill Carus was also detailed as an officer's orderly, and Don Hoppe and Seymour Solomon were transferred from survey to the wire section. Being an officer's orderly at that time actually was not a bad job. My most strenuous task on one day was shining my own shoes with an officer's polish! However, in my thinking then the assignment was downright degrading. "Hey, dog robber, polish my boots!" Phil Hand greeted me one evening when I returned to my section. (Dog robber was a favorite euphemism of officer's orderly.) I was furious. Though Hand had a good 50 pounds on me, I pounced on him from behind and we crashed to the ground together. I got up, but he couldn't. His ankle was broken. Good ol' Phil was quite cheerful about it. He didn't return to our outfit until six months later, after the Battle of the Bulge. Because of that he had to remain in Europe six months longer than most of us. But even that wasn't all bad for him. He served the time in Vienna.

In retrospect, these episodes in far-off Lopscombe Corners might have marked a notch, however small, in my growing up. There was a glimmer of awareness that my attitude and actions were not quite worthy of the army — or of me.

My last few evenings at Lopscombe Corners were pleasant, thanks largely to my acquaintance with Diane, a cheerful, utterly frank, and fun-loving girl I met at a dance at nearby East Tytherly. One night she and her friend Pat met Bill Carus and me outside the camp and together we romped in a haystack for some time. Romp was all we did but it was fun! It was my first and only frolic in a haystack and the last time I saw Diane.

Our outfit moved to Marshaling Area CP-16 near Romsey, a suburb of Southampton, early on the morning of 15 August. I was on KP that last morning, scrubbing pots and pans in the dark, while others were stumbling into foxholes on their way to chow. At the marshaling area my duties switched to motor pool guard. We were issued live ammunition for the first time. All afternoon the day after arrival, we loaded vehicles and equipment onto the Liberty ship, *Amos C. Throop*, and then boarded it ourselves around 6:30 p.m. The ship steamed down the river estuary and anchored for the night. It was about 9 a.m. when we weighed anchor. Through the fog our large convoy passed on the west side of the Isle of Wight and into the English Channel, where the weather cleared for the day-long journey across. By midafternoon we sighted the coast of Normandy and arrived at Utah Beach, near Isigny, in the evening to anchor for the night. More than 100 ships close by ours were a magnificent sight.

In my diary I noted, "Four decker bunks . . . officers living as men. C-rations and hot water. . . ." Late the next day, we climbed down the side of the ship into an LCT loaded with 12 vehicles. I was in the first vehicle off. The front of the LCT dropped, enabling us to drive onto the beach in blackout and onto winding roads recon-structed by the engineers. We stopped at Area B, where we slept under the stars near St. Germain de Varreville, a short distance from Ste. Mère Eglise. For a boy of 20 it was thrilling to hit the beaches without fear of being shot at or bombed, thanks to all that the combat outfits had done only two months earlier. The next day we camou-flaged our vehicles with those nets we had complained about so fiercely. Attempts to find a field shower were unsuccessful. In the afternoon a heavy rain was followed by a rainbow and a beautiful sunset, brilliant yellows and pinks in large clouds. I read a con-densation of *A Bell for Adano* and answered letters I had received before we left England.

There were things I wanted from home. I listed them — several inexpensive pipes, a book on peace plans by Under Secretary of State Sumner Welles, a good map of France, and a typewritten copy of my book. I sent a copy of the *Stars and Stripes* that mentioned my father as a member of Tom Dewey's campaign team. At the time, General Ben Lear had a penchant for unpopular remarks and actions and was often in hot water. In a recent statement, he had said that many troops in the ETO would be going home via the Suez Canal and Tokyo. That was OK with me but not very popular with many in my outfit, I wrote my folks.

My girlfriend Barbara, according to her letters, was making big plans for her future and mine. It made me squirm. "Certainly I don't think I've ever gone as far as she assumes," I explained in a letter to my parents. "I've tried to tell her I have absolutely no idea what I'll

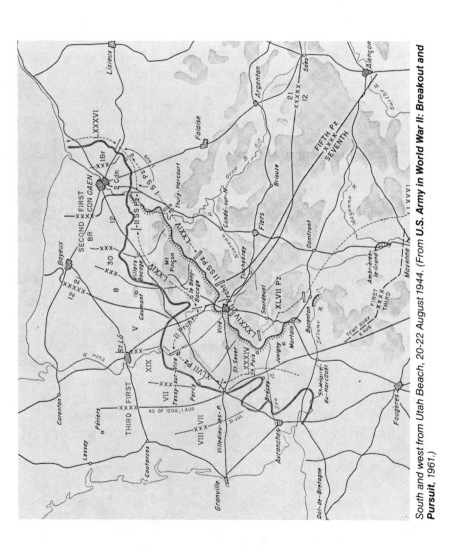

South and west from Utah Beach, 20-22 August 1944. (From U.S. Army in World War II: Breakout and Pursuit, 1961.)

think or how I'll feel when I get back. I don't even think of such things now and have no desire to, because I don't want to be tied down to anyone or anybody for a helluva long time yet. I've really got the wanderlust in my blood now, and it'll take a long time to cure it." In the next sentence, wanderlust aside, I told about the date I had with the girl I left behind in England. "It was the kind of date I've always dreamed of." I left England with a good feeling because of it.

We left in convoy on 20 August from Area C-19, near Foucarville and Utah Beachhead, following a route through Ste. Mère Eglise, Carentan, and Périers. The war had already visited the areas we were traveling through. The center of Périers was virtually destroyed. At Coutances we were routed around the center of the town, and between there and Granville we were treated to a beautiful view of the sea. Skirting Avranches, we saw many abandoned and damaged German convoys and U.S. and German tanks by the roadsides and in nearby fields. St. Hilaire was extensively damaged. We camped in a field near Landean which the Germans had left only three weeks before. The first American troops had arrived only 10 days before. Landean was far into France, east of the base of the Brittany peninsula. Our vehicles were camouflaged as hedgerows and we dug slit trenches. Our C-ration supper was washed down with water and cider brought by farmers in the area. For the most part we stood up in our vehicles as we traveled from village to village, the better to see the many people along the highways. On a Sunday a number of churchgoers threw flowers, apples, and onions as we passed. After two days on the road, our battalion was attached to VIII Corps Artillery for mission in the Brest Area. We drove in convoy halfway across Brittany to the bivouac area at Pluagat, a village west of St. Brieuc.

Notes in my diary sketched our route through Fougères, Antrain, Le Boussac, Dol de Bretagne, and Dinan, where I noted a high bridge that had been repaired by U.S. engineers. There also, we were attracted by sidewalk cafes. At Jugon a sign stretched across the street said "Welcome at (sic) our Liberators." Beyond Lamballe, at St. Brieuc, a small girl threw an onion our way and shouted sweetly and in perfect English, "I love you." Many shouted, "Vive l'Amérique!" Almost everyone waved, threw kisses and gifts of food — eggs, apples, tomatoes, onions. One little girl tossed two slices of buttered bread. A pack of cigarettes from the troops brought a bottle

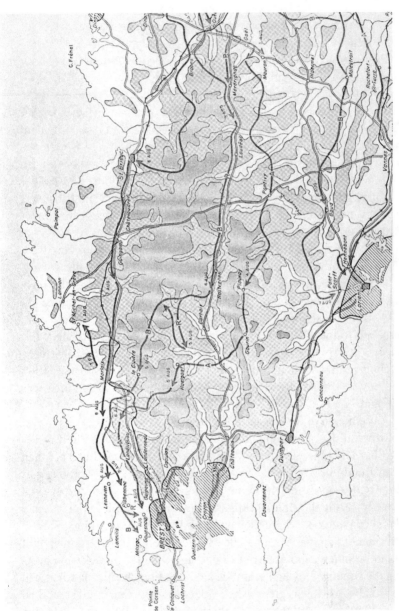

Brittany, where the Sixteenth stayed until 26 September. (From U.S. Army in World War II: Breakout and Pursuit, 1961.)

of "white lightning" in return. In addition to cigarettes, we tossed sugar, dextrose tablets, and lemonade powder to greeters along the way. The day ended with a miserable night at the bivouac area west of St. Brieuc, where we were rained out of our pup tents.

Pushing on toward Brest, we followed a route through Guingamp, Belle Isle en Terre, and Morlaix. From the road we saw the encampments of the French underground, whose members were guarding the bridges. Peasants came to offer cognac in exchange for gasoline. Continuing through Lesneven and Landerneau, we set up permanent bivouac near Landerneau for the Battle of Brest. A and B batteries were put on night sound and flash ranging. The wire section was also assigned night duty. My assignment was to 20-hour, .50 caliber machine gun duty with two other soldiers, McNamara and Broskie. I had never fired a machine gun before. There was frequent shelling of Brest by our artillery from a wide arc. One point of firing was near us. No fire came in return from the German positions. Germans were reported to have held Landerneau up to three days before our arrival. It was thought they were three miles to the south of us. "The flash from our guns was great," I scribbled in my diary, "a continued red glow from Brest during the night." Headquarters and B Battery were attached to the 174th Field Artillery Group, which was assigned to Task Force B with a mission to clear Daoulas peninsula by providing support to advancing infantry units. The Daoulas peninsula lay across the bay to the southeast of Brest. The main town in the area was Plougastel.

A confusion of feelings gripped me during the first week in France. Sorrow on the one hand and exhilaration on the other. The tragedy was in seeing the war-destroyed homes and churches. I had not then seen London or other devastated cities. Seeing a bombed-out port facility did not bring the same feeling, the same sense of personal tragedy, as did the sight of ruined homes where people had lived, and wrecked churches where they had worshipped. At the same time, no President in an inaugural parade ever felt more exhilarated than did I standing in a weapons carrier (a one-and-a-half-ton truck) and hearing the shouts of joy and gratitude from the French citizens who lined the roadways. It was great to be a liberator! It was not until sometime later that I reflected we were only the followers of the real liberators — the dogfaces of the infantry and armored divisions. But, for the moment, the war was exciting. I had not yet experienced any of its

Lesneven, in Brittany. The Sixteenth was stationed near this town during the Battle of Brest, August-September 1944. (Postcard, Editions "Gaby".)

real horrors, nor had I begun to worry about going to the Pacific after the European war was over.

Rereading my diary entries and the official battalion reports of our first week in Normandy and Brittany showed me the unreliability of memory. For years, I had a vivid remembrance of seeing the magnificent Mont St. Michel, the medieval abbey standing at the end of a causeway just off the north coast at the base of the Brittany peninsula. In my mind's eye to this very day, I can see it quite clearly. Alas, it is an imaginary vision, perhaps from a long-ago dream after seeing a picture of Mont St. Michel. Our route of travel after leaving Avranches took us nowhere near it.

We remained in the Brest area for more than a month, first on the Daoulas peninsula and later on the Crozon peninsula to the south, in bivouac (living outdoors and sleeping in pup tents). The Allied command had not anticipated either the number of German troops or their fierce resistance, led by Lieutenant General Hermann B. Ramcke, Commander of the elite Second Parachute Division and a hero of the 1941 battle for Crete. U.S. intelligence estimated 16,000 German troops in the area, whereas eventually 38,000 surrendered. General Troy Middleton, U.S. VIII Corps commander, had at his disposal the 2d, 8th, and 29th Infantry Divisions and Task Force A, plus considerable air support. These combat forces suffered almost 10,000 casualties. The Port of Brest was destroyed and was not usuable by Allied forces after they captured it. Historians have concluded that it would have been far wiser to have used a smaller force to bottle up the Germans while employing the remaining forces in pursuit of the Wehrmacht across France and Belgium. All this, of course, is hindsight. We GIs, as usual, had only a vague idea of what was going on.

I didn't go out with a survey party until five days after our arrival. In addition to observing shelling and bombing of enemy positions and the return fire by the infamous German 88mm guns every day, I made friends wherever I could. After taking a field bath from spring water, I talked to a Frenchman who apparently owned the field. He promised to bring his 22-year-old daughter who spoke English on the following evening. He didn't show up and neither did she, but I managed to get six eggs and a large half-circle of bread from refugees from Brest at a nearby farm. I hung around to show a French girl my ''Blitz French'' book. On a Sunday two days later Bill Carus and I took a five-mile hike on the south side of the Elorn River, which runs from Landerneau west to the harbor of Brest. We went past the impressive Blue Infantry command post and watched shells landing on the north bank. Had we been older and wiser, we wouldn't have been so daring and foolish.

I was driving a weapons carrier on my first day out with our survey party when I saw my first dead American, an officer. His body lay down an embankment. It was a sobering moment, a rite of passage into war. Heavy cannonading by tanks and TDs (tank destroyers) continued. Most members of our party proceeded cautiously with an eye out for booby traps. There were appalling sights all around us. One day we saw a convoy of three badly battered German vehicles, escorted by jeeps, drive into the collection station. Rain fell intermittently for several days. At the end of a soggy afternoon of computing, I found some diversion. My diary reported sketchily, ''Marie Thérèse, 17-year-old baker's daughter & fat friend, Simone, 26, brought bread, carrots, & onions. Extended conversation with them.''

In my first letter home from Brittany, I explained that I was putting my ''Blitz French'' book to good advantage in trading cigarettes and sugar for eggs, onion, bread, and cider — and one bottle of cognac —

and noted the Germans had pretty well stripped the area. I gave my parents my approximate location by using a code I'd worked out with them. I wrote, "You might also get sheet No. 58 of the Michelin road maps ($5.00) from the Field Artillery Association — just keep it until I get home." The Michelin sheet No. 58 covered the Brest area. My mother might have been better off not knowing where I was much of the time, but she always wanted to know. I used this code for the remainder of the war. Much later I learned that the large-scale Michelin maps, reprinted, were used as official army maps.

I slept in one day in late August and had myself breakfast in bed — cheese, crackers, and carrots. While on survey that day, I collected two German helmets, a razor, ammunition, and a Mauser rifle from FFI (French Forces of the Interior). When I came in, I discovered McNamara had picked up a stock of food and a Bretagne (French spelling for Brittany) pitcher from Marie Thérèse. Several days later, he scored another triumph, trading 36 packs of cigarettes and sugar for a Mauser pistol. Most of us went a little crazy collecting Breton and German army souvenirs. We sent some items home, but most of the stuff was ultimately discarded. We traded with the local residents for the items we wanted. In Brittany there was little stealing from the friendly population. War's proverbial looting did not begin until we entered Germany the following winter. The German enemy was known by various names — Jerries, Boche (from the French), Krauts, and Huns. We used the last term when we intended to sound rough and tough.

The French Forces of the Interior formed a guerrilla army of sorts without uniforms. They were armed and still much in evidence. The English and French pronunciation of the letter "I" created some problems. When we said FFI to a member, we were promptly corrected: "No! No! No! — FFE," they insisted. One fine evening I observed firsthand a striking cultural difference between France and the United States. A young Frenchman was standing by the roadside with his girlfriend. One of his arms encircled the girl while the other one was employed in relieving himself. On the day we moved to a bivouac area closer to Plougastel, which had been captured on 29 August, I saw my first dead German. He had been stripped of his valuables. As in most wars, stealing from the dead was accepted practice.

Our survey party didn't go out on 1 September, and I used the day to write a "two-page summation on the causes of war." I elaborated upon what I then considered the two basic causes of war — unequal distribution of the world's resources and human greed and lust for power — and suggested some solutions. In conclusion I wrote, "These suggestions are simple. They require very little deep thinking. They probably have been thought about in one way or another by millions of human beings in the course of history. Yet they are seldom clarified. They cannot be acted upon until they are clarified in the human mind. War is truly hell. It can be prevented. These suggestions are a step in the right direction, even if they take a thousand years in their fulfillment. Our alternative to them is the four horsemen of the Apocalypse." My early feelings of exhilaration as a liberator faded with each dead soldier I saw.

When we got mail for the first time in three weeks, I had something to brag about. In all I received 56 items, "as much as anyone in the battery," I noted. Of course, almost half of the letters were from my parents. I immediately wrote a five-page response to them, summarizing my present life in the army by telling about pitching pup tents in any convenient cow pasture. Except for being rained out a couple of times, it was fairly comfortable. Four blankets were none too many on most nights. Our standard diet consisted of K- and C-rations. The K-ration, which came in three Cracker Jack-size boxes, provided something more than 3,000 calories a day and contained a can for each meal (meat, meat and eggs, processed cheese) plus biscuits, crackers, dextrose, soluble coffee, fruit and chocolate bars, and lemon juice. The C-ration provided more calories but it was bulkier because it consisted of cans. The canned meals were better when heated but that wasn't always possible. It wasn't unusual to eat them cold from the can. Occasionally, we got 10-in-1 (U-ration) which provided a day's supply of food for 10 men. We supplemented these rations with anything we managed to pick up from the countryside. I made a point of mentioning that while I hadn't had a shower since we landed, a few creeks had provided reasonable substitutes. I found a number of mine detonators in one creek, but no mines. By this time, I was beginning to look like a superduper superman, outfitted with two German helmets and a Mauser rifle complete with bayonet.

Two letters from Irene, it seemed to me, were "more than cordial" and did a lot to lift my morale, not to mention my expectations. I was less thrilled by a full dozen letters from Barbara. I had every intention of making it perfectly clear that I wasn't making any decisions about anything until the war ended. My mother sent me a poem which I promised ''to keep with me always.'' My intentions were sincere but the poem was soon lost. Also in that avalanche of mail was a typed copy of my book. I had little more to add to it but I appreciated having it with me. Being a person who plans ahead, my mother was bugging me about what she should send for Christmas. Impatiently, I wrote, ''It doesn't make any difference what you send or whether you send anything at all.'' But I listed some things — a few good books, soap, a pipe, and pipe tobacco. ''No doubt by the time Christmas rolls around I'll have access to all these items, but I have no way of knowing,'' I added.

A letter from my father, dated 18 August, uncharacteristically gave me a bit of encouragement and advice on the subject of romance. He agreed that Irene, from all he'd heard, was a fine girl. Keep writing her as I had been and then after the war, he said, there would be a chance to see whether ''the real comes up to the ideal.'' He added it wouldn't hurt to let her know how I felt about her. That gave me a real lift. He jumped from Irene to a discussion of peace plans, saying he didn't know if the conference to be held at Dumbarton Oaks between the four powers would amount to anything more than a preliminary meeting. But, he noted, as fast as things were moving the Allies would have to be making some decisions about what to do with Germany, whether the war lasted one or three months longer. ''Whatever the settlement may be, it looks like it would probably fall considerably short of the plans you've outlined in your book. However, they will be steps in that direction.'' He wanted to know what news I was able to get so that he'd have a better idea of what to write about.

Back in Kansas, my mother wrote almost daily. The big issue to me was whether or not she would see Irene there. ''Looks like fate's against you where Irene is concerned,'' she said. Irene was still in Colorado, it seemed. Mom was pretty upset because one of our anti-Catholic relatives was fretting about the possibility of my marrying Irene. My ''romance'' was getting more attention than it merited. A letter from Diane, who called herself ''Dinah,'' was a gem: ''Have you found a nice wee french girl yet. We had a party at home on Saturday. Boy oh boy what a time I had. Is there any hay stacks in France or where ever you are. I am going to have a picture take of myself would you like one, have you any of yourself to spare a little English one.'' She signed it ''Love.''

A polarization in attitude toward the French people developed in our outfit. There were those who arrogantly viewed them as stupid — ''They can't even speak English.'' And then there was the friendly, if naive, faction that took an opposite view — ''Gee, are these people smart! Even the little kids can speak French!''

Unlike me, there were some men in our outfit who were adept at nearly everything. Tom Fourshee of Cadiz, Kentucky, was one of them. He built a small wood-fired cooking stove on which we heated our rations and boiled fresh eggs. Tom could fix almost anything, and so could ''Okie'' Henderson from Texas. I came to appreciate their skills in the fundamentals of living in the field and also their even approach to whatever came up in the army. Spending time with these men contributed to my growing up.

Waiting for the infantry to take Brest, our survey section had little to do for a period of 10 days or so. I caught up on my sleep. One day I slept until noon; on other days I took afternoon naps. We picked blackberries, visited with French civilians, had long bull sessions in the evenings, and, making use of the abundance of fallen apples all around us, we staged a few apple fights. My diary noted 13 September as a red-letter day: I had my first shower (in a tent) in a month. It was quite a sensation. Waiting around didn't sharpen our soldiering. A new man in the outfit, drunk on cognac, approached Colonel Lushene to ask him for a tank to go to Brest. On guard, another man fired at a moving horse from eight feet. He missed. On two successive Saturdays I attended Protestant church services conducted by Captain Stainbrook, an VIII Corps chaplain whom we would see fairly frequently until V-E Day. He was, I believe, a Lutheran. My most vivid recollection of his service was being served communion wine for the first time. Up until then, I thought all churches used grape juice!

Dave McNamara of Montello, Wisconsin, and I became pup-tent mates during our stay in Brittany, and we continued to share a tent or other shelter for most of the rest of the war. He was a pleasant person to be around. On the surface, he seemed relaxed and laid back, but underneath he was as much of a bitcher and rebel as I. Sometimes he got into trouble by his association with me. With a burrhead haircut, he reminded me of a friendly black bear. He had a wry, dry humor, and his quaint remarks often sized up situations precisely and relieved tensions considerably. Once, in the middle of the night, we were awakened by German shells whistling overhead. Mac rolled over, sat up, and asked calmly, "Hope, do you have any foot powder?" Early on in France, he nicknamed himself "Bruno" and me "Gunther."

Frequent visitors to our field kitchen were two French women who came for handouts. They were suspected of being collaborators with the Germans. As I remember them, they were on the unattractive side and one was obviously pregnant. We called them "Preg-Nancy" and "Susie the Troj" (short for Trojan horse).

Major Cameron and Lieutenant Tyler, our survey platoon leader, returned from a reconnaissance survey of Lorient. The battalion after action report regarding it said, "General conclusions were that the Nazis were strongly fortified at Lorient and it would be a tough nut to crack." Years later, Ed Kahner told me Tyler had disguised himself as a French civilian in order to check German gun positions there. Later that year, Red Tyler became the first man in the battalion to receive the Bronze Star. His citation read in part: "As survey platoon leader during operations against Port of Brest, (he) did display courage, coolness, skill and disregard for personal safety. . . . (He) always reconnoitered ahead and made certain that all avenues for survey were free of mines and small arms fire prior to entrance of his survey parties . . . real leader of his men. . . . (His) act of gallantry erased all signs of nervousness, anxiety and fear from his platoon. . . . He had inspired his platoon to a pitch where fear practically is non-existent."

All of us admired Red and he did inspire us. But neither he nor anyone else could erase "all signs of nervousness, anxiety and fear."

My letters home during September definitely relayed my concerns. I let them know that while the general European picture might be getting better, it wasn't true that the Huns were surrendering en masse everywhere. GIs could testify to that. My saying so was a reaction to what I felt was a diminishing of American patriotic fervor brought on by a belief that the war was almost over. "In reality," I wrote, "it could last for months more with a few fanatic Nazi commanders in the right places." Furthermore, I went on, the armistice itself would be only the beginning of more problems and certainly not an occasion for any letdown at home. I felt we had the wholehearted friendship of the French but I feared it might be lost if everyone got wrapped up in "returning to normalcy." The men in my outfit really blew when they heard of the Murray-Kilgore bill with maximum unemployment insurance for war workers of $35 per week for two years. On a more congenial note, I attempted to give my mother some help about Christmas. I asked her to send three Modern Library books — *Poverty and Progress, The Theory of the Leisure Class,* and Aristotle's *Republic* — along with *Black Record* by Lord Vansittart and *A Primer of the Coming World* by Leopold Schwargachild. Those were just suggestions, I insisted. Anything or nothing at all would be OK. And then I added I could use more writing paper.

In France as in England, we got marmalade and the bees that it enticed. I joked, "These (bees) over here don't understand English so that makes it worse." Recalling an Ernie Pyle story in which he said that French children were the prettiest and cutest he'd ever seen, I wrote about an 11-year-old girl, Marie, who lived near our camp. She had the sweetest smile I had ever seen. Some of us had a picture of her and we intended to have reprints made for everyone in our section. Marie always wore a peasant costume. I got a cap like the one she wore to send home. While my mother's fussing about Christmas annoyed me, I found myself thinking of it, too, as I collected souvenirs and shopped for gifts to send home. I had German, French, and English coins and stamps, a rosary, postcards, and some items I didn't name in my letter. They were to be surprises. I got the rosary for Irene, some combs for Barbara, and color books of local scenes for my young cousins in Kansas. For myself, I picked up a German overcoat that was a perfect fit.

We moved to a bivouac area near Argol in the Crozon peninsula, south of Brest, early on 18 September. Once again I was in trouble. Bruno (McNamara) and I did not have all of our equipment ready to go at the appointed hour. Although others were equally late in packing, the lieutenant in charge and our section chief, Staff Sgt. Gordon S. Thompson, gave me and Mac hell. I lipped off to them. Thompson really let me have it. He blamed me for virtually all of the faults in the section within the past year. Poor Bruno, who said nothing to the lieutenant or to Thompson, suffered extra duty along with me. His own comments, plenty pungent, were made in private.

As we surveyed, we saw the most Germans to date. They were prisoners in the city square of the town of Crozon. Always conscious of the distinction between officers and enlisted men, I noted in my diary that the German officers were very well dressed. We also saw massive German fortifications in complete ruins, burned and blasted beyond recognition. All fighting ceased on the Brest Peninsula on 18 September, and the last German units on the Crozon Peninsula surrendered the next day. *Yank* magazine said of the battle: "The siege of Brest, largest of the three Brittany garrisons, probably never will receive the world-wide recognition it rightfully deserves. Tougher than Caen, it is said to have been one of the hardest battles fought by American infantry in Europe since 1918." As for our part of it, sound and flash did a job that earned the battalion commendations from group and corps commanders. Everyone griped about survey, but the plots were amazingly accurate.

We left for a regrouping area near Lesneven to the northeast of Brest on 20 September, and the next day we were told of our assignment to the newly formed Ninth Army. For the next week we cleaned equipment, saw special service shows, bathed and washed clothes in creeks, and generally messed around. One day Seymour Solomon and I went to a French home in Lesneven to get two coifs (close-fitting caps worn by the women and girls) as souvenirs. The people wouldn't accept francs in payment. They wanted sugar, coffee, and things like that. They put the coifs in a five-in-one ration box. When their child started crying, they explained that "bébé" used the box as a doll house. It made me feel like a heel, especially since I had only two packs of cigarettes to give them. The next day we came back and made things right, returning the "doll house" filled with bouillon, coffee, lemonade powder, cigarettes, sugar, and whatever else we could get our hands on.

Meanwhile on the homefront, my family was back in Washington after being in Kansas. They called the office on arriving there and learned there was an airmail letter from me. "Didn't take us long to get out there to get it," my mother wrote. It was not until I became a parent myself that I realized how much more letters from children are valued by parents than are letters from parents to their children. Mom's letter reflected the optimism current in the States. She wrote, "Daddy is going to try and get you a map of Central Europe. He thinks you'll need a map of Germany before one of France will even catch up with you."

By the time she wrote again, she had received a later letter from me and was filled with fear. She assumed from my letter that I was in actual combat. Her response was flowery, sympathetic, and complimentary. Reading it really embarrassed me. At the same time, it was comforting to know my family still loved me, especially at a time when I knew not everyone in my outfit did. My father's letters started again on 16 September, after his arrival back in Washington from his trip on the Dewey campaign train. At that time he thought Tom Dewey might have a chance of defeating F.D.R. He had surmised that we were in the Brest area. That brought back World War I memories, because he had sailed from Brest to return to the States.

My long-distance romance of sorts with Irene hit a high point in September. She had started to use her nickname, Renie, in signing her letters. That seemed significant to me. She was then in her senior year at St. Mary College at Notre Dame. She hoped that along with the horrible things I was seeing there were some beautiful things, and that I'd be back soon so I could tell her about everything. I hung on every word she wrote and was especially thrilled to learn she was sending me a St. Christopher medal to wear. Her insight into the war sounded brilliant to me: "This demobilization problem is going to be a great one I can see. No matter how it is figured out a great number of people are going to think it's unfair. I'll be as patient as I can, and I'm glad to know you'll accept the worst without feeling you've been wronged even though you might be."

In a third letter within the month, she wrote, "Cliff, I don't know just exactly what you think about the Catholic religion, but I know you believe in praying and I want you to know that I say a rosary for you every night without fail even when I do miss Mass and Communion sometimes. I don't tell you all these things to make you think I'm overly pious or that I'm making big sacrifices for the war effort. It's just that I want you to know I am praying for you because I think it will make you feel better. I know it would me, no matter who was praying for me — Catholic, Protestant, or Jew."

Chapter 5

Sitzkrieg in the Ardennes

On the morning of 26 September our battalion headed east and then northeast on a four-day motor convoy to the combat zone at the Belgian-German border. The first day we retraced our route of the month before as far as Dinan, then headed southeast to bivouac in a large green pasture near Sens-de-Bretagne, a small village northeast of Rennes. "Hope and McNamara!" Sergeant Thompson called out just as soon as our convoy halted for the night. That night and for several nights thereafter, Bruno and I were assigned as latrine-diggers, more punishment for my smarting-off that morning several weeks before. Customarily, a three-holer was dug for a hundred-plus enlisted men, and a two-holer for a handful of officers!

Alençon, which we reached on the second day, marked the end of the now-familiar hedgerow country. The gentle, rolling land was divided by fences. The people along the route were friendly. The familiar communiqué, "railway junction destroyed," took on real meaning when we came upon the railway yard at Alençon. It had been bombed to smithereens. We bivouacked near Chateauneuf on a giant estate rumored to be the home of Napoleon's first wife. While we slept in the woods to the rear of the large house, the officers slept inside on sheets. "Col. Lushene had four rooms," I noted pointedly in my diary. The estate's gardens, although neglected, were magnificent. Pear trees were trained along wires as they are at Mt. Vernon.

The next day was notable in that it took us past the palace at Versailles and through Paris. We went through numerous parks, crossed the Seine, and had barrages of apples thrown our way. One hit me squarely on the cheek. The scenery was great and I made mention of an important part of it in my diary: "Beautiful and

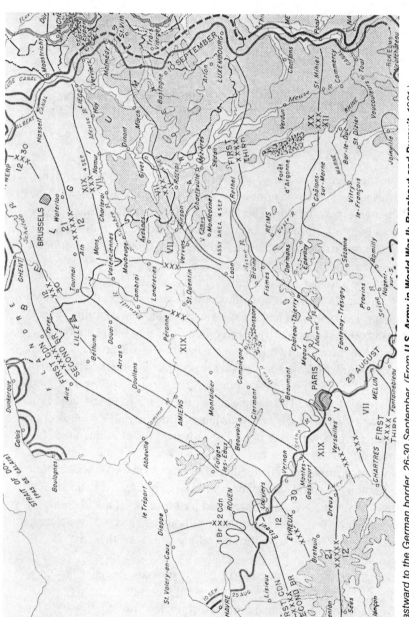

Eastward to the German border, 26-30 September. (From U.S. Army in World War II: Breakout and Pursuit, 1961.)

friendly women, and I ain't kiddin'.'' We saw three truckloads of German prisoners, many of whom appeared to be Japanese and Mongols. From Paris we went northeast through Senlis, Compiègne, and Noyon. It seemed to be official policy for our convoy to travel at normal speed through the countryside but to speed up through all the towns of any size. The better to keep us out of trouble, I supposed. As we were swishing through Noyon, Ed Kahner, suffering from an acute case of the GIs, had an urgent need to relieve himself. There was no stopping the GMC truck. Some of those with him in the rear of the truck located an empty cigar box. Using it with admirable accuracy, he did what had to be done.

After spending the night near St. Quentin, we set out on the fourth and last day of our travels. It turned out to be our most glorious day as liberators. Heading east and north into Belgium, we were treated to many interesting sights and experiences. Our vehicle was given half a loaf of molasses bread in Mont DeOrigny and a bottle of hard cider in Petigny, and between Petigny and Vireux I was kissed on the cheek by a Belgian girl. A woman in the same area gave us hot coffee. We saw steel mills and other signs of heavy industry in Belgium. Our route followed the canyon of the Meuse River from Givet to Dinant. Old fortresses lined the top of the canyon walls and there were burned-out houses along the roadside. I was struck by the peculiar architecture of the churches. The Belgian stores seemed to be well stocked. We crossed the Meuse River at Dinant to arrive at the bivouac area around 6:30 p.m. at the end of a long, pleasant day. Naturally, the highlight of the day for me was the quickie kiss, my first kiss since leaving Diane in England. I was standing in the back of our weapons carrier when I saw the girl by the side of the road. "There's a girl who wants to kiss someone and it might as well be me," I said to myself. I practically hung by my heels out of the vehicle to reach her and she had to run alongside. The mission was accomplished. Short but sweet.

Our camp that night was near Neffe, three kilometers east of Bastogne, in a tall spruce grove. We entered the forest of the Ardennes, little realizing that we would remain in that region for the next four months. The situation in the Ardennes that autumn of 1944 has been well described by Charles B. McDonald at the conclusion of *The Siegfried Line Campaign* (one of the volumes in the army's Green Book series):

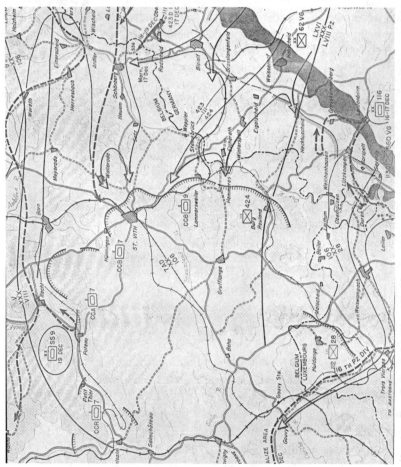

Headquarters Battery area from 1 October to 16 December. (From U.S. Army in World War II: The Ardennes, *1965.)*

The VIII Corps front in the Ardennes was at once the nursery and the old folks' home of the American command. To this sector came new divisions to acquire their first taste of combat under relatively favorable conditions. Here too came old divisions licking their wounds from costly fighting like the Brittany peninsula and the Huertgen Forest. The front ran from Losheim, between Camp d'Elsenborn and the northern end of the Schnee Eifel, southward generally along the Belgian and Luxembourgian borders with Germany. Eventually it stretched all the way in the southeastern corner of Luxembourg. It extended into Germany at two points: along the Schnee Eifel, where the 4th Division in September had pierced a thin sector of the West Wall, and near Uettfeld, where the 28th Division had driven a salient into the West Wall. The mission of the VIII Corps was to defend the long front in place, deceive the enemy by active patrolling, and make general plans and preparations for attacking to the Rhine.

The information our officers had at that time, as set forth in our battalion's after action report for 1 October, was that the enemy, situated behind the Siegfried Line, was preparing a "do or die" stand along the line. The terrain along this sector, the Belgium-Luxembourg border, was a high plateau with small streams and wooded areas throughout. The Germans were using "poor quality convalescents and aged" to fill the fixed fortifications (machine gun and antitank forts), while good quality troops remained in rear areas to counterattack in case of a breach in positions. The estimated enemy strength in the sector was about 30,000 men and 40 tanks. Because of a severe shortage in armor, the enemy refrained from using them offensively. Included in the force were 14 battalions of artillery. The enemy was believed to have 6,500 men for a tactical reserve and a maximum reserve of two divisions, made up of either newly mobilized forces or units withdrawn from Scandinavia, for a strategic reserve. An entry in my diary for this period said the Belgian underground seemed to be very similar to the FFI. Members wore black, yellow, and red armbands and rode around in low-built black sedans, not unlike Chicago gangsters.

Headquarters Battery moved to a new bivouac area in another spruce grove on October first. It was quite close to the German border, near the village of Grufflange (the French, Michelin-map spelling; the German spelling is Grufflingen). We soon learned we were in a German-speaking area and among a number of Nazi sympathizers. I made the comment that the men looked like A. Hitler and the women like Mrs. Pruneface (a Dick Tracy character). The weather turned cold and rainy. One morning Okie Henderson, Bruno, and I decided to dig our double tent in. We finally gave up, realizing all we were digging was a mudhole. For two days in a row, I had to dig sumpholes for garbage. Six members of one party and Lieutenant Tyler went deer hunting, after learning that the 17th FOB, whom we were replacing, had shot 17 deer.

"What a life for civilized men to lead!" exclaimed Phil Grathwol, our battery philosopher, as he contemplated tent life in the rain. That summed it up for most of us. The only access by vehicle to our camp was by a steep, muddy road. Vehicles had to shift into low gear before beginning the ascent. Grathwol called our bivouac area the Götterdammerung. Those of us riding in the weapons carrier picked up the theme, humming "The Ride of Valkyries" as loud as we could during the muddy climb up to camp. Survey work began in the area east of St. Vith on the day after our arrival, but the weather kept us from going out much of the time. Within a few days we were into our first looting. From burned-out houses, we picked up three stoves and an empty pewter bottle. Thompson got a bed. We placed our finds on the floor of the weapons carrier so the MPs wouldn't see them. Because we were still in Belgium, looting was officially forbidden: "Thou shalt not steal from thine allies."

Spurred by our acquisitions, we went to work to improve our camp accommodations. When survey didn't go out the next day, Okie, Bruno, and I started to build a log cabin. We took the weapons carrier to gather logs and stakes. The cabin was four log thicknesses high, topped with two shelter (pup) tents. We put a stove in the center of one side of it. Buried in the ground, it succeeded only in filling the tent with smoke. We worked for two days to refine and improve our hut home. Mac and Henderson made a small stove out of a cocoa can. It was all right except that it required constant feeding. After I drew a sketch of the hut, we christened the place "Chateau of the Ardennes." The nearby sumphole was labeled "mass grave." We managed to heat water for tepid, if not hot, cocoa and warmed K-ration meat which we ate on crackers. With water heated on our stove, I took my first bath in the cabin-chateau. A line from my diary documented that "my bottom half was inside but the top half was outside." Our humble hut became an evening gathering place.

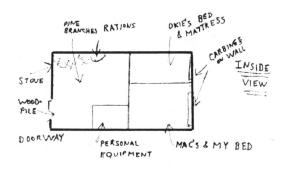

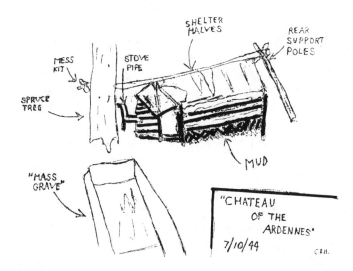

"The Chateau of the Ardennes," in which the author, "Okie" Henderson, and "Bruno" McNamara lived during October 1944. This was the author's drawing in his diary.

It was 7 October when I settled down to write my first letters home from Belgium, one to my parents and one to Irene. I told my parents about the tremendous amount of good will the people of the liberated countries showed toward America. Willkie was right in calling it a "reservoir of good will." You had to see it to realize how great it was. It would all be worthless though, I said, unless definite postwar plans started shaping up. "Plenty of good can come out of this war, if the right things are done." Living in the forest was conducive to writing, and within a few days I replied to several more letters from my parents. They had sent copies of a number of speeches, including some given by Roosevelt. I shared these with Winsor, Gross, Kahner, and whoever else expressed an interest. There seemed to be a general apathy in the camp about the election back in the States. Most who cared at all favored Dewey, but only a few talked about it. Those who hadn't already voted by state ballot and could vote by federal ballot did so on 10 October. For a wonder, I felt the army was handling the election very well. The battalion after action report stated that every man was asked whether or not he wished to vote and was given the opportunity if his home state was one that had approved the Federal Ballot system. The report didn't mention that ''every man'' meant ''every man 21 or over.'' Being old enough to fight did not mean being old enough to vote. However, at the time, 21 was the almost universal voting age, and as I was already bitching about so many other things, I gave little thought to being disenfranchised.

Having just heard of the death of Willkie, I asked my father if he thought it would have much effect on the campaign. Wendell Willkie was my first contemporary political hero. His 1940 Republican National Convention dark horse victory was a great satisfaction to my father, who had been one of his early supporters in Congress. Shouting ''We want Willkie'' from the north balcony of the convention hall and working in the campaign of the months following had been the most exciting time of my life up to our landing on Utah Beach. So there I was out in the forest, reminiscing at the ripe old age of 20! I continued to ponder the causes of war. To the two I discussed a month before in Brittany, I added a third: ''Man's indifference and apathy toward his fellow man.'' This, I reasoned, was expressed primarily in every individual's great concern with his own small, petty world to the exclusion of all else.

Meanwhile, back in the real world of Götterdammerung, we discovered a large hunk of steel wool in the bottom of the coffee pot we used to heat water for our delicious cocoa!

On a drizzly day when our survey party didn't go out, we dug a sumphole for the kitchen. ''Privates did two-thirds of the work,'' I groused in a diary notation. ''We must write 'Ode to a Sumphole' sometime.'' I attended Protestant services, and then had Grathwol and Winsor over for an evening bull session.

After a round of rumors and false starts, and after we had added two logs to our chateau, our winter quarters were moved to Aldringen, a small village a short distance to the west. A typical Belgian-German farm village, Aldringen was unchanged in appearance from decades past. The mud in the streets and GIs walking down the middle of the lanes reminded me of pictures taken in France during World War I. The lanes were composed of a mixture of cow manure and mud. Every farmer had a manure pile in his front yard. After chow, we drove to an old schoolhouse that had apartments upstairs to spend the night. We slept on the floor in a classroom littered with German textbooks and Nazi Party propaganda. That stuff looked like good pickings to me.

The night was fitful. Amid Schlusing's teeth grinding, Hall's talking in his sleep, and a symphony of snores and grunts, Bruno shook me awake. "Hope, do you know what this sounds like? Like feeding time at the zoo." With that, he rolled over and went back to sleep, but not for long. "Take that light out of my eyes, Gross, or I'll pound you into the floor!" Bruno's voice boomed throughout the classroom as Gross roused him for guard duty.

After the kitchen brought us breakfast, we went on detail back to the Götterdammerung to get our stove, the command post tent, and other items left behind. We lunched near the schoolhouse and spent the afternoon getting straw to sleep on. Survey Party Two took the third floor of the school; Okie, Mac, Winsor, and I were in what had been a kitchen; and Grathwol, Peltz, and Thompson were in an adjoining room. We hung our clothes on the stove at night. Eight men shaved at one table with water heated on the stove. We drank cocoa and ate sardines and fried potatoes. The beds and bed rolls took up most of the floor space. "From the Götterdammerung to a New York East Side tenement in one day," Grathwol observed.

I had a field day sorting through the library books and pamphlets in the *volksschule* (primary school). One book, published in 1941, was entitled *Das Amerikanische Ratsel* (The American Enigma). The enigma was none other than President Roosevelt. A large collection of photographs at the end of the book portrayed everyone with a Jewish name in FDR's administration. Included were Secretary of State Cordell Hull and his "Jewish wife" and Mayor LaGuardia, the "half-Jewish mayor" of New York. Another small book, *Horst Wessel*, was a short biography of the Berlin storm troop leader who was killed by the Communists in street fighting in 1930. Wessel wrote the words and tune to the "Horst Wessel Lied," which became the official song of the Nazi Party and later the second official anthem, after "Deutschland Uber Alles," of the Third Reich. Horst Wessel was further immortalized as a great folk hero by Dr. Goebbels' propaganda. I stashed a good bit of the schoolroom literature in the bottom of my duffel bag.

Although we talked of living in a New York tenement, the schoolhouse was considerably warmer and drier than the Götterdammerung. Okie and others built bunk beds for all of us. Often we fixed our own supper rather than make the trip to the official battery mess facilities in the neighboring village of Maldingen. The school provided a good place for nightly bull sessions. Early on, Bill Gross and I discussed writing a book about our outfit. It's just as well for all concerned that this masterpiece never got beyond the discussion stage. To celebrate having "come in out of the cold," Bruno and I went to Mass at the village church on Sunday, 15 October. Then a group of us took showers in the shower tent operated by an engineer battalion at Gouvy. While there, we bought schnapps and wine and returned to our schoolhouse for a dinner of fried chicken, french fries, and creamed corn, prepared by Tommy Fourshee, Emery Bliesmer, and Okie. It was some party. We had bottles of all shapes, sizes and contents and every one of us, man and boy, got drunk. Two days later, in preparation for escorting General McMahon of VIII Corps Artillery to Luxembourg City, we gave the vehicles a thorough washing at a farmhouse pump. I washed and shaved. It was first time in months I didn't scare myself when I looked in the mirror.

Within the next week we drove to Luxembourg City and back twice. The scenery was beautiful, the terrain honeycombed with small, swift streams. On the second trip, we returned by way of Arlon, Belgium, stopping there for about an hour. Arlon was a clean, small city. The stores resembled those back home. I bought postcards, maps, steaks, three scarves, a buffet piece, and, most important of all, a small dish of ice cream. It was the first ice cream I'd had since Fort Bragg. Along the way, we checked out the farm girls of the region. Some of them looked strong as oxen. I saw a girl pulling a four-wheel wagon. They had to be husky. Some of the men sized them up as "13 axe handles wide."

Our fun and games ended on the following Saturday when our survey party was ordered to the Mompach-Berbourg area of eastern

Luxembourg, close to the front. A few minutes after we entered Berbourg, German shells landed a few hundred yards away. Shortly after, medics carried two bodies past us. We heard that six more soldiers were wounded. That night we billeted in a house left by Luxembourgers. There I found a number of Nazi postcards and German and Luxembourg geography books. There were virtually no civilians left in the town but it still had running water and electricity. I found myself wondering who was paying the utility bills.

In the morning we began surveying just east of Berbourg. I was front rodman. Most of our survey paralleled the front. In many places there was a deathly silence punctuated at intervals by an American infantryman poking his head out of the woods. Winsor made the observation that the proximity to the front could be ascertained by the amount of wire laid. We saw only one thin strand that day. Traverse continued the next day up to the crossroads; one spur led to Dickweiler and the other to Osweiler. A German shell landed near Osweiler just as we started there from the ridge, so survey was postponed for a few minutes. We ate a hot meal, brought from an infantry outfit, in a hotel in Osweiler. The hotel had obviously been left in a hurry; everything in it was left intact. I picked up several guidebooks and postcards and an excellent cardboard wall map of Luxembourg. As I pillaged through the hotel, I felt it was a sad and strange thing to be doing, even if the proprietor had been a Nazi sympathizer. No wonder the Germans love war when they can continuously pillage, I thought. It was an addiction which I had not escaped either. Although the Grand Duchy of Luxembourg was our ally, we considered it okay to loot from the houses of Nazi sympathizers. Returning to Aldringen four days later, we had 12 live chickens in a coop and numerous and sundry other items in the back of a weapons carrier.

At the end of the month, there was a report of a German radio transmitter in the kitchen building. Thirty men and the command post and wire sections were called for reinforcements to surround the house. The "radio" turned out to be a leaky valve on a stove. In my diary I editorialized about the incident: ". . . strongly indicative of general incompetence, stupidity and exaggerated fear in outfit." As I was not yet 21 and had few responsibilities, it was easy for me to comment on everything with great wisdom and perception.

My sister, Martha, got some big brother advice from me regarding her school homework in a letter I wrote to the family. "Don't let it worry you," I wrote. "You'll look back on it as relatively unimportant and only part of a bigger picture. Life is too short to worry about little things. Do your best and then forget about it." This, from me, who constantly worried and bitched about "little things"! A perfect example was my reaction when I learned the basement in our Washington house had flooded. Possible damage to my war propaganda collection stored there was my immediate concern. "You mentioned mopping up the water around my boxes in the basement," I wrote. "For God's sake open the boxes and try to let that stuff dry out in case you haven't already." Using the code I had devised to tell my parents of our general whereabouts, I asked them to send me Michelin Map. No. 4, which covered southeastern Belgium and Luxembourg. The rains continued so we were thankful to be sleeping inside, I said. "I suppose you saw the news that the weather here from June through September was the worst in 80 years. October seems well on the way to upholding the record. Everything not hard surfaced is a sea of mud."

Campaigning for his re-election back in Kansas, my father took time to write a long letter on the last Sunday in October. He gently prodded me to write my mother as often as I could "even if you haven't anything to say except that you're all right." She and my sister were alone in Washington. From the war news, he assumed our front was getting ready for a big push soon and hoped we could "finish the job before winter." He said it looked as if the Jap fleet was nearly taken care of, "so that ought to hurry things long in that quarter." Many people asked him about me as he went around the district, and he said he was proud to tell them I was in Belgium. Many of his constituents told him where their boys were in the war. From some came the sad news that their boys had been killed. He said he appreciated learning from me about the good will toward Americans and he agreed it had to be preserved. My father's optimism about an end to the war before winter was shared by many people, including some in the army. In October some wit or wits went so far as to write and distribute an official-looking document entitled "Indoctrination for Return to the U.S." (It is included as Appendix 1.) It includes tips on such subjects as how a civilian should and should not use a helmet, a polite way for a returning soldier to disagree with his civilian associates, and an explanation of pajamas.

I spent some of my spare time in late October and November continuing my great thoughts, rehashing the causes of war, and writing more about human nature. Most of it was repetitious. Hitting it in spurts and spells, it was hard to remember what I had or hadn't written. My writings were stuffed into my duffel bag which contained all my worldly possessions in the ETO.

Our general situation remained virtually the same, one of maintaining the breaks in the Siegfried Line between Auw, Germany, and Heinerscheid, Luxembourg, and containing the Germans in the Siegfried Line, south of Heinerscheid along the Our River to the boundary line of the First and Third Armies. This summation was the substance of the battalion's monthly report of battle activity for November 1944. Most of our survey was in the area east of St. Vith, toward Schönberg, and south, near Burg-Reuland. But in the first week of November we again went to Luxembourg, working in the Flaxweiler area east of Luxembourg City. In three days, we were in Belgium, Germany, back to Belgium, Luxembourg, France, back to Luxembourg and again back to Belgium. That isn't as impressive as it sounds. The total distance involved would be equivalent to traversing a couple of the larger counties in Kansas. The Grand Duchy of Luxembourg is about the size of Rhode Island.

Usually a letter from home arrived in two and a half to three weeks, but sometimes it took six weeks. I wrote home that airmail was arriving faster than V-mail. I was able to assure my mother that I did have long underwear. We had brought all of our winter clothing across the channel with us, in contrast to the boys who landed in June.

For several days my diary thoughts centered around election day, 8 November, in the U.S. The weather was turning colder, and days of inactivity gave us a sense of claustrophobia. Between political discussions, I read *Mrs. Parkington.* Buzz bombs whizzed overhead most of the evening of 7 November and the building shook as one landed nearby. I was feeling low, discouraged about the future in general, and concerned about Dewey's probable defeat. My appetite was poor, to some extent because of the bad chow. Election day was a downer. For a few fleeting moments I listened to false rumors and thought Dewey had been elected. That made the letdown even worse. I was restless and disturbed, but I managed to write home in a couple of days and comment on Dewey's defeat. "I didn't have too many facts available, but I rather expected the results to be what they were.

I think it's a sad commentary on a great democracy when a majority
of the voters accept the 'indispensable' theory, but I guess it's just a
fact that has to be accepted.''

Franklin Delano Roosevelt had a landslide in electoral votes, 432
to 99, but a popular majority of only 3.6 million out of 47.6 million
votes cast. A noted historian would later write that in retrospect it
seemed remarkable that a 42-year-old governor with experience in
neither war nor diplomacy could come so close to toppling a world
leader at the height of a global war. There was some comfort to my
father that Dewey carried Kansas by 61 to 39 percent of its vote. As a
Republican in the New Deal era, my father was accustomed to
disappointing national elections. In his own race for Congress, he
was reelected by a wide margin.

Back at the war, the routine of several weeks was broken by
assignment to a week of KP. At the end of the first day, I found
myself scrubbing pots and pans after supper in the dark with rain and
sleet beating down on the tarpaulin. On the second day, an VIII Corps
lieutenant colonel dropped in for inspection. There was the usual
''mess-kit rattling,'' my diary said. This was the way we referred to
the anxiety caused by the sudden appearance of an inspecting officer.
Twelve men in the battery left for 48-hour rest camp at Arlon. This
was supposed to be a continuing policy, so I had something to hope
for. The week of KP was helped by a good discussion of politics and
economics with Gross and Anfuso one night. We didn't reach any
conclusions but I found myself pretty well agreeing with Gross on the
laws of economics. His basic argument, of course, always boiled
down to his fundamental belief that the moneyed classes are most fit
to rule. Anfuso, on the other hand, had excellent theories, but his
''everything will turn out all right in the end'' philosophy seemed to
regard violent revolutions and the human misery they bring far too
lightly. My fundamental point was that constant change, that is
evolution, is absolutely necessary and to be preferred to revolution.
Naturally, I was prejudiced in favor of my own arguments, I admitted
to my diary, as I rated the discussion one of the ''most elevated'' I'd
ever heard in the outfit.

Within the space of a few days, I received three packages from
home and opened them at once. ''I suppose it'll be a disappointment
to you that I didn't save it all until Christmas,'' I wrote my parents.
''It wasn't curiosity so much as the fact that I thought they would be

easier to carry around and less likely to become lost that prompted me to open them." Included were a Sumner Welles book, a pound of Bond Street tobacco, a tobacco pouch, and pictures. I wrote Martha that I especially like her picture and would rather have it than anything else. Whenever I asked for something to be sent, my mother marked the margin of the letter. (I saw this when I went through the letters years later.) Then she moved heaven and earth to get the item. If she couldn't, she always let me know it was unattainable.

My family got a full report on my KP duties. The pot washing was done outdoors even though it was snowing all week. It hadn't been cold enough to freeze the ground, so there was considerable sliding around in the mud as we juggled the cooking utensils in the dark. As it turned out, I didn't make it through the week. Late one night I began getting chills and a fever. Sergeant Thompson called Captain Lemberg, the medical officer, and tried to talk him into coming to see me. Lemberg refused, so an ambulance was called to take me to the aid station. My temperature was a little above 103 degrees. The next day I was sent to the 10th Clearing Station in Trois Vierges (Three Virgins), Luxembourg. Along with the fever and chills, I developed an upset stomach and dysentery. I felt fairly miserable. Although I didn't like our section chief, Sergeant Thompson, and he knew it, he went to bat for me as he did for all of his men when they were in trouble.

Four days in the hospital seemed like an eternity. Between stomach pains and vomiting, I felt pretty good. I read *Time for Decision* and *Yank* magazine. A Red Cross Clubmobile girl named Betty, from Johnson County, Kansas, brought doughnuts in the afternoon. By the fourth day, I was so restless I begged to go back to the Sixteenth although I wasn't entirely over the GIs. I figured I could handle that better than the claustrophobia and going without mail and a bath. So I was "home" a few days before Thanksgiving Day. I went to church services at Oudler that day with Winsor and came back to a complete turkey dinner. "Best meal I've ever had at Hdq. Kitchen," I told my diary. The kitchen crew had gone to great lengths to prepare this dinner, complete with a mimeographed, folded menu with a turkey sketched on the cover.

Carus, Leman, Andrews, Atkinson, and I decided we were bored with seeing the same GI faces, so on Thanksgiving evening we visited a farm home west of Aldringen. In addition to the parents,

MENU FOR THANKSGIVING DAY
Thursday, November 23, 1944
Cream of Tomato Soup
Dutch Roast Turkey
Cranberry Sauce
Creamed Giblet Gravy
Buttered Sweet Potatoes
Escalloped Corn
French Peas
Cabbage and Apple Salad
Layer Cake
Apple Pie
Peach Pie
Bread — Butter — Coffee
Assorted Candies

PREPARED BY

Mess Sergeant .... 1st Sgt Buren H. Jordan
Cooks .... Tec 4 Makstaller
Tec 4 Dallavalle
Tec 5 McMillen
Pfc. Sorg

there were three daughters and a Belgian boyfriend. The other guys didn't stay long, but I hung around until past midnight. The conversation, conducted through the medium of my small French-English dictionary, was sparse and slow but I enjoyed it. I passed out chewing gum and tobacco. During our remaining weeks in Aldringen, I returned several times to visit the family. I was interested, of course, in the girls, who were plump but pretty. We called them the Three Virgins. To the best of my knowledge no one in our outfit changed their status.

At about this time I was assigned as one of three guards for a member of the outfit who had been courtmartialed and sentenced for "fraternizing." At that time, fraternizing meant association, alone, with a girl or woman. It was not at all uncommon. But this poor private was caught at it and was, I believed, serving time as an example to the rest of us. He was a man I knew at Fort Bragg. For the most part, prisoner and guards had a pleasant time of it. We were quartered in two upstairs rooms in a house in Maldingen. For several mornings I took the prisoner in the pitch-black dark to fire up the stove in the mess hall and scrub tables. I accompanied him to chop wood, go to the dentist, and to get typhus shots (fleas and flea bites were a problem in the camp). In the evenings we reminisced about the good old days at Fort Bragg. In our informal arrangement, we guards slept through the night instead of taking shifts to guard our prisoners. That changed, however, when new restrictions were announced for the prisoner. Recalling the number of courtmartials in our outfit, we decided it'd be a good idea to stand guard.

My intermittent frustration and impatience prompted me to think about asking for a transfer to the infantry, but Ed Kahner, in his usual logical and patient manner, talked me out of it. He said I wouldn't be contributing any more to the war effort there than where I was and, while my job in the outfit was insignificant, a replacement would have to be found for it. He also warned the infantry would mean long hours on guard at outposts.

The end of November was notable only for a trip to the 102d Evacuation Hospital at Ettelbruck, Luxembourg, for X-ray and possible extraction of a wisdom tooth. The dentist decided that filling the tooth would suffice for the time. The electric power was off that day so the "power" for the dentist's drill was provided by a Tec. 5 assistant pumping a treadle, much the same as on oldtime sewing machines. After the visit to the dentist, I wrote in my diary that the nurses at the hospital were a "sight for sore eyes." Having seen only the Three Virgins and other girls who looked much like them for some weeks (except for the Red Cross girl), I thought every nurse looked like a beauty queen. A visit to the farm with Carus and Jim O'Connell the next week to see the virgins confirmed that observation. The parents, as always, stayed up. We showed them a copy of *Life* magazine and explained war maps to them. After everyone yawned for about a half-hour, we decided it was time to leave. It was all of 10:30 p.m.!

My love life was at a low point. I was phasing out Barbara, and Irene was phasing me out. I wrote home about Irene, complaining I hadn't heard for a long time. I decided it was for one, or both, of two reasons: "1) She's pulling a Helen (or a Sallie) on me and will wind up with some obnoxious Naval ensign or something horrible like that or 2) I might have accidentally mailed her a letter written to some other girl." I could've slipped up like that, I rationalized, although I did try to be careful. My mother concluded a long newsy letter with expressions of agonizing concern and flowery praise. It made me feel guilty. After all, the autumn "sitzkrieg" (sitting war) of the VIII Corps was in sharp contrast to the "blitzkrieg" (German for "lightning war"). She carried on about how difficult it was to go about her daily tasks and live a normal, comfortable life while I was out there doing so much for mankind. She asked to hear about as much of my activities and hard times as I was allowed to tell. "It's a thousand times easier to know than to imagine what you are doing."

I took my mother to task for having written about a family friend who had washed out as an aviation cadet and would now be transferred to the army ground forces. She made it sound as if this was a terrible demotion. "It seems to me," I pontificated, "you rather belittle the Army Ground Forces. After all, it's still the infantryman that wins wars — and a look at the casualty lists will prove it. And he does it in mud and snow and cold without the benefit of pinks and hotel rooms, etc. All the high-powered publicity of the Air Force can't subtract from that either. I just don't think there's enough realization that the infantry is still the queen of battles." Still fired up the next day, I wrote a short, critical essay on "The Theory of the Indispensable Man." This was occasioned by F.D.R.'s reelection. I also wrote a short piece on "What I Have Learned About Life from Being a Private in the Army in the United States and Europe." This consisted of my observations and excuses for being only a pfc. after 21 months of service. That writing was without literary merit or redeeming social value.

There was a private in one of our survey sections who had been in show business in some capacity, and he surely did know how to put on a performance. My diary noted that he had "everyone rolling in the aisles with his jokes and recitations of limericks." I didn't copy down any of his material but one limerick I could never forget. It went something like this:

> There was a soldier named Arter,
> Who was known as the world's greatest farter,
> He could fart anything
> From God Save the King
> To Beethoven's Moonlight Sonata!

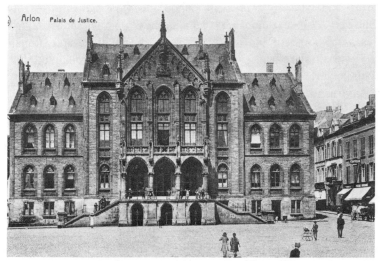

Palais de Justice in Arlon, Ardennes, Belgium, where the VIII Corps rest camp was located in the fall of 1944. (Postcard, Ern. Thill, Bruxelles.)

R and R (Rest and Recreation) for us GIs in the fall of 1944 was provided on two levels. The lucky ones received three-day passes to Paris. The second-class passes were for two days at the VIII Corps rest camp at Arlon, Belgium, a pretty town south of Bastogne on the Luxembourg border. I envied those who had been to Paris. There were, I later learned, some things to do in Paris besides shacking with hookers and boozing, but cultural activities got scant mention. Most married GIs had little to say upon their return from Paris but the single ones, especially those of my age, were interrogated endlessly. Back then, Paris probably was the easiest place in the world for a young soldier to lose his innocence, all for a thousand French francs and no floundering around, fuss or bother. "Well, I met this poor unfortunate woman who needed money," was the way one young buck put it. My longing for a trip there was dampened somewhat by another young returnee who came down with the clap several weeks after his visit. Nonetheless, I continued to dream of an evening or two in Paris.

A two-day pass to the Arlon rest camp, designated Chateau Monarch, was what I got on December first. I wrote a sanitized version of my experiences there to my parents. For the camp, the army had taken over a girls' school near the outskirts of town. Showers, blanket delousing, clean clothes, a barber shop, and movies were some of the amenities offered. All that, and ordnance cleaned our carbines! I was just beginning to get acquainted with a Belgian girl when it was time to leave. Reports of inflation in Europe were true. I spent about 1,200 Belgian francs in two days and had little to show for it. There was all the difference in the world between the French-speaking and the German-speaking regions of Belgium. It was a relief to get to the rest camp and away from a village where huge piles of cow manure seemed to be the main features of all residences. My most vivid recollection of those two days is of drinking one cognac after another in the Golden Ball Cafe while listening to an ancient, scratchy record player grind out, over and over, "It's a Sin to Tell a Lie" and "The Cowboy's Wedding Day" on the flip side. I met the Belgian girl, Emilie, at the Golden Ball. She appeared to be about 16 going on 25 but I left Arlon as innocent as I had arrived.

I didn't spend all of my time in Arlon drinking cognac and trying to go astray. On the second day, I wrote my father just to bounce off some ideas. They were extensions of ones I had already expressed, but I wanted to share them. "Going on the assumption that unconditional surrender and/or armistice terms have been definitely agreed upon," I began, "it's still fairly logical to assume that much remains to be done along the line of planning practical peace machinery." I explained that none of my ideas were exactly original, but they seemed more concrete than anything I'd seen. I enclosed eight and a half hand-written pages, making a special effort to make a left-handed scrawl legible. The title was "Plan for a Limited Government of the United Nations." I spent considerable time during the fall formulating those plans from what I was able to read and think about. I did not know that the Dumbarton Oaks proposal for a United Nations had been published on 2 December.

On 11 December I acknowledged receipt of the *U.S. News & World Report* that contained the United Nations organization proposals. "They rather supersede those ideas of mine which I sent you about 10 days ago, but of course I hadn't seen the Dumbarton Oaks proposals then," I wrote in another letter home. Actually, I was really surprised at what I perceived to be the close parallel between them. The following January, Representative Ed Rees of Kansas had my proposals published in the appendix to the *Congressional Record*, thereby proving that then, as now, almost anything may be published in it if one can find a cooperative member of Congress.

Our survey section officer, Lt. George Jones, left on 5 December to help form a new observation battalion. We were sorry to see him go. Like Lt. "Red" Tyler, he had not "acted like an officer." He had visited with us about our interests and problems, and he brought us his supply of Scotch when he left. Officers received periodic liquor rations; enlisted men did not. He even went to the same shower with us. Jones' departure left Staff Sgt. Gordon S. Thompson in charge of our section.

Bruno returned from Paris the day before I got back from Arlon. I wrote to my parents that "as with all the other boys who've been there, he hasn't been quite the same since." I added plaintively, "I guess Paris is still Paris and I hope to be able to find out for myself sometime." I recorded in my diary Bruno's report of a man on the street in Paris picking up cigarette butts by flashlight at 3:30 a.m. "Don't knock yourself out — here, have one," Bruno said as he grandly offered the man a fresh cigarette.

The monotony of the continuing sitzkrieg was alleviated by visits to more homes in Aldringen. I went with Don Gindele, Anfuso, Bruno, and Jim to the priest's house. The priest turned out to be quite a character. A roly-poly man, he was 66 years old but seemed much younger. He spoke German, French, and some Italian and could read and understand Spanish. He had the best home in the village and a large, well-trained German Police dog. The same night, we went to another home to listen to records, including German marching songs. The residents got faraway looks in their eyes as they listened. I took this as a prime example of the psychology which governs the German race. The marches are "action-compelling," a diary note said. I wrote, "I'm just damn glad I wasn't raised here or I too would undoubtedly be goose-stepping with the rest." A V-mail letter home that week closed on a melancholy note: "I don't know when you think the war will end; I don't even think about it anymore myself."

The military situation in our area in early December was summed up in the after action report:

1 December 1944
This battalion remained in position in the Belgium-Germany-

Luxembourg sector on the VIII Corps Front. There was virtually no change in the military situation during the preceding month. The VIII Corps was committed to a holding action, the objective of the Corps being to maintain their positions along the German border and their penetrations inside the Siegfried Line. The primary missions of this unit remained the same; namely, to sound and flash range on enemy installations and carry survey control for gun battalions.

From 9 December through 14 December several units from the battalion participated in a special mission in Luxembourg under VIII Corps direction in response to orders from the First Army. The purpose was to fake a buildup of strength in the hope of drawing enemy units from the Aachen sector. A few lines in my diary alluded to a "great hush-hush about 9 men from Party 1 and Peltz going someplace on D.S. (detached service)." Except for the participants, who were sworn to secrecy, most of us GIs never knew the purpose of the exercise and heard only rumors about what happened. It was not until I got the after action reports from the National Archives in 1981 that I learned the details. The units from the Sixteenth worked in the Graulinster-Beidweiler (spelled Birdweiler in the official report) area of Luxembourg, near the highway running northeast from Luxembourg City to Echternach.

The report, entitled Special Mission, started with the date of 9 December. To conceal its true purpose, the incident was called "Mission to Moscow." It had many odd features — officers were given temporary ranks to place the mission on the level of a higher headquarters, and vehicles were re-marked with new unit numbers and given new code names. The primary mission was to carry survey control for field artillery units of the VIII Corps. Their secondary mission was to put in a "blind" sound network. Vehicles were to cruise through the adjacent towns displaying the new unit designations. After the mission was completed, the mission unit identifications were obliterated. No information was to be disclosed concerning the mission. The last paragraph of the report, dated 13 December, stated, "An unforeseen accident marred the entire mission. The nature of the accident was pending investigation at last reports. Two enlisted men were killed and one command and reconnaissance car was a total loss." What the official report treated rather casually were the deaths of Tec. 4 Gordon Priebe and Pfc. J. Michael, driver of the vehicle. Somewhat later, it was reported that a cable was stretched across the highway and Priebe and Michael were ambushed. The official battalion history, compiled after V-E Day, does not list Priebe and Michael as being either killed or missing in action. In fact, it does not make any reference to them or to Pvt. Joseph Turansky, who was killed in a carbine accident on 13 October.

My diary entry for Friday, 15 December, was: "Very blue today — extreme restlessness." Little did I know then that in the days to come I would forget about restless and become even more blue.

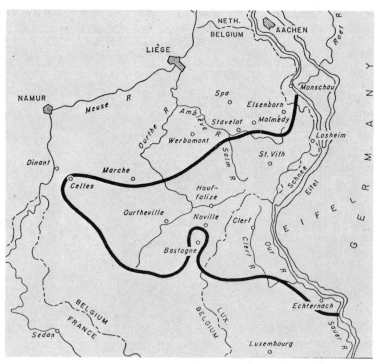

The limit of the German advance during the Battle of the Bulge, 16-26 December 1944.

Chapter 6

Retreat! Back and Forth across the Ardennes

Many books and articles have been written, and are still being written as new source material becomes available, about the Ardennes campaign, commonly known as the Battle of the Bulge. The "bulge" was the huge gap blasted through the VIII Corps sector by three German armies. By Christmas Day 1944 it reached to within four miles of the Meuse River near Dinant in east-central Belgium. The story I am going to relate concerns what happened to our rather obscure battalion (it is not mentioned in any history of the Bulge that I have found) and more particularly to those of us in the survey sections of the Headquarters Battery. It also concerns what my parents were thinking and doing in the first terrible days of the Bulge.

But first, a brief description of the situation in the VIII Corps area on the morning of 16 December. Allied intelligence had rated the Germans as having no capacity for a counteroffensive anywhere and most especially not in the Ardennes. The front of 145 kilometers (88 miles) was held by three green or tired infantry divisions, plus part of the inexperienced 9th Armored Division and the 14th Cavalry Group. In the area of northern Luxembourg, the 28th Division, decimated by battles in the Huertgen Forest and needing 3,400 replacements, arrived on 19 November. To the south, the 4th Division, also weakened in the Huertgen battles and needing as many or more replacements, arrived on 7 December. To the north of the 28th was the green 106th Division, which had gone into the line only five days before the Bulge began. It occupied the Schnee Eifel just inside Germany and a part of the West Wall (Siegfried Line). The Eifel area of Germany was an extension of the Ardennes in Belgium and Luxembourg, heavily forested, with many streams and ravines. A

(Able) Battery of the Sixteenth was headquartered in Auw, Germany, just west of the Schnee Eifel; it had observation posts on the Eifel. B (Baker) Battery was headquartered at Binsfeld, Luxembourg, to the south with observation posts to the east. Headquarters Battery was stationed in the villages of Aldringen and Maldingen, Belgium, southwest of St. Vith and west of the Schnee Eifel.

Altogether on that Saturday morning in 1944 the VIII Corps had 68,822 officers and men, including us, holding a front three times the length that American military doctrine prescribed for a force of this size. On 15 December, the battalion after action report stated, "The military situation was unchanged. Our Sound Outposts reported enemy armor massing along the Schnee Eifel ridge. Unusually heavy enemy patrol activity indicated that the Germans were preparing for a counteroffensive." Few of us soldiers knew that on that day, however. Because of the detailed written records, my diary notes, and a number of letters written during this period, my account for the remainder of 1944 will be on a day-to-day basis.

Saturday, 16 December

"The enemy opened a large scale counteroffensive along the Schnee Eifel ridge," the after action report stated. "The attack was preceded by 1-1/2 hours of artillery preparation. The enemy reached the town of Auw by 0900."

Going out to survey that morning just west of Schönberg, I was rear rodman. The artillery fire was very heavy. German shells were landing just over the hill from us. Lieutenant Tyler came out shortly after noon to bring us in just as two buzz bombs, one very low, exploded near us. We were told to get all personal equipment ready and loaded into vehicles.

In the meantime, A Battery was ordered to evacuate its installations, and within a couple of hours the convoy began to move toward Maldingen. Colonel Lushene left for VIII Corps Artillery to speak to the general about withdrawing the battalion to a safer position. He returned late in the afternoon. By the end of the day, the after action report recorded, all men in A Battery were accounted for and safe, with the exception of nine men missing from two flash observation posts (OPs). Missing were the entire crew of OP #2 — Sergeant Buchanan, Private Bogart, Private Drosin, and Private Bunten — plus Corporal Van Houten, Sergeant Goldberg, Sergeant

Eleks, and Private Mosheim from Lieutenent Bryan's OP. The ninth member of A Battery not reporting was Private Triplett, who was last seen driving a vehicle. It was believed that the two crews had been surrounded and captured before they could escape. It was apparent that A Battery also lost a lot of equipment.

Amid reports and rumors, the day of confusion ended in complete bewilderment. The power was off and lights were out. The word had gone around that the 106th Division, nicknamed "the Hungry and Sick," and/or "General Allan Jones' Three Ring Circus," had numerous lights on the night before and that the officer of the day (OD) had a flare sent up to inspect the guard. As night fell, our retreating tanks and 155mm howitzers were massing at road junctions. There were many flashes and much heavy firing all through the night.

It is difficult to describe my feelings that evening. To say "shock and dismay" would be an understatement. I had seen training films on every conceivable subject, I thought, but never one on how to retreat. As noncombat troops, we were sorely unprepared. At least I was. I still had never fired a machine gun. I fired one round on a bazooka at Fort Bragg, and perhaps threw a hand grenade there once. I had not fired a shot at anything since qualifying on the Fort Bragg firing range on the Enfield rifle in 1943 and on the carbine that last spring in the U.S., which seemed so far away in time and space. The "mountaineers" from West Virginia and Kentucky and others in our outfit were skilled hunters. They were always firing at something, or so it seemed. I had never hunted anything. I enjoyed basic training on the 105mm howitzer but the battalion didn't have any of those things around.

That night, unaware of the counteroffensive, both my parents wrote to me. My father was in Chicago attending hearings of the Special House Committee on Postwar Economic Policy and Planning, commonly known as the Colmer Committee, which had been established earlier that year. My mother wrote in some detail of the family's preparations for Christmas. She told about decorating the house with pine branches and cones, red ribbons and candles. "We're doing things for Christmas just as we would if you could be here with us because we know that's the way you'd have us do. And of course Daddy and I owe Martha a Happy Christmas even if we can't give you one."

Sunday, 17 December

Any thought that the counteroffensive might be only a small-scale affair was dispelled. "It was now apparent," the after action report spelled out, "that the enemy counteroffensive was an all-out attack supported by about fourteen divisions, including five armored divisions." Our 106th Division, on Schnee Eifel Ridge, was surrounded. Its position was critical. The enemy had made good progress toward Bastogne in the 28th Division sector. Some corps artillery installations were overrun.

My own account of this Sunday in December was written two days later. By then, I wrote, I had had "a very sketchy, yet panoramic, view of the American Army in retreat." The rumor of the day before that the Germans had been driven back to their starting point was all wet. Both of our survey parties went out on the Prum road beyond St. Vith to put in a sound base, only to be called back in by Lieutenant Tyler in about two hours. Withdrawn from the front, 9th Armored Division tanks were massed in the forest and some were firing from open fields. There was considerable air activity as well. A 4.5-inch gun battery moved into the back of the schoolhouse in Aldringen at noon. Survey went out again in the afternoon, this time to the Crombach area to put in another sound base. Again, we were called in after two hours. By now, retreating 155mm howitzers were moving into Maldingen. There was movement everywhere, all of it moving back from our sitzkrieg positions. I carefully stuck my Michelin Map No. 4 inside one of my leggings. Who knew how long we'd be together as a unit? In blackout, we hastily packed, loaded the vehicles, and headed for Langlir. Shelton drove our weapons carrier into the ditch twice on the way and also hit a Belgian gendarme on a bicycle. After waiting around in a field for a considerable length of time, we bedded down in a barn. Langlir was a small village directly west of our starting point and north of Cherain and Houffalize.

We soon learned that 17 December was indeed Black Sunday. Kampfgruppe (Combat Group) Peiper, a part of the dreaded 1st SS Panzer Division, the Adolf Hitler Lifeguard Division, led by Obersturmbannfuehrer (Lieutenant Colonel) Jochem Peiper, had begun murdering prisoners. To the north of us, the Kampfgruppe shot 19 unarmed Americans at Honsfeld and another 50 at Bullingen. Then, at a crossroads south of Malmedy, they intercepted B Battery of the 285th Field Artillery Observation Battalion. This battalion was on its

Retreat to the west, 16-20 December. (From *U.S. Army in World War II: The Ardennes*, 1965.)

way to join ours; its advance party, in fact, was already with us. About a 150 GIs were marched into an open field and mowed down by machine gun and pistol fire. At least 86 were killed. This was the infamous Malmedy Massacre. The war continued to worsen.

Monday, 18 December
The retreat continued with all VIII Corps installations withdrawing. The bulk of the 106th Division, hopelessly trapped on Schnee Eifel ridge, continued to hold out, and St. Vith remained in our hands. But German paratroopers dropping behind our lines inflicted much damage, especially at the supply point of Gouvy. Bastogne was almost surrounded but was being held by the 101st Airborne Division, which had been rushed up to the front.

My survey group started the day by going out to put in a sound base beyond Bovigny, but we came back in immediately. On the road we witnessed the pitiful sight of refugees with their meager belongings. American sympathizers, they now were in danger of being turned in to the Germans by their neighbors. We heard that the U.S. 7th, 11th, and 12th Armored Divisions were to be thrown in to stop the German drive. The night before, we saw the Seventh massed in fields near our former battery command post. One bright spot was having Ed Kahner back with us. He had been at 102d Evacuation Hospital at Ettelbruck and escaped just before its reported capture. He had ridden with a mail orderly to Bastogne.

In the afternoon both survey parties went out to put in a sound base. Party One was about two miles from Bovigny when it met refugees who reported that the Germans were there. The party beat a hasty retreat, meeting my party on the road down to Cherain. Together, we returned to Langlir, where we found the battalion preparing to evacuate. The battalion closed all installations at Langlir by early afternoon, and an hour later enemy tanks were reported at Cherain. Upon hearing this, Colonel Lushene ordered the battalion to move back toward La Roche. According to my diary, we were waiting

---

Opposite: A section of one of the Michelin Map sheets (here reduced slightly) used by the U.S. Army. This particular map was carried by Ed Kahner during the Battle of the Bulge, and the route followed by his unit was marked on it. The author's own map disintegrated after being stuffed into his duffel bag or leggings for many weeks, during which it was consulted frequently, soaked when he crossed streams, torn by the wind, and otherwise roughly used.

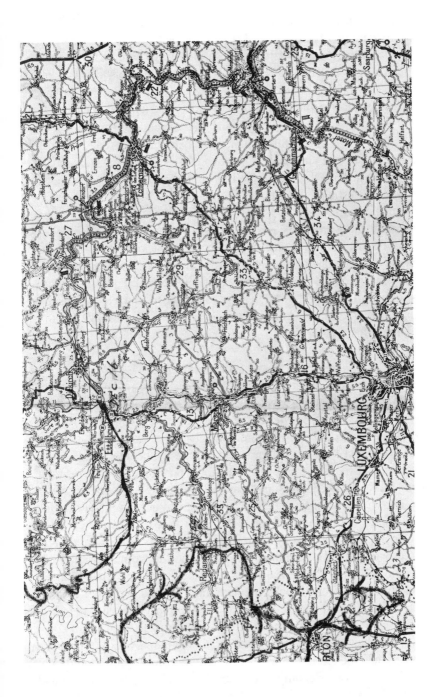

around in the field when we heard that paratroopers were in Cherain. There were no officers around. Everyone became more tense by the minute. Vehicles were stuck in the field. Firing could be heard about four kilometers from Langlir. A German machine pistol was heard down the road. Perhaps that was what got us moving. At last we moved out to get on the main road to La Roche.

I shall never forget the expression on the faces of the people of the first village we passed through on the way to the main road," I wrote a few days later in my diary. "An expression of utter amazement and hopeless(ness). Oh God! I shall never forget it!"

Heavy traffic made progress agonizingly slow. The convoy turned from the main road toward Houffalize and went three kilometers before turning around. Confusion reigned. There was a liaison plane burning in a field. We reached La Roche in blackout after about four hours on the road and went to a wooded area 10 kilometers beyond on the road to St. Hubert. There we spent the night, sleeping while sitting up in our vehicles. It could have been worse. Our turning around on the road to Houffalize was fortuitous. Houffalize fell into German hands that night!

Tuesday, 19 December

We spent all day in the woods. The enemy offensive continued with increasing intensity but details were obscure. There was nothing we were sure about. After being on road guard for two hours, I left with the others at dark for Champlon. Champlon was a small village a short distance southeast of the woods where we spent the night. It was just east of the important road junction where the Bastogne-Marche and La Roche-St. Hubert highways intersected. We stopped at a nice house with a wonderful family and were just getting ready to drink chocolate and clean up when all of us in Party Two were called to form a road block east of town. Bruno, who was left behind on KP, told us the family stayed up all night, and the woman cried at our leaving. Enemy armor was reported to be driving on Champlon. In addition to the road blocks, the battalion set up a perimeter defense for security consisting of bazooka teams and machine guns placed at strategic intersections. The mission was to provide security for corps artillery headquarters, also located at Champlon. I took a bazooka position to the left of a side road, watching from 10 p.m. to midnight and 2 to 4 a.m., sleeping, after a fashion, in blankets on the ground nearby between shifts. It was chilly and damp. All through the night the enemy was reported to be drawing closer.

Unlike much of the area, the terrain on either side of our road block was open, bare field. There was no snow but the ground was frozen. We tried to dig slit trenches (foxholes) of sorts with picks and shovels. It was a futile effort, because several inches below the surface we hit a shale-like formation. The picks hitting the shale all across the field sounded a lot like the "Anvil Chorus," I thought. During the preceding months our bazooka rockets, encased in cardboard cylinders, lay on the floor of the weapons carrier. We stepped on the cases often as we jumped in or out the back end of the vehicle. As I sat there in the open field holding a bazooka, I wondered if the thing would misfire and blow up, taking me with it. That could have been spectacular — I had hand grenades attached to my jacket. Rumor had it that we were awaiting the arrival of the 1st SS Panzer Division and perhaps the Kampfgruppe Peiper. Not a happy thought. Later we learned that those thugs were still to the northeast, west of Malmedy at the north edge of the Bulge. However, the 2d SS Panzer Division, the Das Reich Division, was in our general area. It was as tough as the 1st.

Not everyone in our outfit was on duty that night. Word got around about an officer of our battalion who was found, bottle in hand, drunk in the bell tower of the church. It took four men to bring him down.

Wednesday, 20 December

Survey Party One, led by Staff Sgt. Robert H. Mason, relieved our party in the morning. Bob Mason was a West Virginia mountaineer, tall and slender and only a year or two older than I. He was a natural leader, especially in time of crisis, yet he was warmhearted and had a good sense of humor. Because he had perfected an imitation of Donald Duck, he called himself "the Duck." By Bob's recollection, they had two bazookas, one 50-caliber machine gun, 38 pounds of high explosives, and various small weapons. He remembered, "We dug into the farm trail's rutty tracks and planted 19 pounds of the explosive under each track a tank could crawl over. The explosive was wired to a small battery which I held in my hands. It was of sufficient voltage to set off the charges. We had a forward observer, in the fog, about 600 feet ahead, to listen for approaching enemy tanks. There were rumbles and gunfire beyond our station, but nothing appeared in our vicinity. At some time, just before dusk, our first sergeant rode up in a Jeep and cleared us out.'' Lieutenant Tyler and Mason's group were the last to leave Champlon. The rest of us, under orders to continue our retreat, left about noon. Everyone was mad and disgusted at having to retreat after making efforts to halt the enemy.

The Germans continued to make progress on all fronts, although the flanks were holding firm south of Bastogne and north of St. Vith. While the situation in the center remained confused, it was definitely established that one enemy spearhead was driving on La Roche. The battalion moved back to Bande, a few kilometers to the northwest, in the most disorderly convoy yet. On our way we passed the 740th Field Artillery Battalion. They had two guns left. At Bande the battalion vehicles were regrouped, and at dusk we set out for Neu-villers, several miles to the southwest. The unit drove blackout most of the way, arriving at the destination shortly before midnight. We slept in a barn that night. We learned later that ragtag groups of noncombat GIs all over the Ardennes battle area delayed or stopped the Panzers, much to the Germans' surprise. At the time I thought we would have been slaughtered if the Panzers or armored infantry had arrived, but in retrospect I believe we, too, might have given a good account of ourselves. Although many of us were scared, God knows we were also plenty mad.

Meanwhile, back in the States, my father had a traumatic experience. It began on 18 December and I am sure it was experienced by the families of almost everyone in our outfit. It wasn't until after V-E Day that he told me about it.

''I didn't worry a lot at any time except during the Ardennes battle. . . . I figured you were able to take care of yourself pretty well and would pull through O.K. But I wasn't that way during the Ardennes battle. No one, not even Mother, has any idea of the agony I went through at that time.'' He was in Chicago at hearings held by the Post-War Committee, he explained. Finishing up, he started back to his hotel. Newsboys on the street were crying out, ''Nazis murder U.S. captives.'' He bought a paper and was horrified and then stunned. ''When I read it was an observation battalion,'' he wrote, ''everything just about went black in front of me, because I felt sure you must be somewhere in the neighborhood, and I knew there couldn't be a lot of observation battalions in that small area.''

It wasn't until two days later, when he had returned to Washington, that he was able to verify the Sixteenth was not the observation battalion which had been massacred. Fortunately, my mother, at home in Washington and terribly worried about the Battle of the Bulge, had not seen the massacre story and did not learn of it until my father was able to give her the details.

Thursday, 21 December

While the general military picture remained obscure, the enemy continued to make progress. But this date marked the high point, or perhaps the low point, of our five-day retreat. It was over. It was also my 21st birthday. I was tired and dirty but alive and thankful. I was in good spirits as I went out with the survey parties to put in a control for gun batteries which turned out not to be there. We were called in to move with the outfit, leaving Neuvillers to head for the French border. We picked up all the gasoline we could carry in a dump in the woods to our south. The convoy proceeded by a roundabout route to Matton in France, arriving about 4 p.m. Matton was far behind the front lines. The battalion was to get rehabilitated and reorganize for combat. I went with Schlusing and Bruno to a house where we washed and shaved for the first time in five days. That evening we received our first mail, including Christmas packages, since our retreat had begun. We were grateful, of course, but the gifts added to all the stuff we were lugging around. I muttered about that to myself. There was a toilet kit from Irene. It didn't seem to matter that much. The Bulge had advanced me another notch in growing up.

On 20 December my father wrote me a birthday message which was warm, sentimental, and filled with encouragement. He commented that it looked as if I would be celebrating my birthday by fighting in the greatest battle of the war. ''Your mother and I certainly didn't think it was going to be this way when we held you in our arms 21 years ago and were so happy that we again had a baby boy after losing our first one.'' (Edward Hope died at the age of five months in February 1923; I was born ten months later.) Although the war interrupted my plans, he suggested that perhaps the experiences I was having might be just what I needed to round out my life and character. ''Tomorrow for the 22nd time, I'm going to bring your Mother a beautiful poinsettia plant. You've been here every other time. You'll be here tomorrow as far as loving you, thinking of you and wanting you can bring you here," he concluded.

My mother wrote on December 21st, again carrying on about my "suffering and hardship." She said she was thankful she had been spared seeing or hearing the news of the Malmedy Massacre until my father returned home to tell her.

Friday, 22 December

Retreating into France wasn't as dramatic as it sounded. Matton was barely across the border, southwest of Florenville. It was raining when we awoke in Matton. Captain Carter gave us an orientation lecture on all available reports on the situation. The enemy was still unchecked, although the flanks of the line still held firm. St. Vith was still held. Bastogne was cut off. Units of the III Corps under General Patton's Third Army had started a counteroffensive to reach the isolated units still holding Bastogne. It was still hoped that the 101st Airborne Division there could manage to fight its way out. Three-fourths of southern Luxembourg was overrun.

The battalion spent the day taking equipment inventory and preparing lists of shortages. All vehicles were checked and repaired. Our outfit moved at dusk in convoy through Florenville east on the main road to Arlon and then turned off on a side road to Selange, nine kilometers south of Arlon. We arrived around 10 p.m. and were immediately attached to the III Corps of the Third Army. We bedded down on the floor of a bowling alley, next door to a tavern. Five cognacs before retiring eased five days of tension and assured a sound sleep.

Saturday, 23 December

Rehabilitated, the battalion was once again committed to combat. Five battalion survey parties, two from Headquarters, two from B and one from A, went out to survey, working in the Nagem, Luxembourg, area to carry forward corps artillery survey control. We went through Arlon and within one block of Cafe Boulder on our way to the Redange headquarters of the 26th Division. Less than a month before, I had spent a large part of a two-day pass at Cafe Boulder. We surveyed a loop from Redange toward Hostert through Aspern and back to Redange. Shortly after noon the battalion closed installations at Selange and moved northward to Oberpallen, Luxembourg. After installations were set up, Bruno and I went to a house to wash and then, after standing guard with Winsor and Bruno, I made my way to a barn to sleep.

Sunday, 24 December

The Third Army counteroffensive continued to make good progress north and occupied several towns. On the northern flank of the German drive, however, St. Vith fell to the Nazis. Morning in Oberpallen found us out on triangulation survey near Ospern to the benchmark beyond. A German patrol of six men was brought in from the woods near the benchmark soon after we got there. Two Messerschmidts strafed the 561st Field Artillery Battalion on the west edge of Ospern near us, but no casualties or damage were caused. There was plenty of machine gun fire around us. At some point during the day, we went into a house and took over the diningroom for awhile to get warm, and then seven of us went back to the house where Bruno and I had washed the night before. All of us got to wash with hot water, quite a treat for Christmas Eve. Okie's rejoining us was another cause for rejoicing. He had been on KP at VIII rest camp at Arlon, the rest camp naturally having been disbanded. He brought candy and peanuts, appropriate treats for Christmas Eve. This was the first time since 16 December that we'd spent two nights in the same village.

Monday, Christmas Day

We awakened early Christmas morning to the sound of a generator flashlight carried by the old man of the house as he walked through our room. Bruno said he thought a motorcycle had passed among us. Compared to the days that had preceded it, Christmas Day was not bad at all. The counteroffensive by the III Corps was going according to plan. The 101st Airborne Division still held Bastogne, and it appeared probable that the III Corps would soon relieve them and drive into the city. The weather was clear, giving the Allied air forces an excellent opportunity to destroy the German armor.

"Very tasty," I noted in my diary about the powdered eggs we had for breakfast. Where had my complaining gone? My party ran traverse from two kilometers below Hostert to Oberpallen in the morning. In the afternoon our command post was closed at Oberpallen and moved northward to Redange Attert, Luxembourg.

(Attert was the name of a small river.) This was only a short distance northeast of Oberpallen, but it was an advance, however small. Installations were set up and survey went out again. On the outskirts of Redange there were several chateaus. Bruno, Okie, and I along with several others made ourselves at home in the livingroom of one of them. There was a large fireplace with Chinese pottery on the mantel. Good copies of old masters hung on the walls. The place had class. It was a real change from what we had become accustomed to.

"What a lot I have to be thankful for this Christmas," I wrote in my diary. "I only hope the folks at home have not had their Christmas spoiled by undue anxiety." I received four packages and several letters. There was bright moonlight on Christmas night. I noted the contrast to the eerie fog we moved in when we were holding the line at Champlon. The artillery fire shook the windows of our cozy chateau, a reminder of the war that did not stop for holidays.

My first letter home since the retreat began started: "Christmas Day, somewhere in Luxembourg." I apologized for not being able to tell them much but guessed they probably had more news of the war than I did anyway. "Tonight, believe it or not, I'm writing this in front of a large fireplace in a sizeable mansion, something I wouldn't have believed possible a few days ago. Of course, it won't last but it's very nice for Christmas. Naturally, we didn't have a turkey dinner today, but we may have it tomorrow." On that night my mother and father were writing to me and my sister added a postscript. They shared Christmas Eve with an unexpected, but welcome, visitor, Rellis Eastman, a lonely 18-year-old Marine from Liberal, Kansas. He took my place in my parents' home that Christmas.

Tuesday, 26 December

The deepest German penetration into Belgium was stopped four miles from the Meuse River opposite Dinant. The counteroffensive of the American III Corps on the southern flank of the German salient progressed excellently. It appeared that relief was in sight for the beleaguered American garrison at Bastogne.

We left the magnificence of our chateau for the cold, crisp outdoors. A light snow covered the ground. We began survey at Martelange on the road to Arlon until we met B Battery survey parties, and then took off on the road to Bastogne. I was set up with the front rod on a hilltop with anti-aircraft halftracks below me when two Jerry-manned P-47s began a bombing and strafing attack. A bomb dropped on a hilltop about four hundred yards away, throwing earth two hundred feet in the air. It wrecked a trailer, killed one man, and wounded several others. I was sure the Jerry would be over on our hill next and was damned sure I'd be a goner. But both planes took off after releasing three more bombs farther east. The halftracks near me fired until they ran out of ammunition. We continued down the road to within seven or eight miles of Bastogne. Along the way, we saw a GI killed by a bomb, several German helmets, and two wrecked American halftracks. The road ahead of us was being strafed just before we turned back. Battery headquarters moved to Obermartelingen (the German name for Haut Martelange) in the afternoon to be closer to the front lines and to the artillery units advancing northward.

During the Bulge, the Germans made extensive use of captured equipment and arms. The P-47s that bombed us on this day were American fighter planes. This served a dual purpose for the enemy: it confused us in the first days of the offensive and it bolstered their equipment, which was in short supply. For our part, when we were attacked, we were frustrated in being armed only with carbines and having to depend upon the arms of other groups for our survival.

In my diary that night I wrote, "We had belated Christmas turkey dinner in a darkened machine shop, but naturally it tasted very good." We slept that night in the office building of a slate corporation. It was bitter cold. Back in Washington, my father was writing to me: "You're probably seeing more action than any Hope ever has in the history of this country." And then he proceeded to trace Hope warriors back to the Revolutionary War. He suggested I keep a diary or at least some notes of what I was doing if I had time. His comments about the action we were seeing continued to embarrass me. It seemed to me we were only observing it, not participating in it. I could not respond to his suggestion about keeping a diary for fear my diary (I was then on page 99) would be confiscated by a dutiful censor.

Wednesday, 27 December

The official word on this date had the Allied air forces continuing to inflict heavy losses on the enemy forces. The Germans were making very little headway in pressing toward Liège. The 4th

Battle of the Bulge aftermath. This is a German army photograph found by Lt. "Red" Tyler.

Armored Division finally broke into Bastogne to relieve the isolated 101st Airborne Division. Watching supplies dropped to Bastogne and taking a sponge bath were the highlights of the day for me. One hundred and thirty C47s, in three formations, dropped supplies over a period of a half-hour. It was something to see.

Our survey parties went out late in the morning after taking a tour of the slateworks building. In the basement we discovered two Mercedes Benzes and a Packard with red leather seats. We continued to survey on the road to Bastogne then moved off to the west beyond Warnach for triangulation. "I don't mind saying," I confided to the diary, "that I was a little uneasy on the hilltops as P47s were overhead again and again." But the bath, my first in two weeks, at the end of the day made me feel like a new man. Bruno had his own high for the day. He had a reputation for always running into generals. This time, as he told it, he was holding a red and white survey rod at the edge of the Arlon-Bastogne highway when who should wheel up but George Patton himself. "What are you doing, soldier?" the general asked. "Survey, Sir!" Bruno answered crisply.

The General drove on, perhaps muttering to himself, "What

now!'' in the manner of a later-day general in the comic strip ''Beetle Bailey.''

Thursday, 28 December

The enemy advance was being contained along the entire front. The Americans recaptured Echternach and surrounded a Nazi panzer column near Calles. The Germans were seriously hampered by a lack of gasoline. Our survey parties went out in the morning to continue work in the general direction of Bastogne, but we came in before long because of the dense fog. B Battery managed to survey in four microphones on their new sound base. Our survey group moved into a house in which Bruno and I shared a beautiful bed in a very cold room. Reading the most current copies of *Stars and Stripes*, I learned that all the places to which we had retreated up to Matton in France were now in German hands. I ended the day by writing to my parents and Irene. There wasn't a lot I could write about, but I let them know ''my hatred toward the Germans increases hourly.'' I had trouble writing, as my ink was half-frozen. ''Those Kiplinger predictions on the end of the war certainly were wacky; I hope all his dope isn't as inaccurate although I realize he's only reporting opinion.''

Friday, 29 December

We moved west to Petitvoir, a village west of Neufchateau. The III Corps had begun to consolidate its gains along the Belgium-Luxembourg border, and the VIII Corps was preparing an offensive to retake St. Hubert and the area to the northeast. Our battalion was switched from the III Corps and returned to VIII. Survey parties went out for triangulation west of the Bastogne highway in the morning but soon were called back. In the afternoon we went through Fauvillers to Neufchateau, doing triangulation near Tourney and returning to Petitvoir for the night. I was rodman for ''shooting Polaris'' in the evening. I never did understand why we ''shot Polaris'' with the transit periodically. All I knew was it seemed to happen on clear and very cold nights. After an hour on guard duty, I joined five others to spend the night in the livingroom of a house occupied by a nice family with three children.

Saturday, 30 December

The VIII Corps opened an offensive along a line between St.

A German army photograph of military personnel during the Battle of the Bulge, found by Lt. "Red" Tyler.

Hubert and Bastogne and made good progress during the first day. The enemy counteroffensive apparently had stopped at all points. We surveyed on the main highway from Neufchateau to the Recogne road junction and from there down the highway to Bouillon and Sedan, and we stayed all night in Petitvoir again. Our family treated us to cocoa.

Sunday, 31 December

New Year's Eve and we were geographically in almost the same place we had been on December 20. The difference was that we were advancing, not retreating. The VIII Corps offensive was progressing. Rochefort, at the tip of the German salient, was recaptured by American Third Army troops. A day of survey took us from the Recogne road junction to within five kilometers of St. Hubert. That night we moved into a schoolhouse in Libramont. There was a stove but, as usual, no lights. Libramont had been bombed often in the past week or so. The old year ended, not with a bang but a whimper in my diary: "My feet are finally beginning to feel the effects of prolonged cold. My toes hurt whenever my feet warm up. Quite a New Year's Eve. Dead tired and no cognac. I should think of something more

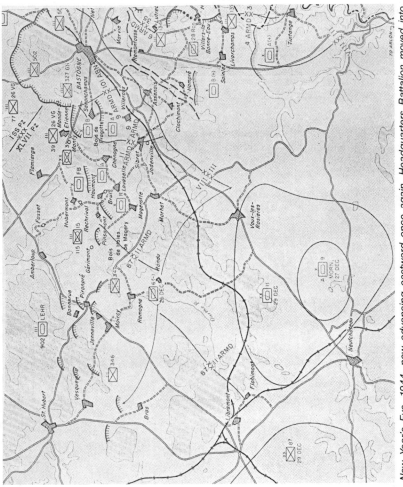

New Year's Eve, 1944, now advancing eastward once again. Headquarters Battalion moved into Libramont. (From U.S. Army in World War II: The Ardennes, 1965.)

worthwhile to say, but am too exhausted to do much more than stare stupidly into the gasoline lamp on the table before me.''

My father wrote a last-day-of-the-year letter. By this time, he had read news accounts of the first days of the Bulge: ''. . . Some real information as to how the breakthru occurred and what happened during the first three or four days when we were all in the dark over here as to what was going on.'' He said Wes Gallagher of the Associated Press had a good story in the paper that day which gave a good explanation of the situation. They still had not heard from me, of course. He guessed, ''We think that if your outfit didn't get trapped like some of the others in the actual breakthru that you've come thru in good shape.''

Our battalion was luckier than most. Since landing in France in mid-August, we had suffered three killed and nine missing in action, a low casualty rate statistically. But that was little comfort to those men and their families.

Chapter 7

From the Ardennes into the Eifel

On New Year's Day 1945 the Battle of the Bulge was far from over. By the official records, it lasted 25 days longer — until the Allied lines were in approximately the same position they were in on 16 December. But, except for local counterattacks, the Germans were in retreat and we were slowly advancing. The battalion was assigned to the VIII Corps of the Third Army in the first days in 1945. The primary mission, as outlined in the after action report, was unchanged. We were to continue sound and flash range on enemy targets and carry survey control for the field artillery units of the VIII Corps. The immediate aim of VIII Corps was to retake St. Hubert on the southern hinge of the German salient in the Ardennes. The eventual objective was Houffalize, a road junction northeast of St. Hubert.

In our outfit there were two events that didn't get into the official report that day. Tom Garos and a crew from our supply section were in Arlon to get rations for the battalion when about 15 German aircraft appeared suddenly and bombed the area without opposition for at least 10 minutes. Tom and his men scurried under nearby rail cars and came out unscathed. Others were not so lucky. And I started the new year on the wrong foot. On survey from Morhet to Sibret to the southwest of Bastogne, the weapons carrier I was driving slipped off the icy highway, hit a tree, and landed on its side in the ditch. I climbed out with only a scratched knee. About five minutes later, Sergeant Thompson came by and gave me hell. Then 15 minutes later, he returned to ask if I was hurt. This was truly typical of the kind of guy he was. I waited around for a maintenance truck to arrive. An

armored division wrecker already had come along to pull the
weapons carrier out of the ditch. It was after 8:30 p.m. when I got
back to the schoolhouse at Libramont. In addition to suffering a royal
ass-chewing by Thompson, I was humiliated because this accident
resulted in the loss of a needed vehicle for some time, causing
inconvenience to everyone in both survey sections. Of even greater
concern was the fear that I might be forced to sign a statement of
charges, agreeing to pay for the cost of the weapons carrier. For some
days I worried that I might have to stay in the army for years making
payments from my paltry $65 per month pfc. wage. That did not
come to pass, but I was not allowed to drive a vehicle for some time;
and that was all right with me.

The next day brought excitement of a different sort. In the evening
we moved east to Wideumont Gare and into a house filled with
Belgian refugees. Never one to go to bed as long as anyone else was
up, I went to the basement to get hot water from the stove. The room,
dimly lighted, was full of civilians whom I could barely see. In a
friendly manner, someone asked me to sit down on the floor. Just as I
did, a beautiful feminine voice across the room exclaimed, ''Oh, my
aching back!'' Thus did I meet Christine, the very pretty 19-year-old
niece of the owners of the house. Christine, from Arlon, was trapped
in Wideumont during the high tide of the German advance at Christmastime while she was visiting her aunt and uncle. Not only was she
pretty but she was also a nice girl, by my mother's standards, and the
kind with whom I could, and did, immediately fall in love. Much to
my consternation, and no doubt to her amusement, she became the
sweetheart of almost everyone in my age bracket in the outfit,
including Marvin Elting of the medics and my good buddy Bruno.
That first night was the height of my romance with Christine, I
suppose. The family brought out good coffee and bread and jam. I
distributed cigarettes, chocolate, and anything else I had to give in
return.

My diary entries for the next several days contain a curious mixture
of reports about Bastogne and its environs, the snow and bitter cold,
and, of course, Christine. On the third day of the year, survey started
out in the morning but dense fog turned us back before we had gone
more than a block. ''Spent the day doing nothing — what a heavenly
feeling,'' I told my diary. I also spent a lot of time with Christine and
her aunt and uncle. At midnight I stood guard for an hour out in the

cold, a strong wind driving the falling snow. In a heavy snowfall the next day, we surveyed from previous stations into Bastogne. I carried an umbrella for Peltz, who was operating the transit. Bastogne was pretty well wrecked. About half the buildings were destroyed or damaged beyond repair. It was extra sad to see a town, which you once saw intact, in ruins. The day's chores and the devastation of war were forgotten that night as Christine and I danced to the music of our section's record player. She was quite a good dancer but my feet were so frozen they seemed like two stumps. As I wrote in my diary, "I had a helluva time dancing."

While we were putting in a triangulation base near Bastogne the following afternoon, 10 to 15 shells landed on the road a few hundred yards behind us. As notekeeper, I stood next to the transit operator to record the angles turned and the distances taped in the surveyor's book. At the end of the day back in Wideumont, Christine's aunt and uncle, with the help of Elting, pulled a great gag on me by telling me Christine had gone back to Arlon. I'm sure my reaction amused them, but Christine and I danced to records again and we managed to escape the surveillance of Christine's aunt for about 30 seconds. Just long enough to give her a kiss — Christine, that is, not her aunt!

It was midafternoon when we went the next day to turn three angles north of Bastogne to tie in to the 101st Division Artillery. There was dancing again in the evening but no such luck as the night before. For my big moment, I had to settle for being asked by the aunt to go across the street to get Christine for supper. It was late afternoon when we started to Bastogne on January seventh for a couple of tie-in shots. As it was getting dark when we got there, we couldn't locate the forward point. Then guns cut loose with about the greatest artillery barrage I had heard so far. We spent about half of our time hugging the snowy ground. No one was hit. Back at our temporary home, I spent the evening in the kitchen with Bruno, Elting, Christine, and her aunt and uncle. For a couple of days, we just kind of hung around, wondering when we'd be moving on. One night, Elting began moving in on Christine. "I guess I must be losing my grip," I confided in my diary. "Of course his knowledge of French has something to do with it." We surveyed for three kilometers on the Marche road out of Bastogne on the morning of 10 January. In the afternoon we moved to Sibret. Elting impressed Christine again. I left Wideumont with a heavy heart. I told all about it in my diary:

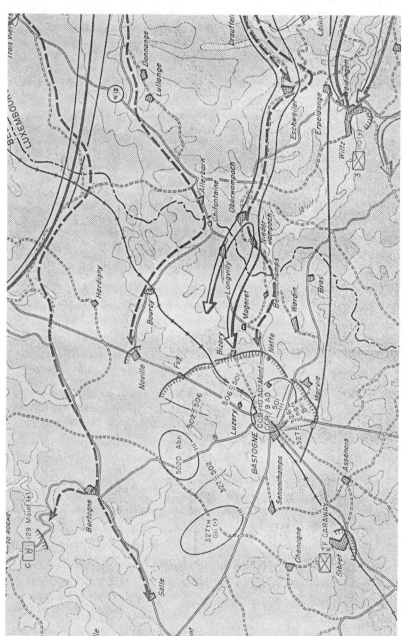

Sibret to Trois Vierges, 10 January to 26 January. (From U.S. Army in World War II: The Ardennes, 1965.)

"Elting starred with Christine again, and I muffed an opportunity for kissing her goodbye. I don't know how to say it exactly, but I really fell for Christine — beginning with that first night until the very end when Elting 'took over' and I was more or less put in the shade. It was an experience which I'll not forget for a long time. My meager knowledge of French and inability to jitterbug, which she loves, gave me an inferiority complex which I just couldn't seem to break. I have a lot to learn I know, and I seem to act more childish over things like this than anything else. But believe I can truthfully say that she 'struck' me like no girl since Irene, and in the same way. I suppose I'll never get over being a romanticist and consequently will probably continue to have my heart pushed around quite a bit. I suppose it's all over now. There's nothing to describe my feelings except that I'd like to butt my head into a wall."

Although we had plenty of spare time at Wideumont, I wrote only one letter home from there and it was mostly about how cold it was. I said my toes were always numb that assured my folks it wasn't anything to worry about. I also went on about my increasing admiration for the people of Belgium. Of course, the Belgian getting most of my admiration was Christine. I did not mention her to my mother however. I had a feeling that beyond the war itself, my mother's biggest worry was that I'd bring home a foreign bride. It wasn't that she felt superior to other peoples, but the feeling was, I believe, that a European girl in the family would upset the tidy, well-ordered world she envisioned for herself and the whole family. That world included my marrying a clean, wholesome, religious, *American* girl! Our stay in Wideumont lasted for eight days, the longest in one spot since the Aldringen schoolhouse. Sibret, our next stop, was to the northeast and just outside Bastogne.

Mixed in with my dreams and frustrations about Christine were growing feelings of dislike, approaching downright hatred, for Sergeant Thompson. My diary caught a barrage of the bitterness. Thompson came in the first morning at Sibret and abruptly announced that he was going to take the bed Bruno and I had. Later he tried to make out he was only kidding. I thought he had a "fuhrer complex." I vowed I wouldn't take the bed back for a million dollars. Instead, Bruno and I took a mattress and put it on the floor in a room that had a stove. My mood wasn't helped by the fact that Elting went back to Wideumont for medical supplies and, naturally, saw Christine. There was some consolation in being able to listen to the radio again. A special photographic unit in the rooms below had a generator that we were able to hook onto. If we could have found 110-volt bulbs, we could even have had lights! We didn't have sleeping bags, only blankets. Bruno and I somehow managed to accumulate a total of 16 blankets. We slept on eight of them and used the other eight as covers. This bunch of blankets made a huge bedroll to load in and out of the weapons carrier. It became a source of irritation to Sergeant Thompson and others. Yet another officer got some angry words in my diary. Party One had a refugee mother and six little kids at their house. The officer ordered them out of the house, but the GIs there made room for the kids in their beds.

With Christine no longer around and surveying curtailed by snow and fog, I wrote a proper letter home reporting the noncensorable items I had noted in my diary. I cheered the landings in Luzon in the Philippines and asked my folks if they could send a camera soon. But the main thrust of my letter concerned my feelings about the Germans and the Belgians. "The trouble with those bastards," I wrote, "is that they obey the rules whenever it is to their advantage and throw them overboard when it isn't. There is ample evidence that they haven't been paying much attention to the rules since their counter-offensive began." I ventured that if the majority of our boys had their way, we wouldn't be taking *any* prisoners. I was pretty upset by editor Gervais Reed in a November issue of *The Garden City Telegram*, my hometown paper. In it he referred to the two wars — "the gentlemen's war in Europe" and the "brutal war against the Jap animal."

I fumed, "If these Huns are 'gentlemen,' then I give up. I don't think it can ever be emphasized too strongly. The only difference I can see between the Germans and Japs is that the Germans are much better propagandists and their cruelty is simply more brutally calculated. For my money, I think the world would be much better off if every last German — man, woman, and child — were shot. But, of course, that's impossible and perhaps something can be salvaged from all the wreckage." I cautioned my folks not to think I was becoming too hardened and went on to tell of the good people I had encountered in Belgium. "In the last place we were, the people treated us wonderfully. A girl even mended my socks. . . ." The girl was Christine.

Tanks and armored vehicles rumbled by all night long on 13 January. When we didn't go out on survey in the morning, I sawed wood. Two men from the photographic unit downstairs were seriously wounded the day before when they were taking pictures atop tanks in a battle near Foy. One suffered head injuries, and the other, the one who had taken our pictures only the night before, got it in the back. One day after going out on the Marche road from Bastogne, we came upon Mande St. Etienne, a thoroughly wrecked town. There were 17th Airborne Division units in town. Equipment, ours and the Germans', was strewn about. Cows and sheep were flattened on the road like so many bearskins rugs. In the afternoon, I was computer with Bliesmer and Anfuso when we went to Longchamps for several shots. We saw numerous destroyed buildings on the lee side of the hill near the edge of town. A company of tank destroyers passed us on the road to La Roche. One of the destroyers stopped on the crest of a hill. At about the same time a German anti-tank or mortar shell landed on the other side of the road. Shelton got a small shrapnel wound in his back but no one else was hurt. Bricks and shrapnel fell on Captain Carter's command car, flattening two tires. Many planes were flying overhead and the Germans were sending up a lot of flak. Once again we were lucky to have escaped, and I knew it; but at the moment I was thinking more of Elting's luck. He and Kiser were sent to Wideumont to get the command car's tires and, sure enough, he managed to see Christine again. According to his and Kiser's reports, she was really sweet on him. "Well, I guess I can't have everything," I wrote in my diary, "although, I could still really go for the kid. My feelings are so deadened however that I can almost pass it off as I have so many things of late . . . C'est la guerre."

That day we heard a rumor that the Huns had slaughtered the citizens of Bande. Years later, I learned details concerning the execution. Bande was the village to which we had retreated on 20 December 1944, after we were ordered to abandon our roadblocks at Champlon. Earlier, at the time of the German retreat across Belgium in September, the Belgian resistance movement (Armée Secrète) ambushed German troops in the nearby St. Hubert forest. On 24 December troops of the Second SS Panzer (the Das Reich) Division were in Bande. With them was a group from the Sicherheitsdienst (SD), the security service of the SS. On Christmas Eve, the SD began rounding up male civilians, interrogating them about the Armée

Secrète. Then 32 young men, including four seminary students, were shot, one by one. It was then the villagers remembered the vengeful shouts of the Germans as they left in September: "We'll be back!"

On 15 January I poured out my thoughts, filling several pages of my diary. Once again, I admitted our good fortune. We had just learned that the main German spearhead had reached Champlon several hours after we left on 19 December. What a slaughter there would've been had we remained another night! But I was in a surly mood — Gindele, Abney, and Bruno found a variety of reasons to go back to Wideumont. There wasn't room for me in the jeep. Bruno managed to get himself a farewell kiss from Christine. She and her uncle and aunt asked about me and wondered why I hadn't come. That helped a little. My diary mirrored my frame of mind: "I'd like to get back there just once more. . . . I don't know why I write all this stuff — like hell I don't!!!" I pulled out of the dumps long enough to wash out a pair of socks and a handkerchief. That night Elting went to Wideumont again and came back bragging about how Christine was head over heels in love with him.

Love is hell and so is war. So I decided to write about war for a change. "The stupidity of it is increasingly brought home to me day after day. Heard two more reports of the beating the 17th Airborne Division is taking, not from the Huns, but from battle itself. Kids of 18 and 19 look like they were 50 . . . Oh God! if only the human race could rouse itself sufficiently to cast out this scourge forever. Let me always remember — let me always bear uppermost in my mind — that the cause of peace — just and durable peace — is the greatest cause in the world."

Returning to the immediate, I wrote, "It's strange what a galaxy of human emotions war and its close association of men brings. The men in survey section No. 2 represent (to me) a very vivid cross-section of humanity. The things we argue about — the different values each of us holds as of the utmost importance. How a simple little matter like Christine's affections (?) can cause so much petty bickering. I have to watch myself. My temper on many things is becoming very short these days. . . . War creates little Caesars, each seeking to extend his own domain over the lives and fortunes of free citizens," I went on, making a case in point of "the officer" who deliberately picks out uncalled-for survey regardless of danger to the survey parties, and suggests men would be "toughened" by moving

The author with Bruno and others on a disabled American Sherman tank.

to the field from buildings in the middle of winter. In our own section, I mentioned, "the monster (who needs no identification)" sought to control even the minds of his men. I thanked God that it was impossible for him to do it. I went to bed in a froth that night.

The next day we were out to survey from Longchamps to Recogne in the morning and early afternoon. Since Bliesmer was down with a cold, I computed with Giulio, and didn't do too badly, considering it was my first real try at it since Plougastel. Everywhere there were remnants of German and American battle lines — shell holes near the road, a knocked-out Sherman tank. The 11th Armored and 101st Airborne Divisions were occupying the towns. None of the U.S. tank fire was returned by the Jerries. We saw our white phosphorus shells landing near Noville, which was still held by the Germans, and we passed a knocked-out Tiger tank when we returned by way of Foy and the Bastogne-Houffalize road. Houffalize and Cherain had been recaptured. Being busy helped us all. The arguments about Christine subsided somewhat. On guard at midnight, I was aware of ambulances driving by in the dark night. I turned in, hoping we'd get a chance at the 101st AB Division's showers the next day.

While surveying in the morning and early afternoon from Foy to

The grave of a German soldier in Belgium, early February.

Noville and off on a side road to Vaux, we saw some disturbing sights. There were numerous deserted Tiger Mark IIIs and IVs and Sherman tanks. Noville, for all practical purposes, was destroyed.

Hitler Jugend (youth) signs were in evidence everywhere. Giulio and I saw what appeared to be a trash rubble pit near a shell hole at the side of the main road. In it was a battered arm, all that remained of what was once a man. On the way to Vaux, we came upon many dead Germans. Private Blank, the GI I had guarded two months before, acted like a madman as he tore around looting the bodies. "That guy!" Giulio commented wryly, "I expect to see him howling at the moon some night."

My hands and feet felt frozen as I went back toward Wideumont in the late afternoon with Shelton, Bruno, and Elting. Supposedly we were to pick up a tire and get things out of our duffel bags. The real purpose was to see Christine. On the way we met battery vehicles moving up, and about 100 yards from Christine's house we encountered a motors truck with the tire we needed. Seeing all the movement of vehicles, we thought we would be moving too, so we returned to Sibret at once only to learn that survey wasn't moving. C'est la guerre! In my diary I recorded, "I wrote Christine to let her know I wasn't angry which she probably thinks because I never returned. . . . How long can this war go on?"

My life as far as girls were concerned was in a slump. But despite bombings and shellings, snowdrifts and frozen feet, I thought of them constantly. I hadn't received a letter from Irene for weeks and surmised she had found someone else nearer home; and I had lost Christine, if I ever had her, probably to Marvin Elting. To top it all, in January I received a beautifully written letter form Barbara. It was dated the day after Christmas and was in response to my "Dear Barbara" letter written in early December. Barbara said she was dumbfounded at my letter and found it hard to believe. She explained she had no reason to hold me . . . "but you did tell me you loved me and I believed you . . . and I can't simply say that I don't love you anymore." She said she appreciated my frankness in saying what I did, but, she went on, "If you're telling me this because of a warped sense of anxiety of war, please realize that we at home are trying to do our share by sharing the worries and having faith in people we love. . . . If it is something we might iron out, it would be tragic to mar both our lives over a misunderstanding. But if you're sure in your heart of what you say, then the sooner I start forgetting the better it will be." Once again, I was guilt-ridden about my fickleness. Why, oh why, in moments of temporary sincerity, had I told her I loved her? It had not been, as is so often the case with professions of undying love, to take advantage of her. I respected her. Here was a girl not yet out of high school with maturity and wisdom concerning affairs of the heart the likes of which I would not possess for years.

A bottle of Paris perfume I intended to send home weeks before was about half evaporated. I wrote my folks that I was looking for some "suitable Belgian girl" to give it to since I didn't have proper packing to mail it home to them. In the meantime, I joked, I was carrying it in my pocket "which helps some — in that I haven't had a shower for five weeks!" I mentioned that I hadn't heard from Irene in a while and then casually added I met a girl in the last village who reminded me a lot of Irene. Back to the war: "The death and destruction under a mantle of snow presents many grotesque scenes. Can't say that I haven't been affected by it all, but I'm still safe and sound."

Numerous letters from home, 15 written between New Year's Day and 17 January, were arriving. My mother, an only child, corresponded regularly with many of her cousins and often wrote me detailed accounts concerning kin I barely knew. She never let up on writing about the importance of trusting in God. I resented some of her lectures about God and all of her lectures about girls, but one letter really touched me. "There is no need in spoofing you any longer. I might as well confess that writing to you now is the hardest thing in the world to do. Not knowing where you are or under what conditions you'll be when you get your mail — for you see we can't help but think that you may be wounded or in a prison camp — as much as we believe down deep in our hearts that you are alright the terrible fear of these other possibilities creeps in. We are living under great anxiety and that's why its difficult to write you a light airy letter. I trust, Son, you do not tire of my mentioning that you must ask God's help to see you through. I can understand that it can easily seem to you that God doesn't enter into the picture very much just now. Yet you must see that our entreating God to be with you is *all* we can do to strengthen and sustain you."

Two days later my father wrote saying he wished there was some way he could take my place for the coming year. He said most fathers felt that way about their sons in the service but had to realize the army would think them just "a bunch of tired old men and a mighty poor trade" if they tried to take our places. Like other fathers, he said, he took pride in the part I was playing in the war for him and the rest of the family. He sent a pamphlet published by the State Department on the Dumbarton Oaks Conference. "The whole foreign situation seems to be deteriorating, but I don't think it's hopeless yet," he said. "A Roosevelt-Churchill-Stalin Conference should certianly (*sic*) be held as soon as possible. We're certianly (*sic*) in a much less favorable position for insisting on our ideas than we were at Teheran. I think Roosevelt has let his big chance go by to be a big factor in the peace."

He told me he had reread my peace proposals and found them to be well thought out. "If the final world organization plans are as well worked out it will be surprising. It's like the old story they used to tell on Uncle Joe Cannon (the legendary speaker of the House of Representatives). Someone proposed him for President and he said with becoming modesty. 'Well, they could go farther and do worse and probably will.' That's about the way with your proposals."

My mother wrote on January ninth that Admiral Ingram, Commander-in-Chief of the U.S. Atlantic Fleet, said a token bombing of either New York City or Washington by means of robot missiles launched from submarines was possible and probable within the next 30 to 60 days. "There was a time that would have worried me, but when I think what you and your buddies are going through, I guess we could stand a bomb or two." My mother was always better able to handle big concerns than small ones. In another letter she was off on a guilt trip for the "many times I've punished you severely, because you were so self-willed. . . . I pray the Good Lord that that determination is still strong in your heart. God will give you the added physical strength and moral courage that you need when you have the will to use all of your own."

On 11 January my family received my Christmas Day letter telling them I had survived the worst of the Bulge. "What a terrible fear it has alleviated," my mother wrote. My father was in Topeka to make a speech when the letter arrived, so she called and read it to him. In a letter to me she named the 18 other people she had called immediately to tell them I was all right. As I was sure she would, she commented on what I'd written about hating the Germans. Hating them was the only way I could be a "good soldier," she supposed, but "it hurts to know that you must have hatred in your heart." She suggested I direct the anger at "the things for which they fight and for all they were doing to me and my buddies.''

Pop (I called my father by that name for some years, but I did not use it when mentioning him to other people) wrote a four-page letter on 17 January. Although our mail home was censored, the incoming mail was not, and that made it especially welcome. He wrote, "There hasn't been a lot of comment in the press or elsewhere which attempted to place the blame for the breakthrough. What there has been has been rather critical of the high command, and it's pretty hard for anyone to understand how the Germans could spring the surprise they did if our intelligence was even half way on the job. I think most people think we did pretty well to stop the drive as quickly as we did, but they are giving most of the credit to the GIs instead of the generals. However, there's been some praise of Bradley and Patton for getting into action as rapidly as they did, and I presume that when the story is finally written there will be credit enough for everybody as far as stopping the drive is concerned. I hope that sometime we'll get the real story of how we were so badly taken by surprise.''

We moved from Sibret to Rouette on 18 January and I was back to bitching in my diary. I could see no logical reason for the move to the partially destroyed village northwest of Bastogne. We were still about 10 miles from the front, no closer than we were at Sibret. Elting, Okie, Ziegler, Bruno, and I had a room above the aid station, about a block away from Thompson and the rest of the party. Okie nailed up a window and we sawed wood for the stove and got a coal oil lamp. A lot of the time we just sat in the room and stared into space. I decided we were all beginning to suffer from a sort of fatigue. The weather was terrible. Standing guard for an hour or more in the dark in a blizzard wasn't anybody's favorite thing. We'd start out to survey, drive about a half-mile and come back. The visibility was 20 feet or less. In between attempts to go out, I read *Time*. On 20 January my party surveyed from the cut-off on the Bastogne-Houffalize road to Rochamps. The road was under German observation but everything was quiet. It was extremely cold out in the blowing snow. Back in the room Okie gave me a haircut and I looked forward to taking a sponge bath, waist down. The next day I stayed in with a temperature, but I sawed firewood in the morning and afternoon. That evening I received three copies of *Life* magazine, something new to read. Our party stayed out all the next day, surveying beyond Rochamps. Winsor's face got scratched by debris from a tree that was accidentally hit by a tank shell.

When I wrote home, I asked the folks to save clippings and reports on the breakthrough so I could read them when I got home. All we got were short radio reports or stories of fighting by individual divisions in *Stars and Stripes*. I said the blizzard we'd just had was the worst I'd seen since one in Kansas in 1931. The worst summer and fall weather in 40 years had been followed by an equally bad winter. Belgians told us there had been very little snow last winter. "All eyes are centered on the Russians now," I wrote, "and it's beginning to look as if we might meet them on the Rhine." Our Rouette room was fine. We had two beds, a good stove and two portable "closets." I actually got my feet warmed up but my nerves were frayed. I was becoming more irritable all the time. I tried to read to get a grip on myself, and an article in *Life* on William Penn helped temporarily.

We moved again on 24 January, this time to Tavigny, northeast of Rouette and a short distance southeast of recently recaptured Houffalize. This move dispelled rumors that the VIII Corps was moving to Strasbourg or the Riviera. Our party shared two upstairs rooms and it was really crowded. After the beds or mattresses we had in the last three villages, the floor was very hard. The temperature slipped to two degrees. We had to melt snow to have water. Bruno, Elting, Ziegler, Okie, and I missed the setup we had at Rouette. In my diary I wrote that Kindel was driving everyone crazy with his imitation of Ned Sparks. "Everyone's becoming slightly wacky anyway."

The official end of the Battle of the Bulge was 25 January, the day when the American lines were restored to approximately the same position they were on 16 December. Of course, we didn't know this at the time. Our party didn't go out, so I chopped wood, washed, and shaved for the first time in three days, bringing water from the pump at the mess hall about a quarter of a mile away. Spots in front of my eyes, probably from the snow, made reading impossible. The man and woman in the house where we stayed said the Germans stole all their food, looted their household possessions, and burned what they didn't take. They also killed good livestock and shipped it to Germany. From various reports, this apparently occurred everywhere in the Bulge as a matter of policy.

We put in a full day of survey near Limerle to Hautbellain. I computed with Giulio. The 87th (Acorn) Division, which we last saw at Libramont, was moving up in convoys all day. When we got back to Tavigny, we found the battery had moved east, into northern Luxembourg, to Trois Vierges, where we were to stay into early February. So, in blackout convoy, we moved too. At Trois Vierges, we quartered on the second floor of a good house — it had only a few bullet holes. The family was still there. Bruno and I shared a single bed. It was nice to find Trois Vierges mostly undamaged.

We were out near Huldange most of the next day doing nothing. Gindele and the tapers went back to bring chow for the rest of us. What we didn't eat we gave to some hungry men from a detachment of the 17th AB Division. They said they had 250 men left out of the first battalion. We surveyed on the Trois Vierges-St. Vith highway from Lengeler to Oudler on 28 January. It was very cold and we were stopped once by heavy snow. I did absolutely nothing, nor did the computers, except for going back to bring out chow. "What the sense of all this is and why we didn't wait to come in for chow beats the hell out of me," I wrote in my diary that night. "We have enough men to alternate on plenty of jobs." As we neared Oudler, there was a five-minute German screaming meemie barrage. Infantry men reported that 40 German prisoners were captured in Oudler the day before. By the side of the main road there were 60mm mortars, and the road itself was clogged by the 87th and 90th Divisions moving up with plenty of artillery. We saw a new outfit with tape covering the vehicle markings, giving credence to rumors we had heard about a new secret Fifteenth Army thrown into the battle.

The next day brought us back through St. Vith. We had last seen it on 17 December while it was intact and still the headquarters for the 106th Division. "Saw St. Vith from the top of an embankment — the most destroyed sight I've ever seen," I wrote in my diary. The railroad bridge had been blown up, the track sagging but still hanging together. Engineers were blowing up debris; a bulldozer was hung up on the rubble. It was cold as blue blazes and we stayed out most of the day, although we put in only one station. In doing so we found several of our old stations beneath the snow. We ate partially warmed C-rations. Bliesmer and I were called to Survey Information Center around 9:30 that night to compute four stations.

The mail brought tobacco, two books, film, and my sister's Baby Brownie camera. Although I didn't appreciate it much at the time, the camera was really a boon. I was able to take eight rolls of photos by May. Developed after V-E Day, they provided a photographic record

Just-captured German prisoners on the main road between St. Vith and Schönberg, Belgium, in early February 1945. This was the first photo taken with the Baby Brownie camera sent by the author's parents.

of our experiences from late January on, and I was able to give prints to the GIs in our outfit and to other friends.

A symphony of screaming meemies accompanied our surveying from St. Vith two or three miles along the Schönberg road. We went almost to the roadblock and the place where we were surveying on that memorable 16 December several weeks back. "I think I get colder every day when we go out," I noted in my diary. We drove through St. Vith; the center of town was unrecognizable. Throughout the month, the daily log of the January after action report commented on the slow but steady advance of the VIII Corps. It also mentioned various shellings by artillery and mortars and named those who were wounded as a result. Probably the most spectacular, but fortunate, such event occured on 30 January, when a dud shell landed about six feet from Bob Mason. He was not injured.

When I wrote home at the end of January, I reviewed everyday events — Bruno and I nearly always slept warmly, my feet were all right: "As long as the shoes can be removed at night, there's no danger of trench foot." The cold seemed to make us feel more tired. I explained we were on the move most of the time, "but if we can keep pushing the Jerries back, it's certainly worth it. . . . Everyone here is

A view of St. Vith from the west on 2 February 1945 showing the complete leveling of the town. Even the streets were destroyed.

more interested in the Russian drive than anything else now. I hope by the time this reaches you they'll be at the gates of Berlin but of course everyone has been fooled on that score before and I refuse to make any more predictions.'' As I told my family, I knew certain sections of Belgium and Luxembourg better than I ever knew Kansas, and I joked that I was thinking of becoming a guide for tourists in the area after the war if I couldn't make a living peddling apples or pencils in the States. ''I suppose you saw Stimson's announcement of casualties for the breakthrough including 8,663 for the 106th Division alone,'' I wrote. ''About 15 or 20 of the boys that left Maryland at the same time I did were in the 81st Eng. that helped defend St. Vith . . . but I've never heard from any of them since they came across.'' I ended by asking for a box of cigars. ''It's getting so I'll eat, drink or smoke anything but I haven't felt any ill effects yet — in fact that's one of the few things I have to look forward to.''

Keeping busy and on the move didn't ease my conscience on a matter that was always creeping up on me. As the month ended, we surveyed toward Schönberg, turning off at Setz and the area where we were on December 16th. It was cold, rainy, and noisy — screaming meemies most of the day. I took pictures of seven German prisoners brought in by the 87th Division Infantry. We didn't get in until dark. My toes ached from the cold and my head was weary with a day of regretting that I wasn't in the infantry. But my conscience wouldn't let up on the subject of getting into the infantry. For one who had worn glasses since the eighth grade and who had difficulty sighting a rifle or carbine, my feelings about transferring to the infantry, even if I could have, didn't make sense, but that didn't stop me from brooding about it.

Looking back on the Ardennes battles, I believe our feelings then were well summarized by Russell Weigley in his excellent history, *Eisenhower's Lieutenants*. It was his opinion that victory belonged "preeminently to the American soldier." Charging that the generals failed to foresee the German counteroffensive, Weigley maintained that they also neglected to prepare for it as a contingency "even to the extent they might have if they had been truly calculating the risks in the Ardennes." This meant they had to wait long and work hard before they could recapture any semblance of control over the shape of the campaign. The stubbornness and bravery of the soldiers got the job done for them, he insisted. Historically, American armed forces in wars in the twentieth century were always in possession of such material superiority that doubts could be raised about how well they might do against an equally well-equipped force. Weigley suggested that the American military might be found to be "a paper tiger, too dependent on material superiority to get along without it." The Ardennes battle (like Guadalcanal but on an immensely larger scale) reduced such doubts. In the Ardennes, with material superiority nonexistent or nullified by the weather, the American soldier, temporarily abandoned by many of his generals to his own resources, won the battle. "If the victory was less than complete," Weigley wrote, "the fault lay mainly in generalship's failure to seize fully the opportunities created by the valor of the men at Lanzerath, Clerf, Stavelot, St. Vith, the Baraque de Fraiture, and scores of other places besides the fabled Bastogne."

My father wrote me on 19 January about a letter he got from the mother of a GI in my outfit: "I had a letter from Mrs. Blank today saying they hadn't heard from Blank since Dec. 4th. She wanted to know if we had heard from you and wanted us to ask you if you knew anything about him." The GI was not the world's most frequent letter-writer, I knew that. My father contacted the casualty section of

the War Department, and my mother wrote me on 30 January that
Mrs. Blank finally received a letter from her son. It was dated 2
January.

"Were you anywhere near the 106th Division?" my father asked.
"I notice their losses were about 60%, mostly prisoners. My guess is
that you were pretty close to where they were. . . . If you were, you
were lucky to get out. You were lucky anyway wherever you were."
The news in Washington centered around F.D.R.'s fourth inauguration. My father wrote with obvious amusement, "During the last
two or three days there's been more talk about Elliott Roosevelt's dog
than about his father's inauguration." The dog was shipped from
Washington to Los Angeles in an army transport plane with an A
priority. Three servicemen who had only C priorities were put off the
plane at Memphis when some high priority freight was taken on. One
of the men was going home because of the death of his father and
another to see his sick wife. The dog got the full ride. It created a
storm and the White House was busy making apologies. There was to
be no inaugural parade and no ceremony at the Capitol. The president
was to take the oath on the back portico of the White House. Each
Congressman got two tickets, not transferable, to the swearing-in and
to a buffet luncheon afterward. My father said he and Mom planned
to go.

I did little to mask my misery when I wrote to my parents, and it
obviously came through plenty strong. My mother wrote that she
hoped I had grown accustomed to being miserable so I wouldn't mind
it so much. "I've prayed for you by 'degrees,' " she said. "At first,
until you were in imminent danger I prayed that God would use you as
he saw fit — then when we knew your life was imperiled I prayed
God to keep you safe, then I realized you needed more than that and I
prayed that He would give you added strength and courage, as you
needed it — now, sweet, I pray that you not only be given strength
and courage for your own needs but that you'll be strong enough to
give your buddies help if they need it. And as you share it, more will
be given you!"

A letter from my father boosted my morale. He said I was getting
some good publicity on my world government plan. The Associated
Press apparently picked it up from the *Congressional Record* and sent
out a story on it. He didn't know anything about it until it started
showing up in Kansas papers. I would be surprised, he wrote, at the

amount of radio time taken up with war programs at home. The number of news programs had increased and at least three-fourths of the time on them was taken up with war news and comment. Also, there were more programs like "We the People" as well as a lot of quiz programs that pretty well limited the people who appeared on them to servicemen and women. A number of other programs reenacted battle scenes, and then there were programs like the "Army Hour." He ended, "This all shows how much time people are giving to the war as far as their thoughts are concerned. A pretty large percentage of our families now have one or more members in the service and practically everyone has some fairly close relatives in uniform."

Lu Winsor, notekeeper, and Bill Kiser, transit operator, near Kobscheid, Germany, early February.

Chapter 8

Death at the Siegfried Line

Still at Trois Vierges on 1 February, our battalion continued the execution of its primary mission in general support of the VIII Corps, moving on in a few days to southeast of St. Vith, next to the German border and the Siegried Line, which the Germans called the West Wall. The immediate objective of the corps, the after action report stated on the opening day of the month, was the Schnee Eifel Ridge along the Belgian-German border, one of the first places seized by the Germans during their "breakthrough" launched in mid-December. Resistance was fairly light so far and good progress was reported all along the corps' front. At the German-Belgian-Luxembourg Border, several bridgeheads were established across the Our River.

My diary entries for the next week reported a variety of thoughts, rumors, and events. The good news was the return of unflappable Phil Hand, who had been gone since I broke his ankle at Lopscombe Corners. There was no let-up in my bitching about Sergeant Thompson. I usually referred to him as "the Monster." We had a day of rest "for a change," I noted on 3 February. "We didn't go out and the Monster didn't have us cleaning out vehicles, etc., by some strange miracle." I wrote five letters, a small dent in the list of 23 I owed, according to an inventory I had taken the night before. At this same accounting, I made a list of my correspondents and would-be correspondents and came up with a total of 45. After reading a couple of issues of *Time*, I took a modified bath and put on a clean undershirt and shorts, by no means an everyday occurrence. In the afternoon I took pictures of various members of our party, of Sidy, the girl in whose home we were staying, and of knocked-out tanks at Trois Vierges.

S/Sgt. Gordon S. Thompson and his jeep in early February 1945. The photo was taken about a week before Thompson was killed when his jeep was blown up by a double Teller mine.

The barn southeast of St. Vith in which the author's survey section lived at the time of Sergeant Thompson's death.

We left early the next morning to move to a barn at Wiesenbach, southeast of St. Vith on the road to Prum. Part of the party went out in the rain for triangulation near Amelscheid but I stayed in, going with Gindele to take out chow. A peacock was chased out of the barn when we moved in. Later in the day, my diary noted, ''Some moron from A or B Battery fired about 15 carbine shots until he had killed it. No wonder these people believe some of the things the Jerries tell them about us.'' The fan belt on Kiser's truck broke as we started out for survey near Schönberg on the following morning. It turned out to be a slow, depressing day. I shaved and washed. A new order had been handed down — ''wash and shave everyday — all buttons buttoned, etc.,'' a diary entry said.

Triangulating beyond Schönberg the next day, I kept notes for Kiser. From the Bleialf benchmark, we could see across the valley to the top of a far ridge, supposedly the location of the front lines. At the end of another dismal, rainy day, we were called over to the battery command post to hear a lieutenant read the Articles of War. In my diary, I wrote ''. . . a sad affair. This means the Lt. was a sorry excuse for an officer.'' I closed with, ''How long can this life go on — cheer up, Hope, old kid — only a few more years now.'' Waking again to dreary rain, we returned to the benchmark near Bleialf but soon came back in because of fog. After lunch I went to church over at the command post for the first time in five weeks. Thompson was mad because nearly everyone had taken off. Some in the group, I wrote, "were trying to get somewhere with two babes here." I didn't join in that competition as I was still brooding over Christine.

A tragedy on 8 February was to change the small world of our survey section from that date until the end of the war. What we all believed to be inevitable happened. Thompson and Wagner, riding in a jeep, ran over a mine near Brandscheid about noon. Out working on triangulation, some of us didn't learn about it until four hours later. The jeep was apparently headed down an uncleared road, Mason and Hoppe told us. They and Gindele went to the site. The jeep was wrecked and burned. What wasn't burned had already been looted by GIs. An infantry staff sergeant said his hand pulled off burnt flesh when he first tried to pull Thompson out. Wagner was thrown 40 feet.

"Thompson is dead," my diary stated on 9 February. "He is reported to have died before reaching the hospital, being 75% covered with burns. Sgt. Troy (the supply sergeant) came up today to get his personal effects and clothing. It was a helluva feeling to watch Troy sorting out his clothes. There is plenty I could say about how Thompson was becoming a regular obsession with all members of the party but all this must now rest. . . . Party stayed in all day — read and writing letters and tried to keep warm. We are moving to Bleialf."

A paragraph in the after action report for 8 February gave more details: "The mission of Party #2 was marred by an unfortunate tragedy which resulted in the death of their Chief of Party, Staff Sergeant Gordon Thompson. Shortly after noon, Sgt. Thompson and his driver, Tec 5 Wagner went out on reconnaissance northeast of the town of Brandscheid, Germany. Despite the fact that the area was heavily mined and booby-trapped, Sgt. Thompson proceeded on his mission. Around 1230, the jeep struck a mine on the road, injuring both occupants. Both men were rescued almost immediately by members of a regimental CP of the 90th Division, and treated by medical aid men prior to the arrival of an ambulance. Tec 5 Wagner had been thrown clear of the vehicle and suffered only minor injuries. However, S/Sgt. Thompson had been very seriously hurt and died before reaching a clearing station." In the official battalion history,

Thompson was listed as killed in action and as receiving the Bronze Star award posthumously. And thus, as was the case with all casualties, the official record was closed on Sergeant Thompson.

"There is certainly a perceptible difference in daily lives with Thompson gone," I wrote in my diary. "Everything seems so quiet & one keeps expecting to see him storming in at any moment." Another GI wrote in his diary: "If any of us had to get it, I'm glad it was Thompson. We'll be better off without him." In the months and years that followed I came to see the life and death of Sergeant Thompson in a different and broader perspective. This began after V-E Day, when I sent Thompson's mother a photo I had taken of him at Trois Vierges, soon after I received my sister's small camera. She replied:

Eagle Grove, Iowa
June 28, 1945

Dear Cpl. Clifford Hope:

I just can't put it in words how happy I was to get your letter and the picture of Gordon yesterday; I believe a letter from some of the boys that has been with the one that has to give his life for our country is the nicest thing you can do for the parent. Thanks so much.

I know he was looking forward to coming home and had many plans for the future. God's ways are not ours, and we just have to go on.

Hope you will return back to the States and Good Luck.

Sincerely,
Randa Thompson

A year or so later, after I had been home for some months, I sent the negative to Mrs. Thompson, and she again thanked me. From her letter it appeared evident that no one from our outfit except Captain Carter and I had written to her. Probably no one in our outfit disliked Sergeant Thompson more than I in February 1945. With my volatile disposition, I had constantly bitched about him in my diary and to others. There was no question that Thompson was bucking for any promotion possible, including a battlefield commission, and we all suffered from the intensity of his ambition. All of us were pretty punchy at that time. You could say we had the "rattle of the battle" and we certainly were "fed-up with the setup." If we'd all been working eight-hour days and going home at night to relax as in civilian life, it would have been different. But we had togetherness around the clock. We lived with Thompson's ambition 24 hours a day, just as he lived with my defiance of authority and go-to-hell attitude. I was not the only one with such feelings, but, foolishly, I did less to conceal them than most. Who was I to castigate someone for having ambition? The difference between Thompson and me in that respect was that his ambitions were quite practical while mine were mostly dreams. Thompson's death pushed me on to another milestone in growing up.

In reflecting, I could see that Thompson had qualities of leadership beyond ambition. He was constantly looking after his men, helping them with personal problems. When we landed in France, he drove Giulio Anfuso up and down the beach looking for Anfuso's brother, who was in a port battalion. And, as previously related, he tried very hard to get immediate medical attention for me when I had a high fever in the Aldringen schoolhouse.

More than 40 years have come and gone since Gordon Thompson met a fiery death at the Siegfried Line, years in which most of us have been afforded the opportunity to return home, raise families, and pursue our ambitions, whatever they might be. Just as in the case of some assassinated presidents who were not admired by all, Thompson did give his life, the most that anyone on earth has to give. For that, those of us who survived owe him respect.

In the days to come I had cause to reflect on the vicissitudes of war and the way survivors may profit from the tragedies of others. Within a few days Cpl. Lu Winsor, our notekeeper, was transferred to the 285th Field Artillery Observation Battalion, a transfer which I am certain was occasioned by the terrible losses suffered by the 285th in the Malmedy Massacre. I was appointed to Lu's position and later was promoted to corporal. If Sergeant Thompson had lived, I am certain that would not have happened.

During the first half of February I wrote only one letter home, and that on the day before Thompson's death. In it, I noted I had "finally heard from Irene after a good two months." I was beginning to get her message. I asked my parents to send a copy of my peace plans to my old Garden City friend and fellow world-government planner, Houston Smith. He was then serving as a naval aerial gunner in the

A Siegfried Line (West Wall) roadblock and "dragon's teeth" on 11 February.

Pacific. Two days later I wrote to Al Buckberg, my basic training buddy from Washington, D.C. It was intended that this letter would be hand-delivered to Buck by Okie Henderson, who had a pass for Paris, but Okie didn't get around to making the delivery. The letter contained my uncensored thoughts of that date. Buck was in the transportation corps in Paris but was getting bored and thinking of trying to transfer to the Sixteenth. Strongly advising against it, I wrote, "I've lost all interest in getting a rating except to stay off a week's KP now and then — which is still worth it. I'm still in survey and still officially a rodman, although I'm mainly a substitute computer and notekeeper with no chance for advancement except from casualties, which I don't like to contemplate. Our chief of section was killed yesterday when his jeep hit a mine. A kid with him is in the hospital but not seriously hurt. The only other casualty in our party of 17 men was a slight shrapnel wound which one of the boys got about three weeks ago. We've been very lucky. (I was forgetting the deaths of Priebe and Michael.) Our life is a long way from being as rough as the infantry. We're in a barn now but have had buildings or houses since October except for a few nights when von Rundstedt was running wild."

We moved to Bleialf, Germany, at the foot of the Schnee Eifel, on 10 February, and for the first time were living inside Germany at the base of the Siegfried Line. We stayed for three weeks. It was good to leave the large, cavernous barn with its memories of death. Our party had fairly good quarters in a house in Bleialf — four rooms with a stove in each and plenty of hay from a nearby barn for mattresses. For the first week in Bleialf, my diary reported observations along the Siegfried Line and such matters as washing clothes and taking my first shower in two months. While surveying from the road junction, Grosslangenfeld, to Habscheid, I took pictures of dragon's teeth (concrete barriers) and pillboxes on the side of a hill and two of a Siegfried Line roadblock. A Christmas package from my folks caught up with me. It contained four books and a letter from Pop with the Dumbarton Oaks proposals. Coming in soaked from a day out in relentless rain, I read them and they inspired me to include a few brief, great thoughts among the mundane in my diary: "Wars are the greatest scourge of mankind — if there was ever any doubt in my mind — God knows I know it now. I am more & more firmly resolved to devote my life to any and all attempts to prevent them."

Survey on the following day on the road junction east of the Schnee Eifel, south on the main highway to Prum, was abandoned after three kilometers because the area proved to be under enemy observation. A number of shells landed on either side of the road. The 8th Infantry Regiment of the 4th Division was along the road with mortars. Someone in the outfit asked me when they were going to be relieved. He said the 22d Infantry took two-thirds of Prum just the night before. And then a full colonel stopped me to ask the way to Bleialf. I guessed he was going to pick up supplies that were being dropped by C-47s, escorted by P-47s, just as we returned. In traveling the length of the Schnee Eifel, we saw a number of pillboxes, painted green. Most of them were virtually undamaged, but one, a massive block of reinforced concrete, had been turned up on its side. I took a shower at the 4th Division shower unit in Bleialf in the afternoon, noting in my diary: "What a sensation after two months." The mail that evening brought a few press clippings from Kansas newspapers concerning my peace plans. More supplies were dropped just west of Bleialf the next morning. There must have been about a hundred planes in all. Each plane dropped six chutes of varying colors. Some cartons, breaking away from the chutes, came hurtling down.

Both survey parties were ordered, supposedly by Colonel Lushene, to stay in on 17 February. Having worked out an outline for an
improved version of my book, I started writing the revised edition but
quit after four pages. Upon reading in *Stars and Stripes* the details of
the actions at the Big Three Conference, I decided almost all of it
would be very obsolete by the time I could have it completed.

In a letter home I wrote about the beautiful weather we had enjoyed
for two days, "clear sunshine with few clouds. A week of this
weather would dry up the mud, but as it is it's pretty soupy." All in
all, for me, it was an upbeat letter. I went on, "We're living in a
house now, not badly damaged, and it's been warm enough that we
don't have to have a fire all day. There's no need to worry about
fraternization with German civilians, because there are none here and
I've seen very few in other places. The meals have been generally
very good, particularly the breakfasts. I had an orange this morning.
Incidentally, from what I've seen, I can't see that the great vaunted
Nazi superstate has done much to improve the lot of the Herrenvolk.
The villages here, if anything, look worse than those of the poor,
decadent French and Belgians. The only things here the least bit
modern are the pillboxes, which is a sad commentary indeed. I just
got a pair of shoepacs last night. You've probably read of them.
They're boots with rubber soles part way up and leather the rest of the
way. They eliminate overshoes and are very much lighter. There are
felt pads in the bottom and heavy white wool socks are issued with
them. I could've used them to better advantage about a month and a
half ago, but I'm glad to have them in any event.

"I'm receiving *Time* by airmail now. In our last mail delivery I
received the January 29th and February 5th issues — which is
certainly a great improvement in the service. Incidentally, in the Jan.
15th issue there was an item on the manufacturer Frederick Crawford's report on France to the effect that conditions there under the
Nazis were very good and that in another year and a half of occupation most Frenchmen would've been satisfied with it. It's such
blind stupidity as that that really makes me see red. I only hope that
attitude is not widespread. . . . The February 5th issue's report upon
the feeling of GI's on the western front I thought was about the best
thing along that line that I've seen. The point that the public at home
still seems to hate the Japs more was well taken, I thought. Of course I
suppose I'm prejudiced, but it seems as if most advertising, etc. from

home always mentions the 'Beat the Jap' theme, while ignoring the Nazis' front, where the vast majority of our men and supplies are. However, maybe I'll have a different view after I've been in China awhile.''

It was about this time that each GI received General Omar Bradley's ''Special Orders for German-American Relations.'' I saved my copy. The General issued these seven orders:

1. To remember always that Germany though conquered is still a dangerous nation.
2. Never to trust Germans, collectively or individually.
3. To defeat German efforts to poison my thoughts or influence my attitude.
4. To avoid acts of violence, except when required by military necessity.
5. To conduct myself at all times so as to command the respect of the German people for myself, for the United States, and for the Allied Cause.
6. Never to associate with Germans.
7. To be fair but firm with Germans.

Each order was followed by sub-orders. Order 6-c read:

American soldiers must not associate with Germans. Specifically, it is not permissable to shake hands with them, to visit their homes, to exchange gifts with them, to engage in games or sports with them, to attend their dances or social events, or to accompany them on the street or elsewhere. Particularly, avoid all discussion or argument with them. Give the Germans no chance to trick you into relaxing your guard.

Well intended, the order was soon outdated by the tide of events. Trying to enforce nonfraternization among soldiers was like trying to enforce the Prohibition Amendment for an earlier generation.

During the third week of February, Lu Winsor, Blades, and Cooper left as replacements for the 285th Field Artillery Observation Battalion. I hated to see Winsor go, although, as previously mentioned, it was a break for me because I got his job as notekeeper. It was a definite job in the army for the first time in almost two years of service. On 22 February I worked on constructing a box from some moss-covered boards I'd picked up to ship my German rifle home. There were an amazing number of men down with the GIs, flu, and assorted ailments, I noted in my diary. I heard that the same was true in all outfits. That evening I had a satisfying discussion about the United Nations government plans with John Ziegler; it lasted almost three hours. He had some very good ideas and he had previously read my plans and made suggestions.

On 23 February I wrote myself an anniversary greeting: "Well, Hope ole Kid, this marks your second anniversary of entering AUS (Army of the United States). Can't say you've come very far materially and perhaps you've lost a lot, but you have learned a helluva lot about human nature and such subjects, very much more than you could've ever learned as a civilian. I hope by the time two more years roll around you'll be a little further ahead. In any event, thumbs up and be ready to take what comes."

From 16 December until our arrival in Bleialf, it had been almost impossible to wash our clothes. At least, I hadn't done so. I did, however, create an illusion of clean clothes by carefully folding my dirty shirt, trousers, long underwear, and socks and placing them in my duffel bag (which also contained all letters, my diary, great thoughts, and what was left of my propaganda collection) at the end of each week. Then, I would put on the clothes placed there the previous week, repeating the process each weekend. On the fourth Sunday of February, Bruno and I finally broke down and washed all our clothes except the ones we were wearing. I made proper note of the occasion in my diary. "Bruno and I went to show in afternoon (*"Two Man Submarine"* — questionable merit) and then returned to wash clothes in big pot outside — how we ever drove ourselves to do it beats me. I swear I'll never wash anything again." The pot was a huge iron one. We built a fire under it, filled it with water and threw in some soap and the clothes and brought it all to a boil. We made an attempt at rinsing our laundry, but soap reappeared in streaks on our uniforms whenever it rained for some weeks thereafter; at least we smelled of GI soap instead of dirt and sweat. My reluctance to wash clothes and perform other household tasks prompted my mother, as I was growing up, to tell others, "Clifford is physically lazy." She was right.

"The way GI's will steal from each other is amazing," I commented in my diary, noting that some stole tires and other accessories from jeeps. Although nearly all of us would become proficient in looting from German homes, stealing from other GIs, a common practice, continued to bother me.

Toward the end of February I used regular air mail to write to my parents. Nineteen letters from them were stacked up, awaiting responses. As usual, I started a letter by making requests — for khaki handkerchiefs and a bottle of ink. I had a good supply of handker-chiefs, thanks to my big wash day, but most of them were a very dirty white and the percentage of loss was high. ''Also, of course, anything you want to send in the way of candy or cookies would be greatly appreciated, but don't go to any trouble. If you do send anything, I'd appreciate your sending it in good containers, so that I can send some miscellaneous items back in them.'' I could use more film anytime (they'd already sent eight rolls), I added, but I had an adequate supply of Bond Street tobacco. My watch was still running and my supply of eyeglasses was intact. A dental inspection was coming up, so that should take care of any cavities. It was the kind of letter my mother relished.

At least one person in the family continued to write me every day. On March third, Punkie, Mom, and Pop all wrote. As usual, my father's letter was newsy. He said they were happy to get my letter of 16 February, having just about given up hearing that week. The V-mails had been coming through pretty regularly in about two weeks. I had a lot of mail coming, he said, explaining that there'd been at least one letter mailed to me every day for the last two months. Mom wrote most of them but he was sure he'd averaged two a week. ''Well the war news keeps good,'' he said. ''Looks like a good time to open up on the Western Front and it looks from here like Eisenhour (*sic*) was about ready to take advantage of the situation. Lots of speculation now as to what the Germans will finally do. Current idea seems to be that after Berlin is captured and the Siegfried line broken that Hitler and the S.S. outfits will retire to South Germany and hold out as long as they can and finally go down in a tremendous crash like the old German mythological figures. The general thought here seems to be that when the German war is over most of the ground forces there will be sent to the Pacific. However, they'll go by way of the United States and will be given good furloughs of 30 days or more when they stop in this country.''

On a less serious note, he mentioned that if I were home right then, I might think it was Belgium. The weather was unpleasant and there was a big pile of manure in the back yard. He added, "However, as I remember it, over there they pile their manure in the front yard." There were many current matters he would like to discuss with me, he said, but he felt by the time his letters arrived situations generally would have changed or the subjects would have lost their importance. He wished for a faster method of communication. "If the airmail really went by air, it would help." In closing, he told me, "Stay in there and pitch and maybe this whole thing will be over sooner than we expect."

When my mother wrote on 9 March, she complained about having to go to dinner parties on three successive nights, including one at which Tom Dewey was the speaker. In addition to her aversion to Washington social life, she said she felt guilty. "It hurts me more than you can ever know to be going to dinner parties and having a good time on the surface and knowing all the time what you're going through! Of course, I've reason enough to know we can't help you any by hybrinating (*sic*) but the Good Lord knows we would do it if it would help you any."

In a letter later in the month, my father gave his opinion of *Time* magazine: "It's probably the best way to keep track of what's going on over here altho a lot of its stuff is written from a sensational and smart aleck view to the extent that it isn't altogether reliable. What I mean is that they use so much over emphasis and under emphasis as well which throws a lot of their stuff out of perspective." He said the report in the 5 February issue on the feelings of the GIs on the Western Front, which I had referred to, sounded a good deal like what he expected from what I had been writing in my letters. He asked if I ever heard from Burke. "He's our favorite of all the boys you ever brought home with you, and we haven't heard from him since before Christmas. He used to write to Mother occasionally and we're worried about him." Jim Burke was my best friend during ASTP days. Pop advised me not to try to do too much serious reading and thinking about peace plans until the fighting was over. "No use in going around with your head in the clouds thinking about a peace plan and then stepping on a German mine," he wrote. He was glad, however, that I hadn't lost interest in such things and he expected me to resume "intellectual and educational interests" just as soon as fighting ceased to be the main thing.

Letter-writing took up much of my spare time in February. Almost every girl whose address was in my book got at least one letter. Mail service from the army to civilians in Belgium, France, and England was available again, so we no longer had to rely on the underground mail system. I wrote in French to Emilie in Arlon and received a pleasant reply; however, we never saw each other again. I also wrote to a girl in Brest whom I had never met. I obtained her address from a fellow GI. In the French manner, she replied: "Although Bretagne is picturesque, like you say, I am tired here; I should want to live in a great, large town such as New York or Paris; alas . . . there are some features of my character: I am very greedy, capricious and romantic, sometimes too much — What do you think of that? I hope you don't judge me wickedly — they are defects so much feminine — are they not? I am also very frank — it is better." We never met, and that probably "is better" as well.

The message I most treasured was an anonymous Valentine from Diane (Dinah), the fun-loving English girl:

Open Sesame!
IF ONLY I HAD A KEY
That would open your heart
to me
On Valentine's Day
I just can't say
What happiness mine would be!
Love, (you had better guess). (xxxxxx)

Alas, Diane and I never saw each other again, either.

As February ended, Jeff Peltz was appointed as our survey section leader. Then 36 (I thought of him as middle-aged), he had been a science teacher and head basketball coach at Mt. Pleasant, Ohio, and head basketball coach and assistant football coach at Wintersville, Ohio. We called him "coach" and he liked that. He was soft-spoken but firm and a good leader. Jeff probably was the greatest poker player in the Sixteenth. On every night possible, he and his victims stayed up to the wee hours, usually until Jeff, playing fair and square, won the pot. When asked what he was doing with the winnings he

Peltz and Kindel with transit near Autobahn at Pirk near the Czech border — late April 1945.

sent home, he would smile and say, "Why, I'm setting up a trust fund for the boys (the losers)!"

As for me, as the month ended I continued as notekeeper for our transit operator, Bill Kiser. As I had written in my diary, I was happy to have a specific job after two years. It also kept me off KP!

Across Germany to Czechoslovakia, March and April. (From *U.S. Army in World War II: The Supreme Command,* 1954.)

Chapter 9

Across the Rhine and on to the Czech Border

We were still in Bleialf, just inside Germany, on the first of March, poised to move on straight across Germany to Czechoslovakia. So rapid were the Allied advances during the last days of the Third Reich that we had many moves ahead — eight in March and 12 in April. The feeling of exhilaration we had experienced journeying across France and Belgium in September returned. But with one great difference. Then we were liberators; now we were conquerors. Most of us were no longer repulsed by the sight of dead German soldiers. Their bodies were looted right along with the unoccupied German homes in which we stayed. We saw slave laborers of many nationalities, and some of them were doing their own looting from the Germans. Although the German armed forces were disintegrating, there was still danger of surprise attacks, and we had not seen the end of deaths and casualties.

Many GIs were constantly on the lookout for booze in any form, not for the purpose of relaxing but for getting dead drunk in the shortest possible time. Many also were looking for girls and women. "Kommen sie hier, Fraulein, mit dein hosen gefallen!" soldiers would yell from their vehicles at every female passed along the road. This was gutter German for "Come here, with your pants down!" This attitude came to be known as the Four Fs: find'em, feel'em, f---'em and forget'em. All of us were indulging, to a greater or lesser extent, in the age-old fruits of conquest.

The mission of the battalion remained one of general support of the VIII Corps, primarily by sound and flash ranging on enemy targets and by carrying survey control for field artillery units of the corps, the after action report said. The present objective of the VIII Corps was to clear the area east of the Prum River and gain the high and dominating ground west of the Kyll River. The enemy was on the defensive all along the corps sector, and our troops reported good progress against light to moderate enemy resistance. The objective was still in the Eifel, west of the valley of the Moselle River, which originated in France, flowed past Trier, and joined the Rhine at Koblenz. The major combat units of the VIII Corps at that time were the 4th, 87th and 90th Infantry Divisions and the 6th and 11th Armored Divisions. Our surveying was hampered by the huge convoys of the 90th Infantry, 6th and 11th Armored, and tank destroyers and self-propelled artillery units moving up.

On 3 March we received the report that the 11th Armored, followed by the veteran 4th Infantry, was pushing off to the Kyll River. That same day another memorable, albeit minor, event occurred. We GIs received our first official liquor rations. Historically, I believe ever since the Revolutionary War, U.S. officers had received liquor rations, but enlisted men in the field had to scrounge for their booze. There still was a difference. Officers received hard liquor, we got wine. Could it have been this that set me to considering the pros and cons of applying for infantry officer candidate school in France that night? According to my diary, I held a serious debate with myself on the subject but tabled it until I could learn more details. Ultimately I decided not to apply because I didn't want to miss the end of the war in Germany.

Winter had not yet left us. The following day I wrote in my diary, "Out all day surveying in weather alternating between, snow, sleet and finally rain. I was too wet to go to chow . . . even though it was fried chicken." We moved to heavily damaged Prum, a road junction on the east side of the Schnee Eifel, on 5 March. All of the battery was together in several large buildings. Two of the survey parties settled into an apartment. Ziegler and I cleaned out one room piled high with furniture and rubble. My reward was finding a very good stamp album, von Clausewitz's "Von Krieg," and a guide book to Kreis Prum. The apartment had belonged to a German professor who, judging by appearances, was a very good Nazi. His library contained such volumes as "The War in Poland." I came across a copy of the song, "Just Like Washington Crossed the Delaware, General Pershing Will Cross the Rhine." In a letter home I asked my father if he had ever heard it in the last war. "I don't quite get the connection," I said, "unless they were trying to prove what evil designs we had on

Germany or something like that.''

Manure piles came up again in our correspondence. My father, like nearly everyone in the United States who had a plot of ground, was growing vegetables to help the war effort. And, like other good victory gardeners, he used manure for fertilizer. He wrote that now he had not one, but two, manure piles. I responded, ''Not only would you be a big shot in France and Belgium with two manure piles, Pop, but you'd also be one in Germany. From appearances, the supermen thrive on that sort of work also.'' It seemed to me the Nazis had given up the idea of evacuating their civilians. I saw a number of them in various towns and villages. Most appeared apathetic and some looked almost happy. But I was wary. I wrote, ''I'm still waiting for some old lady to pull a burp gun from beneath her skirts and open up.'' I was joking about the old lady with the burp gun because Mom had written about her worries concerning German civilians plotting against us. Once again I had the eat-drink-and-be-merry attitude which I'd had before the Bulge. But not all GIs were so carefree. On 7 March I wrote in my diary about an older soldier in our section who definitely had ''the rattle of the battle.'' It seemed to get worse by the day. I couldn't think of anything to do to help him. He did keep the room clean and had a good fire going whenever we returned, so he was still managing to make some contribution. It was a typical day for that period of the war when I wrote about him. The misty, rainy weather had a great influence on my morale and that of nearly everyone else. A little sunshine always went a long way toward giving us a lift.

On a ridge near Gonnersdorf that day, we saw three or four explosions of what we believed to be a German ammunition dump miles to the east. A great semicircular, almost transparent, wave came first, followed by a fire-flash and then a large volume of slowly rising black smoke. The ''transparent wave'' was a most peculiar phenomenon. The heavy traffic, including 60 tanks of the 11th Armored Division, made going slow. It took us about three hours to make the 17-kilometer trip back to Prum. Baileys (prefabricated metal bridges), constructed by the engineers, replaced many destroyed bridges. Budesheim, a village directly east of Prum, was our next move. Both survey parties, battalion operations, and others moved in on a houseful of German civilians. ''Very disgruntled at our taking over. T.S.,'' I commented in my diary. (In this context, T.S.,

meant something like "Well, now, isn't that just too bad!") "I feel
no regret in taking their wood for our stoves or even such things as
wiping muddy hands on their curtains," I continued. "They asked
for it. Some of the population naturally appear solitucious (*sic*), such
as a little girl helping me get water and an old man saying 'C'est la
guerre' to Mac."

Many Comz vehicles (big trucks) moved in night and day with
supplies, mainly gasoline. The army was determined not to come up
short again. Shortage of gasoline was one of the reasons we bogged
down after the sweep across France and Belgium in early September.
Comz was short for Communication Zone, the territory behind the
combat area. The Comz GIs were doing a fantastic job of supplying
the front lines.

I got a package of loot together to mail home on 9 March. Included
was the stamp album, all the propaganda booklets I had been
collecting in the bottom of my duffel bag, and a variety of other
items, some of them clearly contraband. But Red Tyler put his
censor's stamp on it.

"If I get into any trouble because of this stuff, your father will have
to get me out," Tyler said.

"Well," I rejoined, "if this package busts open on the way to the
States, probably all three of us will go to prison for the rest of our
natural lives."

POWs (prisoners of war) were much in evidence during the early
days of March. We saw many truckloads of German POWs as well as
released French prisoners going to the VIII Corps PWE (prisoner of
war enclosure). The POW collecting point was jammed to over-
flowing and guards were begging drivers to take prisoners further
back. Some of our battalion vehicles were used to carry them. It was
reported that there were as many as 5,000 prisoners in an open field.
K-rations to feed them were stacked as high as two-story houses.
There was change everywhere. All vehicles were now using head-
lights. Convoys crowded together made the roads look like Main
Street on Saturday night back home. Everything and everyone
seemed to be on the move. Moving on every day and standing guard
almost every night was tiring. Guard shifts were usually one to two
hours long and involved losing several hours of sleep. I was glad to be
young. In the area, there was a regular congress of nationalities. I
made note of Poles, Russians, Yugoslavs, Austrians, Dutch, vir-

tually all nationalities of Hitler's slaves. Some were refugees going back on the roads, while others, such as farm laborers, were patiently awaiting our orders to move on. We moved to Nohm, a village to the northeast, on 11 March for a one-night stand. We were housed comfortably in the upstairs of a German home. The owners were quick to explain their hatred of the Nazis and they eagerly provided warmth and other needs. "The business of non-fraternization is truly a great problem," I wrote that night in my diary. "Time alone can assay its wisdom." Earlier that day we were all but pampered at nearby Adenau. We went in bedraggled formation to the VIII Corps enlisted men's mess, where for the first time since rest camp at Arlon on 1 December I ate in a building — at a table. Leaving Nohm early in the morning, we returned to Adenau to get our orders to proceed to Saffig, a village some distance to the east and directly west of Koblenz. That afternoon we took over a house after waiting for civilians to clear out their possessions. Watching them do it was a pitiful sight, I acknowledged in my diary, adding, "But God knows, they asked for it." The house was a great setup — electric lights, radio, running water. Too good to keep, I figured.

Our arrival at the Rhine made 13 March a day to remember. Seeing the legendary river satisfied a certain longing for me. The sun came out in the afternoon. There were civilians driving horses, milling around, and going about their chores even as our tanks fired in the distance. It seemed an unusual situation to see them as we heard the report of the guns and the shells whistling overhead and landing on the opposite bank of the Rhine — white phosphorus shells landing on an island in the Rhine as we watched deer roaming in the fields! We completed almost eight miles of survey that day, the most we had done in the ETO. Of far greater significance, however, was returning to Saffig at the end of the long day to find we'd been evicted from our comfortable living quarters just as I had predicted we would be. The battery command post, survey information center, and so forth had moved into the place. Everyone was having a violent case of the R.A. (red ass), cussing out everyone else as we took our stuff out. Colonel Lushene was sitting in "his" room hearing every word, I guess. To add insult to injury, we got C-rations for evening chow. When our party was with the rest of the battery, we were usually assured full-fledged meals and mail delivery. Eventually we settled into a

*The author with Bruno on the east bank of the Moselle, across the river from Kobern,
Germany, March 1945. Rocky vineyards can be seen on the hillside in the background.*

house down the street. I pulled guard duty at 5 a.m., and when I came
off I built a fire. Some of the guys objected to the noise I made.
Another day off to a bad start.

Surveying through Mulheim, a village near the Rhine, I was
impressed by a street of white flags, symbolizing surrender. The
countryside was beautiful. At the last survey station a brook babbled
through a green meadow. Most of the village citizens went about
work in their gardens unperturbed. Others had the French and
Belgian habit of hanging out the windows of their homes and staring
at us. The battery went wild again about guard duty, putting six men
on at a time, I wrote in my diary that evening. I had a middle-of-the-
night shift that lasted an hour and 15 minutes. "This might as well be
an MP outfit," I grumbled. "I don't know whether hot chow from the
kitchen is worth being with the battery or not."

The Ides of March (15 March) deserved a note. The term had
fascinated me ever since I read of Julius Caesar's assassination on

that date. Originally I thought "the Ides" was a geographical location instead of a date. On this date in 1945 we saw out first German jet. It came over dropping flares. Then, for a moment, there was a great red glow the sky. Guards up the street said the plane was jet-propelled and the glow was produced when it was shot down.

An entry in my diary said, "Five GIs, riding high, in a command car, asked me if I knew where they could get ____." What they asked was, "Where can we get laid?" Although at that time I was cursing and using gutter language right along with others, I always was careful to use only blanks or initials in my diary instead of the obscenities. As to the question posed, I truthfully did not have an answer, although I was sure others in the battery did.

On the following Monday, we crossed the beautiful Moselle River for the first time on a pontoon bridge at Kobern, southeast of Saffig. High hills on either side were terraced with vineyards for the famous Moselle wines. It was a sunny day and the scenery was terrific. The job I dreaded and thought was behind me forever reappeared on 20 March when Peltz told me I was scheduled for KP. In addition to having no desire to work for the mess sergeant, I was put out at doing a corporal's job as notekeeper for five weeks and then getting thrown into the kitchen. Peltz and Lieutenant Tyler said they'd try to get me off, but I had little faith in them. "It'll take more than that (KP) to bother me these days," I told my diary, adding the usual, "C'est la guerre, Hope ole kid." I escaped KP. At breakfast I was relieved to find Barstow on the job. Perhaps Peltz and Tyler did put in a good word for me but I didn't ask. By this time I had learned to let sleeping dogs lie. It turned out to be another day of sunshine, good for morale. I swore if I didn't have to go on KP, I'd write Dr. Hollister and Rev. Williams of Garden City. And I did. "It almost sounds as if I made a deal with God," I told my diary. "Deal with God or not, I was thankful."

Earlier in the month I expressed a worry (in my diary) at the realization that being an arrogant world conqueror still rode high in my brain. Bruno had the same fantasy. "It almost worries me, but always I am restrained by my conscience and pray to God that I always will be." On 22 March I returned to the subject more specifically. The diary account said, "Bruno and I jestingly talking tonight of an American Army of 400 divisions — 50 Armored, 25

Airborne, 10 Mountain, etc., with an Air Force & Navy of four million and and millions in foreign labor battalions. And although we jest, I almost think we're both halfway serious; after all we've seen and heard, it's a helluva way to feel. It worries me.''

There was no question about it, I had become hardened to seeing death every day. Only the day before I reported casually that in surveying down the main highway for six to eight miles we passed one badly shot-up village with ''75 to 100 dead Krauts stretched out in two neat rows on the edge of a village near the highway.'' Two civilians were using hooks to load them into the wagons. Two more dead men, one with his head blown off, were near one of our survey stations. I ended the account, ''No comment — I've lost all feeling that way.'' Two days later, I wrote: ''___ stopped on way out to take GI combat boots off of dead Kraut near road. I cut SS insignia from his collar and Death's Head from his cap.''

On the morning of 23 March we moved to Emmelhausen, southeast of Saffig but still west of the Rhine. I managed to get a bed in a nice house. There were electric lights and plenty of lavatories but no running water. It was another day of sunshine and everything seemed brighter. We ate at outdoor tables near the kitchen and saw a movie, *Hollywood Canteen*, at Mogul (VIII Corps Artillery Headquarters). Seeing Joan Leslie was a treat but hearing the song ''Don't Fence Me In'' for the first time was a letdown, I noted in my diary. Later that day, by fishing around for them with the help of Hand's flashlight, I found a pair of sandals for myself in a damaged shoe store. Right after writing that, I flipped to a more noble level: ''New thought, possibly naive: Perfection in various fields of human endeavor depends upon various qualities — for example a violinist's hands, a baritone's voice, an industrialist's brain — but perfection in statesmanship is almost entirely dependent upon character.''

Although I had a devil-may-care attitude in general, there still were moments of apprehension. On 24 March we were surveying near Bacharach to the highway near Dichtenbach and Rheinbollen. In looking for a benchmark before starting, we rode up a winding road overlooking the Rhine. It was a beautiful view of the river, but it also was perfect for being observed. A town on the opposite bank was burning. While Peltz stopped for about five minutes to check his maps, everyone became exceedingly jumpy. It was such a naked feeling. I hadn't felt so uneasy since the German-manned P47 dropped a bomb on the Arlon-Bastogne highway. Returning that evening, we saw great preparations underway. There were navy assault boats, and a complete bridge and other materials were stacked in the fields near the main highway. Crossing the Rhine was imminent. A quartermaster outfit was setting up a railroad that would soon be in operation. Although my mechanical aptitude was zero and my desire to learn to do anything with my hands was the same, I was impressed by those who knew how to build.

The next day was Palm Sunday, but the only way you could tell was by looking at the calendar. We cleaned trucks and equipment in the morning, and our party put in a radar station near Pleizhausen in the afternoon. It was another beautiful spring day. There were many navy assault boats on the roads and much traffic was moving north. We surmised it was in preparation for the announced bridgehead between Koblenz and Boppard. Before long we learned that we had received crossing priority for six survey vehicles after 5:30 p.m. the next afternoon. Elated at this word, I settled down to write letters by candlelight. One was to my parents, only the second for the month. I shared the good news of the Rhine crossings and had positive reports about the weather for a change. "Naturally, there's quite a lot of dust," I wrote, "but being an old Kansan, it doesn't bother me — and I'll take it over mud any day."

For my mother's benefit, I made special mention of our chaplain, the Rev. Earl Stainbrook. He came almost every week but he had never yet made it on Sunday. "Sunday," I explained, "is naturally never different from any other day, but that can't be helped." Rev. Stainbrook and his assistant, G. W. Richards, prepared a four-page Holy Week program for us, I reported. The rest of the letter was about tanks. "In regard to our discussion about tanks, I notice that the new T-26 (Pershing) is still not supposed to be a match for the Tiger and Tiger Royal, particularly in maneuverability and armor. Our tank-men are certainly great, but it's their skill and great superiority of numbers that's doing the job. Personally I think it'd be a good idea to keep manufacturing Tigers in Germany after we defeat the Krauts and use them (the Tigers) against the Japs."

Sometime in March Pop wrote a four-page letter. The only letter from my parents written during March that I saved, it gave a good picture of life on the homefront. My father mentioned getting the victory garden started with radishes, lettuce, and swiss chard, saying

The crossing of the Rhine River (near Oberwesel, Germany) was made in the LCVP (Landing Craft Vehicle - Personnel) pulled up to the shore.

it looked as if they might need it more than they had anytime yet because food as well as everything else definitely was scarcer than it had been any time during the war. "The supply of everything is gradually getting a little shorter, so gradually that we don't notice it a great deal." The most serious shortage at the moment was in clothes, especially work clothing and children's clothes. Meat and butter were in the shortest supply as far as food was concerned; chickens were practically unobtainable and canned goods were scarce. Cereals, however, were plentiful and prospects for the wheat crop were good. Transportation of goods was a problem; railroads suffered from a shortage of manpower, and truck transportation was hampered by the deteriorating highways. All conventions were prohibited for the duration of the war except on approval of the ODT (Office of Defense Transportation). "It doesn't approve any unless they contribute to the war effort, and very few do," Pop commented.

Lounge lizards, playboys, and nightclub owners were howling about the 12 o'clock curfew, he said, but no one was paying much attention. The curfew was given credit for lessening absenteeism in war plants. That, in fact, was the real purpose of it, although the announced one was to save coal. "A lot of these high-priced workers got the idea that they were playboys and as long as their money lasted they were working at it harder than they were at their jobs, but," Pop added, "that's no criticism of a large percentage of war workers who really are doing a good job." Drew Pearson, prominent and controversial columnnist of the time, had moved his prediction of the war's end up from "almost anytime now" to 30 days, "so I guess you're going to have to stay and fight a little longer," Pop wrote. He closed with a touching reminiscence about the walks the two of us used to take at the Washington Zoo. "Wish we could take another one in the morning. Anyway, let's figure on one when you get back."

Our long-awaited crossing of the Rhine in a naval landing craft came on 22 March. It seemed incongruous to see U.S. sailors on the Rhine. The navy officers were told that we had orders from the general (McMahon) to get across and survey. We crossed at Oberwesel and from there went down the river highway to Kaub, then over high hills and across fields northeast of Bornich. Both of our weapons carriers got stuck, and a winch cable was broken in an attempt to get them out. An infantry platoon was moving into Bornich at the same time we were. The town was freed the day before, but there were no other outfits there. Oberwesel lay about equidistant between Koblenz and Mainz and also near St. Goar, home of the fabled Lorelei.

Stobert Abney, one of the original members of the Sixteenth, and I went looking for wine on our second night in Bornich. I considered him an "Old Army Man" from whom I could learn a lot. Our search was successful. We filled a couple of helmets with 1944 wine from a basement by pulling out the spigot and letting the wine gush forth. Then we took off through the town collecting about 10 bottles of wine from friendly Russians. "Coach" Peltz frequently disapproved of such activities but that didn't stop us. We took off again, going over the barn roof because he was on guard out front, but our luck had run dry. When we knocked on doors, one resident German after another told us we'd find wine just down the street but not at their house.

By the next day, Holy Thursday, wine and schnapps were flowng freely and Peltz was plenty upset. In my diary I wrote, "Coach saying he'd turn in the next man he caught taking a drink. Meanwhile, most of the rest of the battery seemed very drunk." That day, drunk or sober, we moved northeast to Miehlen and then to Daisbach, north of Wiesbaden. On Good Friday I went to services in the morning. Chaplain Stainbrook was there. It was the first time we had attended services in a church since leaving England.

There were so many Russians and other workers in the German towns that it made me wonder if we were in Germany or Russia. The entire battalion joined us in Daisbach later in the day and I spent the afternoon with Jack Joss, a new reinforcement, putting up two latrines. There was no furniture left in the house we moved into and hence no beds. Ordered to flush out the neighboring woods on 31 March, we found plenty of equipment and clothing but no soldiers — stragglers from the Wehrmacht. A and B batteries, however, captured 17 prisoners. My main diary notation for the day was that five GIs (I named them) were "out in two vehicles at night with at least one Austrian babe." As usual, punishment for the enlisted men was swift. The next day, 10 in the battalion, including some in the above escapade, were reduced in rank to private. One advantage to being a private, I noted, was you couldn't be busted.

Easter Sunday, falling on April Fool's Day, turned out to be a good day for me. After church the Red Cross Clubmobile showed up. With it was that same girl from Kansas, Betty, whom I had met at Trois Vierges when I was at the clearing station in November. Our battery and a field artillery group searched houses in Daisbach in the afternoon, looking for firearms, knives, cameras, radios and a certain mysterious Major Yonki. I found an expensive shotgun in one house in a locked cabinet which I had to get a locksmith to open. Because of various activities of party One, Lieutenant Tyler restricted both parties for one week. We had to be inside at 7 p.m. with lights out at 10 p.m. Our party was really red-assed about it, so a good part of Easter was spent bitching about that. After being on guard in late afternoon, I was called to the battery command post, where I was informed I had made corporal. At the same time, Peltz made staff sergeant. "Buck corporal satisfies a dream I've had for a long time," I wrote in my diary right ahead of a note that mentioned I heard "Rum and Coca Cola" on the radio for the first time.

The promotion was a far cry from my basic training bet that I would be a captain in two years, but the reality of any promotion meant more to me then than any basic training fantasy. Although being promoted put me in the same category with Corporals Napoleon Bonaparte and Adolf Hitler, I realized it was no big deal in the annals of mankind. However, because my return address on envelopes would now have to read "Cpl.," I thought I should mention it to my parents. So I added an ever-so-casual P.S. to my letter the next day: "I was promoted to corporal yesterday and hence increased my allotment from $26 to $40 today."

What our battalion was doing in the war on 1 April was chronicled in the after action report as continuing its "mission in general support of the VIII Corps." In the closing days of March, the rapid advance of the First and Third Armies had pinched out the corps front and created a pocket southwest of Giessen, Germany. By the end of March, units of the VIII Corps had cleared nearly all of the remaining enemy elements trapped within this pocket and were awaiting further orders to move to a new sector of the front lines. Two days later we advanced far into Germany. Leaving Daisbach in convoy early in the morning, we drove 114 miles northeast to Oberaula, a town between Alfeld and Hersfeld. For about 60 miles we were on the famed Autobahn. It was comparable to the Pennsylvania Turnpike, I wrote in my diary. We saw many freed French prisoners, most of them headed south, marching along the famous road. Some were in vehicles. One group was in two trailers pulled by a tractor. Carrying their tricolors, they looked amazingly well dressed in old army uniforms. It was a cold, rainy day, and our outfit was pretty uncomfortable by the time we arrived at our destination.

Of the house we moved into, I wrote, "One babe, 21, living here has (or had) husband in SS Panzers — everyone giving her the eye." She kept hanging around being helpful, showing us how to fix fires, putting disinfectant on my finger when I cut it on a C-ration can. I felt keenly the basic conflict in nonfraternization enforcement. Everyone realized its wisdom, but "it practically drove you crazy to be in a country in which you were supposed to have absolutely nothing to do with the civil population and in which you knew its civilians would hate you no matter how you treated them." The next day we waited around until late afternoon before moving out, going through Hersfeld, Bebra, and Nentershausen. Many Frenchmen along the way gave us the V for Victory sign. Two girls, probably French, laughed and giggled when I gave a "San Antone" yell from the back of the weapons carrier. Bruno and I nabbed a bed in the house we ended up in that night. There were artillery flashes, and a number of planes were heard overhead. Peltz and Don said two Messerschmitts were strafing the Autobahn about dusk. They were on the road, about 200 yards from the strafing, after delivering information to infantry divisions. Also, paratroopers were said to be in the woods nearby. Reports of ambushes persisted. A field artillery battalion commander and his party were rumored to be lost. On 6 April our battalion made a coordinated search of Nentershausen for suspected enemy soldiers and potential weapons still in civilian hands. Aiding us were a group of liberated Polish soldiers who identified several Germans in civilian clothing with notorious Gestapo backgrounds. Twenty-seven prisoners were rounded up and hauled to the corps' prisoner-of-war cage. Because of the danger of an ambush of our survey parties, six GIs from the 6th Cavalry Group were assigned to protect us. Arriving in two jeeps, they were armed with .30 caliber machine guns and automatic shoulder weapons. It was good to have them along, especially the ones who remained sober. I was beginning to have a guilty conscience even about drinking. That night a friend gave me a little gin, and with the help of five other guys we finished off a bottle of wine I had been saving. "This may be a terrible thing to say," I confessed in my diary, "but that stuff has certainly relaxed me from increasingly greater tensions."

We were on the move again the next day to Marksuhl, southeast of Nentershausen and southwest of the city of Eisenach. As we surveyed east of Marksuhl, I was thinking of girls, a more-often-than-not preoccupation. There were women in workers' barracks along the road to Ruhla beckoning for us to come in as we were returning to Marksuhl. It was a temptation. Marksuhl was another overnight stay. The next day we moved to Brotterode in the Thuringer Wald (Thuringia Forest). Bruno and I engaged in exchanging assorted postwar fantasies, including a tour of Europe and plans for a $50,000 home with a large trophy and souvenir room in Maryland on the banks of the Potomac, opposite Mt. Vernon. We also discussed what it would be like to have Germans occupying our houses the way we were taking over theirs.

Moving from Brotterode through Friedrichroda to Ohrdruf, the entire battery was assigned to a castlelike mansion on a high hill at the edge of town. It was built around 1933-1935 by a Dr. Muhlberg. As we waited about two hours for the rest of the battery to arrive, some of us went around taking pictures of the place. Muhlberg was obviously a chemist, an industrialist and a bigtime Nazi. Captain Carter lectured us on looting as soon as he arrived. Bruno and I carried our bed rolls up to a bed we had picked out in the nursery. Amazingly, all the

The castle of Dr. Wolfgang Mühlberg at Ohrdruf, Germany. At noon on 11 April German planes bombed the area around it. Cpl. Tennis Humphrey was killed in the attack.

plumbing was in good condition. Our sense of well-being was short-lived. Shortly after noon, a prolonged rumbling, like a piano being pushed across the floor, filled the castle. Explosions shook the structure. Everyone rushed into the hall. It was filled with plaster dust. Guys were lying on the floor. My first thought was that time bombs were going off. I didn't realize until I reached the basement that Kraut planes had bombed us. "I have never seen such terrified expressions on men's faces in my life (including my own, undoubtedly), as I did in the hall and on the way down the stairs," I said in my diary.

The only bomb that landed near us hit east of an outside wall. It killed Humphrey and wounded Sargent, Sulfleski, and K. P. Thompson. Hurka, who was next to Humphrey, was covered with blood. He told us Humphrey's head was blown off. Ordered to load up, we drove the vehicles into fields under concealment of trees by the side of a small stream. Bruno, Stobert, and I helped load gasoline and then waited a couple of hours in the fields by the stream bank. Moving into a wooded area near Arnstadt, we awaited further developments. "Some of the boys think the caretaker of the castle may have tipped off the Krauts as to our presence, but I personally believe it was a target of opportunity — they undoubtedly thought a corps or division headquarters was housed there (in the castle),'' my diary notation said.

This was the day, 11 April, marked for a second D-Day, for the jumping off of all Allied armies upon what was left of Germany, according to reports. I saw a whole line of white phosphorous shells in the distance as we pulled into the woods. Eventually, we occupied houses along a street near the edge of Arnstadt. I found a little wine in the basement and also canned strawberries, plums, and currants. In spite of Captain Carter's warnings against looting, I took from the castle a small atlas entitled, *"Berlin in der Tasche,"* autographed by Dr. Muhlberg. Much of the other loot I collected I discarded soon after my return home, but I kept that book and have it to this day.

In our haste to leave Ohrdruf, some of us didn't see the infamous concentration camp there, but others in the battalion did and they took pictures of the dead immates. Later in April I wrote home: "I've mentioned before the warped minds of the Krauts — a particular instance of this is the fact that they all seem worried about starving, yet I've seen hundreds of Russian, Polish and French prisoners and workers who are literally skin and bones, which the "good Germans" never seemed in the least concerned about. At one town several stops back, 2,000 workers were murdered just before our forces took it, yet all the townspeople denied knowledge of the atrocity; the burgomeister committed suicide when he was shown the bodies. Everywhere people deny ever having been Nazis, but practically every house looks like a branch of Goebbels' propaganda bureau. Not only that, but most houses are littered with ornate paintings, souvenirs, and trinkets of the war. When you get to thinking about it, it gives you a sickening feeling in the pit of your stomach.''

I did not know the full significance of the village of Ohrdruf until years later when I was researching World War II to place this memoir in historical perspective. A German officer-deserter told of a high-level headquarters or communication center there. This information led Eisenhower and Bradley to direct Patton to roar ahead of the then-front lines to seize Ohrdruf. The village was captured on the afternoon of 4 April by the 4th Armored Division, one week before our arrival. An immense underground communication center was discovered set in deep concrete tunnels with radio and telephone facilities large enough to serve a small city. The center was constructed as a headquarters for the German armed forces high command (OKW) just before the Czechoslovakia crisis of 1938, but it was never used. Then in the spring of 1945 Heinrich Himmler, exercising increasing authority, ordered the facilities expanded as a possible retreat for Hitler, to be presented to him on his birthday on 20 April. Work had hardly begun before Ohrdruf's capture, but the center was being used by Field Marshal Kesselring, then commander of German forces on the Western Front. Kesselring fled less than 24 hours before the 4th Armored arrived.

Only after discovery of the underground facilities did the GIs find the concentration camp (a satellite camp for Buchenwald). It was the first to be liberated by the American and British armies. On 12 April Eisenhower, Bradley, and Patton visited the camp. Eisenhower turned pale and silent, Bradley was overwhelmed by the smell of death, and tough old George Patton vomited. Then Ike ordered every unit nearby that was not in the front lines to tour the camp. He also cabled London and Washington, urging that delegations of officials and newsmen see for themselves the liberated camps, the horror of which exceeded any previous reports.

It was early on the morning of 13 April that we learned of President Roosevelt's death. My immediate reaction was recorded in my diary: "Heard the report that the President died. . . . As with everyone, I suppose, it leaves me feeling as if I were in a huge vacuum. It'll be days before full significance of his death really 'reaches' everyone. I just can't see Truman as President, but for the sake of the entire world, we must all strive to make the best of the situation."

That day both Mom and a Garden City classmate, Bob Jordan, then a Navy V-12 pre-med student in Detroit, wrote me their somewhat different reactions. My mother said that Pop didn't come home to eat that evening, so she and my sister went to the Hot Shoppe for supper. There, a waitress told them of Roosevelt's death. They hurried home to turn on the radio. Just as they arrived, my father was calling to tell them. He had gone to his car to catch the seven o'clock news. He was a few minutes early and he heard an announcer talking about Roosevelt in the past tense. It struck him as strange. But in a few minutes he understood why. "Those of us who did not approve of Roosevelt's methods and policies may find that Truman will suit us better," my mother wrote. "You know how conservative Daddy is in his judgment of people and how prone he is to not criticize — when I asked him what sort of a President Truman would make, he said, 'He has not undertaken anything so far that he hasn't done successfully.' We'll all hope that proves true of his presidency. Surely we as a nation should give him our undivided support until he proves that he does not merit it. God hasn't forsaken us and perhaps He is working out His plan in His own way even though it may look impossible to us. Indeed I do pity Truman to have all the overwhelming responsibilities of the Presidency thrust upon him at this time of crisis. I pity the people who almost worshipped Roosevelt and thought the world would end if he were not elected last November. The radio commentators are profuse in their praise of Roosevelt. They continually compare or liken him to Lincoln and Washington. I can't see that myself but perhaps history will prove that that is true.''

Bob's letter began, ''This is indeed an unhappy day, not only for America but for the world. . . . Cliff, it would do your heart good to see how the American people are reacting now. No one has an unkind word for the President. Everyone acknowledges the fact that he was undoubtedly the greatest international figure of all time in politics, and everyone is concerned, not with how F.D.R. died and how things are for his family, but with the future of our nation. There is such unity and brotherhood everywhere.'' He went on, ''Instead of criticizing Truman, as nearly everyone did at election time, they all have given him their fullest support and have confidence in him. It may be a fickle population, this country of ours, but it is certainly proving its loyalty to the ideals of a nation. It makes me feel darned good to know that we can have such unity of purpose and desire. All the shops, other places of business, etc. are shutting down tomorrow afternoon to pay tribute at four o'clock.''

Several days later Pop wrote that the President's death was a great shock to the country. Although there had been a lot of discussion of his health during the last two or three years, not much had been said about it lately, especially since he seemed to stand the Yalta trip very well. ''I last saw him when he addressed Congress after his return from Yalta,'' Pop wrote. ''He looked somewhat thinner than usual but had a good color, the result no doubt of his sea voyage. ''I suppose that no one has ever lived whose death created so much news or was more widely discussed and publicized. For the last three days Roosevelt-Truman news has practically pushed the war not only off the front page but also out of the newspapers entirely. The networks cut out all their entertainment programs from the time of the announcement of his death until after the funeral today. Everything has been news and commentators and sacred or classical music. A lot of time and space, of course, has been devoted to Truman, because he is comparatively unknown to most of the people. He's really getting a great buildup now.

"I scarcely know Truman, but I've talked to several senators, both Republican and Democrat, who know him well including some who have served on his investigating committee and all of them think he can do the job. It's too bad Roosevelt couldn't have lived to see the end of the war and the beginning of some world organization. However, as far as his place in history is concerned, and that's something which he apparently gave some consideration, he could never have passed away at a better time. There are going to be a lot of disappointments and disillusions during the next few years, bound to be no matter who is at the helm, but from now on Roosevelt will not have the responsibility for them."

Back in central Germany, our eastward advance continued rapidly. We moved five times from 13 to 18 April. The first few hours after we moved into a house on a hill at the edge of Tannroda on the 13th were spent looting, and then we fixed ourselves a delicious supper from what we found — chicken soup, potatoes, string beans, canned strawberries and apples, pickled cauliflower, and coffee. When I found a large basket of eggs under my bed, we added fried eggs to the menu. After the meal, I willingly helped with KP. Captain Carter and Lieutenants Johnson and Tyler came around for a free feed. Johnson became our party's officer on this date. An outdoor "bathhouse" provided the accommodations for my first tub bath since my last three-day pass to Washington in May — 11 months before. There was a long, galvanized tub to stretch out in; water was heated in a large wash pot. It was a great bath.

We moved on eight kilometers to Blankenheim, where we had another homemade supper of rabbit. The 6th Cavalry boys prepared it and I washed dishes again. Bruno and I slept on sheets, supplied by the house, that night. It was a reminder of the good old days. Bruno was a master of spinning fantasies. He carried a picture of Rosemary Lane, a popular singer of the time, in his wallet. That night at Blankenheim he passed it around, saying it was a picture of his wife.

The incident gave me the heartiest sustained laugh I'd had in a long time. He also had two snapshots of himself as a junior high student. He said they were pictures of "his boys." A tub bath, good food, sheets, and humor. Life was looking up, and I was grown up enough to admit and appreciate it.

The battery moved to the outskirts of Kahla on 15 April. We found 10 bottles of wine, brandy, champagne, and cognac in a locked basket in the basement of a house. After standing guard, I had a good German sausage sandwich and washed it down with wine and champagne. When we went to look over an underground plant that made jet-propelled planes at a foreign labor camp in the hills the next morning, we didn't see much. Smoke was pouring out of the side of the hill at the entrance to the plant. Probably the place was being dried out. In talking with a military government officer who was loading western European workers in a truck for transportation home, I learned that 18,000 workers had been employed in the immediate area. The report was that a thousand of them died of starvation during March. Moving on to Triptis, both survey parties stayed in one house. I drank gin, apricot brandy, and cognac with Wagner, Shelton, Abney, and Okie until I went on guard at 2 a.m. "I suppose it's a helluva thing to crave," I commented in my diary, "but it (liquor) really helps relieve the nervous tension." I found a good map of Germany when we looked over several bombed-out factories the next morning, and Bruno gave me a pair of binoculars he got from the burgomeister of a nearby town in the afternoon.

A few notes in my diary describe the way the war was at the time: "Coach raising hell about drinking last night. Party seems more like a Sunday School class every day, but of course it's still a helluva lot better than it was under Thompson. . . . Burning desire to fraternize tonight but as usual I'm repressing it — and I confess it's more from fear of running into trouble than from any moral scruples. ____ expressing contempt for Russians and Poles; it's things like that make all this seem senseless — but I haven't lost my faith that much can still be salvaged from the war."

At our next stop near Alt Neugommla, the house we moved into had already been thoroughly looted. That night we learned that Ernie Pyle, the famous war correspondent, had been killed. To me his death was as great a shock as the President's had been. He was a great hero. Don Gindele, upon returning from Paris, told us a Frenchman,

Phil Hand and the author with German children at Gommla, Germany, in late April.

Tom Fourshee, Jeff Peltz, and Jocko Kindel, kneeling, at Gommla, April.

obviously grieving, showed him a newspaper telling of F.D.R.'s death. The man, and later a French girl, asked Gindele why the GIs were drunk at such a time. He didn't have a satisfactory answer. "I guess," I wrote in my diary, "it's just a trait peculiarly American."

Except for one-night stops of our survey party in Limbach to the northeast and Selb to the south, we stayed in Alt Neugommla until after V-E Day. This village was a short distance northwest of Greiz on the border between Thuringia and Saxony and also right on the Czech border. On 16 April the VIII Corps was transferred to First Army control and ordered to reach the Zwickauer-Mulde River line and "hold their positions." That river line was just west of the Czech border. Awaiting the arrival of the advancing Russians, we were still surveying like crazy although none of us lower-ranking GIs knew why.

A brief diary entry for 23 April noted that it was raining hard on our way back to Neugommla. The top of the weapons carrier was rolled halfway back, and Ziegler, Bruno, and I had a helluva time holding it down. As the loose canvas top pounded on our helmets, Bruno composed one of his many imaginary official army telegrams to his mother: "Dear Mrs. McNamara: We regret to advise that your son David has been beaten to death by a piece of canvas."

There was a GI in our battery who had a knack for finding friendly women immediately upon arrival in a village. It was as if he had a special kind of radar. I called him the "Operator" and I had every intention of learning something from him when I accompanied him on 21 April on his usual mission. We went to the home of a woman who was originally from Texas. With her in the house was her German husband, his female cousin, and his parents. There were also several extra "available" women in the household. Naturally, our being there was a clear violation of nonfraternization rules. What I decided that night was that fraternization with Germans was impossible for me. I hadn't really ever thought it would be possible, but this personal experience convinced me.

"These people, supposedly 'good' Germans, openly welcomed us, but their conversation revealed how warped their minds are," I wrote in my diary. I listed these cases in point and my reactions to them:

"1) They were worried about starving. (But had they never seen Russians & Poles & Frenchmen and yes, even Americans, in the

Riech starving?)

"2) Hans (the babe's husband) said the Germans would never allow a man of Himmler's character to run the country. (My God! what do they think has been going on for the past 12 years?)

"3) Hans also said Von Papen was not a Nazi, that he was one of their most brilliant diplomats. (Of course, he was no Nazi, but he worked closely with them in diabolical schemes for 12 years.)

"As far as I can see," I wrote on, "this entire generation is ruined; their minds are warped beyond repair." Returning to the subject two days later, I made it clear that I declined to go back to the Texas woman's house with the Operator. My excuse was that I wasn't feeling too well. Furthermore, I confided, I was "more or less disgusted with the whole idea anyway. But I was ambivalent. "____ went with him, and they had a quart of schnapps in addition to the usual stuff. I could've gone for the schnapps, but still am glad I didn't go. The whole idea is just no good. Wish we'd get to Czechoslovakia."

So that night, instead of going for women and schnapps, I wrote a long letter home. The weather, I reported, had been generally fair and mild up to the last few days, which turned cold and rainy with sleet and hail for good measure. "I don't know what the effect of weather on national behavior is supposed to be, but if there is any connection I can certainly see why the Krauts have warped minds." I went on to note that the apple blossoms were out. They reminded me that the Shenandoah Valley should be beautiful back home. "I am farther in Germany than I ever expected to be before the war ended and hoping to meet the Russians any day now. It's becoming increasingly apparent that the Krauts will never surrender and I'm still expecting a long drawn-out job of at least several months duration." As for President Roosevelt's death, I wrote that while it was a great shock to everyone here, "outwardly it hasn't seemed to have affected anyone very much." With hundreds being killed every day, one man's death, no matter how important he might be, seemed relatively unimportant, I editorialized.

One of several things I did routinely was to keep track of the number of places I'd slept while overseas. I reported the latest figure: "57 and still going." On another score, I said I hadn't heard from either Barbara or Irene for a month or more, "so I guess I'll have to start all over again when I get back." In answer to my mother's mention of collecting clothes for people of liberated Europe, I said, "From some of the sights I've seen, you can certainly tell everyone that there was never a worthier cause." They could send me more pipes, I advised, because I kept losing them. There was no need for more cigars, however. We found a cigar factory intact. "As a result, the whole battery looks like a bunch of small-time, cigar-smoking politicians, or racetrack bookies, or something."

The next night I was writing again. My diary caught a well-intentioned, if emotional, outburst. "I am very restless again. I read in *Time* of a secret deal for U.S. & Russia at San Francisco conference — such things are sickening. Oh God, why can't the wishes of common men the world over prevail? Must humanity, in decisively defeating the largest combine of evil ever set against it, merely pile power politics upon the foundations of lasting peace and build a structure which must surely come crashing down within a generation? Make men of good will, God! Let them see the light!"

The last week of April we were still surveying and still wondering why and beginning to get on each other's nerves in our impatience with the way the war was dragging on. Sunday, 29 April, brought a good break. Headquarters battery left Alt Neugommla early and picked up A and B batteries on the Autobahn to do control work for the 1st Division and V Corps mainly in Czechoslovakia. At Selb, a German town right on the Czech border, we moved into the office building of a pottery factory. The 17th FOB had just vacated it. We had a great time throwing unbaked dishes, which crumbled in our hands, at pictures of Hitler found in the factory. In the afternoon, our party surveyed across the Czech border to Muhlbach. Vehicles went ahead of us to clear logs from a road block which apparently had just been thrown up by civilians.

In the evening I went with Shelton, Wagner, Elting, and Gindele to the barracks for Polish workers in a factory. About 40 Polish girls and six men, at least one of them French, were there. Abney and some men from Party One arrived later. To my amazement Coach Peltz went over with us, but he didn't stay long. He thought Tyler might be wanting him. The women were very goodlooking, it seemed to us. Some spoke French, so I managed to carry on limited conversations. The tables were pushed back, someone began playing an accordion, and the girls danced with each other at first. Hurka, Elting, Stobert, and I soon joined in. Later, the workers sang Polish songs, including the Polish national anthem. We GIs punctuated their renditions by screaming "Ei-hi" occasionally and it sent them rolling in the aisles. "All in all," I wrote in my diary later, "it was one of the best times I've had since I've been in the ETO."

We returned to battery headquarters at Alt Neugommla on the last day of April. The ride back was very cold but there was a good pork chop dinner awaiting us. It was a welcome relief from C- and K-rations. At a beer hall in town, we saw *Meet Me in St. Louis.* During the movie I thought about those Polish girls who had been in forced labor for four years or more and realized again how disrupting and tragic war was. I finally got a letter from Irene. "It's strange," I wrote in my diary, "but it seems I can never forget that girl."

The after action report summed up the area military situation at month's end, saying the VIII Corps continued its defensive mission of holding its positions along the rail line running north of Chemnitz (since renamed Karl Marx Stadt), then south along the Zwickauer-Mulde River line, and finally southeast to include the western tip of Czechoslovakia.

Toward the end of the month, I wrote Mom a Mother's Day letter. In it I expressed thoughts I had intended to put in writing on her 46th birthday back on 2 March but time had slipped up on me. In spite of my often resenting her advice, I really was thankful to have a mother who cared and who had high hopes for me. I wrote, "I just want you to know that I think you are about the finest mother anyone could have. Since I've been over here, I've reflected time and again upon the many things you've tried to teach me and upon the loyalty and devotion which you've expressed in every letter you've written. I know that I seldom mention those things that you've written, but don't for a minute think they have been ignored and unheeded. I consider myself very lucky in having a mother who cares enough to write such things. All my life my family has given me a standard to maintain and a banner to hold high; I am proud of you for that."

On the very day I wrote, Mom was writing me, carrying on about my promotion to corporal. "If you'd announced that you'd been made a four-star general we couldn't have been more pleased or more excited. It's not the fact that you're a corporal, but knowing that you've had to stay 'right on the ball' in order to get the rating that pleases us most. We're terribly proud of you." She went on in a teasing manner, saying it was inconsiderate of me to change ranks. A friend had obtained pfc. pins for her and my sister. "We've gotten such a kick out of wearing them," she wrote. "Now they'll have to be discarded." She said Punkie read my letter, got up, went to her coat, removed the pfc. pin, and said, "Well, I can't wear this pin anymore!"

Mom also wrote about the postman on Brandywine Street. I still regard that portion of her letter as a treasure. "We've got a nice old man for a postman. And when I say 'old' I mean old. It's all he can do to carry the heavy mail bag, and he's terribly slow. He's also pretty inaccurate, for he's always leaving mail that doesn't belong to us. I figure he is apt to leave our mail some place else. Last week, I said to him (just so he'd be careful about delivering it) 'No letter from my boy? We're so anxious to hear from him.' He tipped his cap and said, 'I'll be happy to deliver it when it comes.' Yesterday morning he rang the door bell and delivered your letter 'in person.' I thought that was swell of him.'' That kindly gentleman was one of thousands of men and women beyond retirement age who volunteered to perform essential services for the duration, often enduring, I am sure, physical discomforts greater than those suffered by most of us in the armed forces.

April was the month of liberation not only for millions of slave laborers within the Third Reich but also for thousands of Allied prisoners of war, most of whom were down to skin and bones. Among them were Bob Van Houten and the eight other men of A Battery. Bob later reported that he was liberated from Stalag 9-A at Ziegenhain, south of Kassel in central Germany. (His story is in Appendix B.)

Seymour Solomon and Ed Kahner have recalled for me humorous incidents which happened somewhere in Germany during the spring of 1945. These incidents, I believe, are typical of experiences of most GIs in our outfit.

As with everything else in the army, rank had its place in looting. Some officers and high-ranking noncoms thought the best loot should be reserved for them. Seymour remembered that a sergeant ordered the GIs in his section to discard the mattresses they had taken for sleeping comfort, but the sergeant looted a bicycle for himself. The GIs had their revenge. With wire cutters, they clipped all the spokes in the wheels.

Seymour gives a classic description of himself as he was in the army: "I was just an ignorant, innocent abroad. I didn't know where I was or why I was there. But I knew who I was. That's the one that gets a lot of folks today. But I knew. I was 18 years old, age-wise. Maturity-wise, maybe 12. Like . . . well, it says in my diary: 'Went into Paris. Looked up the Red Cross right away so I could wash up.' " He would have shaved, too, he said, but he didn't have whiskers! On his return from that trip to Paris, he reported his first experience in a Paris public restroom — "There I was, standing at the urinal when the young cleaning girl started mopping between my legs!"

Seymour kept a diary, too, but it was far different from mine. His could be subtitled, "European Theater." Most of its pages are filled with the names of movies he saw there, who played in them, how many times he saw each one, and whether a movie was good, very good, or not worth seeing more than two or three times. He had the only floor-length raincoat in our outfit. "I couldn't stand having my trouser legs wet and muddy all the time," the six-footer explained, "so I took a coat off this fellow (a German soldier), who was just lying there . . . he was, well, how he was, he didn't need a raincoat. I cut about 18 inches off the bottom of it and sewed it to the bottom of mine."

One day Solomon found himself alone in a bombed-out farmhouse. One wall of the room he hoped to spend the night in was gone. He allowed he'd freeze to death before morning. Suddenly, he said, this soldier straggled in. He was a guy Solomon didn't think much of. He was kind of a rube, big-city Solomon figured. "Cold in here," the newcomer observed. Then he set about boarding up the wall and making a stove with the metal and pipes strewn about. He built a good fire. "Thanks to this guy I first figured for a Klutz, we spent a warm and cozy. night," Solomon said. "I'll never forget him."

Once a cow wandered into the kitchen of an abandoned house where a group of soldiers had holed up, Seymour's diary noted. "We shot the critter on the spot and made steak. It was so tough you couldn't cut the gravy. Then someone noticed the cow had shoes on. We were eating a 'plow cow.' "

Seymour, as did McNamara, made up scenarios. A favorite was his report of a GI returning home to his wife without giving her advance notice. Embracing her in the doorway of his home, the returnee said fervently, "Oh, Honey, I've been true to you," while thinking to himself, "Little does she know about all those babes I had in Europe."

"And I've been true to you, too!" the wife replied with feeling as the iceman was exiting through the back door.

In the days before electric refrigerators when homes had iceboxes to which ice was delivered several times a week, the dalliances of icemen and housewives provided a standard theme for jokes.

Ed Kahner, who alternated with Bob Gray in 12-hour, around-the-clock shifts as battalion clerk, was privy to information not available to the rest of us. His most dramatic recollection concerns the day he was with several officers in a command car in April at a time when there was no front line as such. They had been ordered to Neustadt. Neustadt was a common town name in Germany. As luck would have it, they headed for the wrong Neustadt and suddenly came upon a column of 12 or more German troops a short distance from the highway. The car stopped, and an officer commanded, "Corporal Kahner, accept the surrender of those Germans!" Ed, blind in one eye, obediently advanced. Fortunately, the German officer in charge was looking for Americans so he might surrender his unit to them rather than to the British, the French, or the dreaded Russians.

Ed also recalls Herb Shriner, an entertainer who later became a television celebrity. Herb worked in special services for the VIII Corps and edited a corps newspaper. He had a series of one-liners in each issue. Ed's favorite was, "You can tell the war is about over — the officers are treating us almost human." Herb also had the finest description Ed ever heard of chipped beef on toast: shit on a shingle. This was abbreviated for the weak of stomach as S.O.S.

A couple of examples of the strange quirks of military justice are among Ed's memories. In one, Private ____ passed out drunk while guarding German POWs. The prisoners bundled him up and placed his rifle alongside him. The private was given a special courtmartial and sentenced to six months at hard labor. The J.A.G. Office threw out the charge, stating he should have been given a general court-martial. So he went free! Another incident concerned several men from a quartermaster unit who received long prison terms for selling cigarettes on the black market. General Eisenhower offered pardons to those who volunteered for combat duty. Two such men arrived in the Sixteenth at the end of the war in Europe. Our battalion commander immediately transferred them to a unit going straight to the

Pacific. However, these units went to the Pacific via the U.S.A. As a result, since the war with Japan ended shortly thereafter, they got home long before the rest of us.

My wartime friendships with men such as Seymour and Kahner meant a great deal to me at the time and forever after. Their individual differences, their decency, and their approaches to life gave my life new dimensions. As I had been a loner much of the time in my childhood and not much of a mixer in my teens, the camaraderie I had with these men was a welcome and enjoyable part of my maturing years. Those bonds of friendship, formed far from home under unfamilar circumstances, did not lessen with distance and years. They remain intact and true, holding strong with little more than exchanges of greetings at Christmastime through many years.

On the first of May my Garden City friend, Houston (Smitty) Smith, with whom I had plotted to conquer the world, finished a long letter he had started writing in March. He was then in the Pacific, serving as an aerial gunner in the Naval Air Corps. I later learned of the horrible experiences he had. His letter was in response to one I had written him and to a copy of my peace plans which my mother had sent him. He commented on these things and then concluded on a remarkably hopeful note, "It seems to me that the idea of world brotherhood has gained such favor now that it won't be lost. In the last war the sod was merely broken for the building, the site abandoned, whereas in this war, and in the interval between the two, the value of said real-estate has gained appreciably, the foundation built, and its completion is insured. What have you in mind for the permanent structure to be built from the scaffolding afforded by the limited government? That gets us back to the subjects we discussed the last time you were in G.C. (Garden City), and inevitably, to plans for the future." It was good to know that Smitty had not forgotten our dreams of the past, no matter how tempered by reality they had become. I felt a special closeness to Smitty, because I spent more time with him discussing world government and peace plans than with anyone in the Sixteenth or elsewhere.

Also on 1 May the war in Europe was in its last week, but we GIs didn't know that for sure. Once again, the after action report stated, "The battalion continued its mission in general support of the VIII Corps." During April the corps advanced from the Rhine River across Germany against light resistance and was now undertaking a holding action along the Limiting Line near the Czech border and including the western tip of Czechoslovakia in the Asche area. The enemy was generally unaggressive against the corps sector, and activity was limited to scattered patrolling and occasional artillery and small arms fire. The general support furnished by our battalion consisted of sound and flash ranging on enemy targets and coordinating and carrying of survey control for field artillery units of the VIII Corps. In addition, a radar-mortar detection team was attached to the unit to experiment on mortar ranging by means of radar.

My intellectual friend, John Ziegler, and I had a discussion of ideas on universal education on a day in early May. I took notes which I transcribed and tied into my peace plans. John and I urged that the United Nations Economic and Social Council establish an education commission. "Its duties would be primarily to devise a universal program for the presentation of the social sciences, especially history." We recommended the adoption of such a program by all nations. Throughout our time in the ETO we were fortunate to have a great variety of books available via the army's traveling library service. My reading for that first week of May included *The Prophet* and Aristotle's *Politics* as heavy stuff and *Tales from the Pampas* on the lighter side. The weather was miserable. At one survey station on 2 May we were delayed for an hour because of the blinding snow. It was Wideumont and Bastogne all over again. *Objective Burma* was showing in the beer hall that evening. "What a 'significant' title," I noted in my diary. I decided to let my shoes dry out instead of going. Anyway, the thought of a war picture with no women in it didn't particularly interest me.

Don Gindele and I were back to fraternizing in a couple of days. One evening we took off on a road leading through the woods to Greiz. We caught the eye of a couple of girls and started to follow them. Just as we were about to give it up, one of them came running back to tell us they would meet us after they had eaten. So we waited in the woods and they returned shortly after 7 p.m. We had an enjoyable evening walking around with them. It would have been better without three little kids who kept hanging around and pestering us. We went to the woods to meet the girls again the next night and spent about an hour and a half with them and then stopped by the beer hall on the way back. "This is fraternization pure and simple and I make no excuses for it," I told my diary. "It's merely that I'm getting claustrophobia looking at four walls all the time."

V-E (Victory in Europe) Day finally came on 8 May. I wrote to my parents, "Well I suppose today is a great day at home, in spite of the fact that V-E Day must seem to be an anticlimax. For us, it is just another day with no excitement whatsoever, although I wouldn't say that anyone is unhappy about the whole thing. I'm planning on listening to Churchill's speech in about an hour. I certainly wish I could've been in Washington or Paris or almost anyplace but this village last night. I heard the news of the signing of the surrender terms at 10 last night and then went to bed — that's all there was to it. Of course, there are all sorts of wild rumors flying around now, but I suppose it'll be a week or two before we know anything definite, if then."

My mother wrote a detailed letter on 7 May telling of the news coverage in the States of Germany's surrender. A friend called her that morning to say the Associated Press reported that Germany had signed an unconditional surrender, so she turned on the radio and listened all day to hear it confirmed by a proclamation from either the President or Eisenhower. "Eisenhower had given out the idea that he would not declare V-E day as long as there is fighting going on," she wrote, adding, "American soldiers were killed many days after the armistice was signed at the end of the last war. Eisenhower's idea was to avoid that catastrophe this time. Well, whether V-E Day is today or tomorrow makes very little difference in our concern about you. We'll be anxiously awaiting a letter from you written after V-E Day assuring us you are still alright."

Then she turned to my favorite subject. She was sorry in some ways, she wrote, that I didn't have a girl I felt belonged to me and to whom I would be coming back. She thought it would have been a comfort to me. On the other hand, it might be just as well to be "footloose and fancy free and not pledged to any girl . . . particularly to one who may have changed or lost interest while you've been away." My mother always figured all the possibilities. She ended up saying, "I'm glad you will have a chance to find the 'right' girl without the emotions of war pulling you this way and that." I sure agreed with her about being "footloose and fancy free." At the moment, I wasn't interested in any girl thousands of miles away.

After V-E Day was confirmed, my mother wrote again, an emotional letter filled with effusive sentimentality and gratitude for my "making this day come to pass." In retrospect, I can see it was an outpouring of her thankfulness and relief that I had come through the war unharmed. "Now that your life is not endangered, I can scarcely comprehend it all at once," she wrote. "There is no celebrating going on in D.C. today," she reported. "It was pouring rain when the Pres. issued his proclamation at nine o'clock. Since then it has cleared but Washington seems quite subdued. Leahy, Marshall, King, Eisenhower, Arnold, Nimitz and McArthur all spoke this P.M. and King George made a very stirring talk. We are going to attend church service at our church tonight. God has been wonderfully good to us thus far . . . we must show our gratitude by thoughtfulness and consideration toward others less fortunate than we have been."

I don't remember how many letters were written to me on V-E Day. I do know Pop's youngest brother, Ralph, a Wichita lawyer with four daughters, wrote. He was just overage for military service. I was his only nephew. Another letter was from Dorothy Ann Cochran, whom I had known while attending Kemper Military School. She was then attending Central College in Fayette, Missouri. She was a good friend (the kind of girl my mother liked) who had written me periodically. I especially appreciated her writing on that day with a message of faith and hope:

"This has been an eventful day, all right! We'd been waiting for the news since yesterday morning — hoping it was true and afraid to draw our breath until we were sure. We listened to all the reports we could get, including speeches by Truman and Churchill, in our 8 o'clock class. At 9 the whole town, including the Navy unit, had chapel. We meant the thanks we gave God for the victory, but we also meant the prayer for strength to finish the fighting and the building of a true, good peace. We all are proud of all of you. We can never understand all you've seen but we do know you did your share of the fighting and we feel part of the responsibility — lots of it. I've thought about so many people today and the effect the news will have on them. You, fighting and now knowing at last immediate victory over the foe. Those whose boys have paid the price. Those in the South Pacific and the ones at home, knowing they have such a long way to go. The English and all of Europe — to know that the bombs and robots (V-1 and V-2 missiles) have ceased now — they need be afraid of the skies no longer. The space is running out. I just wanted you to know that I'm there with the rest of America, right behind you, not only in the joy of the victory, but in the work that is still to be done. Here's to complete victory!''

The after action reports for 7 and 8 May gave the official army version of Germany's unconditional surrender:

7 May 1945

The offensive along the southern part of the corps was halted as reports were received that the enemy had surrendered uncon- ditionally in Western Czechoslovakia and Austria. No aggres- sive enemy action was reported opposite the VIII Corps Sector. All Corps troops passed to Ninth Army Control. . . .

8 May 1945

With the official announcement of ''Victory in Europe'' day, hostilities ceased all along the front. The Battalion remained in bivouac to await further orders. It had completed its final mission of the European War.

On 9 May battalion headquarters issued a one-page summary of statistics entitled ''Cumulative Summary of All Battalion Oper- ations.'' But, as was the case with the battalion unit history issued in July, only a few GIs saw it; it was stamped ''SECRET.'' Since 23 August 1944 the battalion had operated 50 flash ranging bases, 58 sound ranging bases, surveyed 1,728,505 meters, and captured 138 prisoners.

Of more significance to us GIs were the statistics in the unit history. Eighteen had received the Purple Heart for wounds not requiring hospitalization. Eleven had received the Purple Heart for wounds requiring hospitalization. Chuck Wagner was in both cat- egories. Nine were missing in action, all as prisoners of war. Most important of all, in a battalion of approximately 500, five were killed. Gordon Thompson and Tennis Humphrey were on the official list. Joseph Turansky was killed accidentally, and Gordon Priebe and J. Michael were killed either by enemy action or by enemy sympathizers.

One in a hundred is, of course, a low mortality rate when compared to the infantry or other combat forces, but not when compared to the total number of men and women serving in all the Armed Forces. And when one considers that four of the five dead were serving with

Headquarters Battery survey, numbering not more than 30 or 40 GIs at any one time, we in the survey sections had good reason to give thanks for being spared.

On V-E Day most of us were expecting to be sent to the Pacific to a war some thought might last as much as three years longer. Hence the expression, "Golden Gate in '48." What I did not know then was that while millions in Europe and the Pacific would be suffering in the aftermath of the horrible war, for the next seven months I would be having the most carefree days of my life.

Part Three

The Army
of Occupation

Those were the days, my friends!

Chapter 10

Landkreis Eisenach and a Girl Called Gyp

With the thought of early transfer to the Pacific war, most of us adopted an eat-drink-and-be-merry philosophy in earnest. Rules against fraternization, still illegal, became unenforceable. Most GIs began chasing girls, both Polish DPs (displaced persons) and Germans of all ages. Many of the girls did not need to be chased. I continued to have frustrating and often humorous experiences in the pursuit. We remained in Alt Neugommla for only two days after V-E Day. Many years later Jeff Peltz recalled being directed to continue surveying on 9 May. He said some GIs from another outfit asked him, "Are you surveying for the next war?" The rumor of that day, reported to us by German civilians, was that Hitler had escaped to Japan on a U-boat. Also, on the same day, our Third Army Commander, the one and only George S. Patton, now a full general, issued General Orders Number 98, which read in part:

SOLDIERS OF THE THIRD ARMY, PAST AND PRESENT
   During the 281 days of incessant and victorious combat, your penetrations have advanced further in less time than any other army in history. You have fought your way across 24 major rivers and innumerable lesser streams. You have liberated or conquered more than 82,000 square miles of territory, including 1,500 cities and towns, and some 12,000 inhabited places. Prior to the termination of active hostilities, you had captured in battle 956,000 enemy soldiers and killed or wounded at least 500,000 others. France, Belgium, Luxembourg, Germany, Austria, and Czechoslovakia bear witness to your exploits.

All men and women of the six corps and thirty-nine divisions that have at different times been members of this army have done their duty. Each deserves credit. This enduring valor of the combat troops has been paralleled and made possible by the often-unpublicized activities of the supply, administrative, and medical services of this Army and of the Communications Zone troops supporting it. Nor should we forget our comrades of the other armies and of the Air Force, particularly of the XIX Tactical Air Command, by whose side or under whose wings we have had the honor to fight. . . .

During the course of this war I have received promotions and decorations far above and beyond my individual merit. You won them; I as your representative wear them. The one honor which is mine and mine alone is that of having commanded such an incomparable group of Americans, the record of whose fortitude, audacity, and valor will endure as long as history lasts.

Even I, rebel that I was and no admirer of Patton, had to admit that sounded great! Two days later, our soft-spoken battalion commander, Lt. Col. Joseph P. Lushene, issued separate commendations to each of our three batteries. The one to Headquarters Battery read in part:

All of us will remember your courageous stand during the Ardennes Offensive and the subsequent feats of arms to the Rhine River. At the most difficult sector of the Rhine, you established new records for Survey and Communication in a most bitter lesson to the enemy on mobile warfare.

My sincere thanks to those Officers and Enlisted Men of your command now living and my humble reverence to those deceased, who, by their devotion to a cause and to duty made our magnificent victories possible.

The after action report officially announced our next move, almost directly west, from one end of Thuringia to the other. Colonel Herriott, 203d FA Group, visited the battalion to confer with Lushene on its designated mission of occupation and organization of the sector of Germany near Eisenach. Captain Carter went at once on recon-

Sidney Davis, Okie Henderson, Bruno McNamara, and the author, standing; Corporal Nesset and "Dishface" O'Connell, kneeling; in front of house at Höztelroda, near Eisenach, in late May 1945.

The schoolhouse at Höztelroda used as a mess hall by Headquarters Battery in late May.

naissance for a battalion bivouac area in the proposed occupation zone. The entire battalion moved in convoy on 11 May to Stregda, a village north of Eisenach, within the area of the Landkreis, somewhat analogous to a county in the United States. The area in and around Eisenach, a city founded in the twelfth century, was our location for most of May. It lay at the western boundary of Thuringia in central Germany. On a hill above the city was the Wartburg, an ancient castle, where Martin Luther was sheltered by the elector Frederick III of Saxony in 1521-1522. Eisenach also was the birthplace, in 1685, of Johann Sebastian Bach.

My fraternization attempts began immediately. Another guy and I climbed over two fences to talk to a couple of girls on an adjoining street late that night. I ripped my pants getting over the fence. The next day I wrote in my diary that I should certainly be ashamed of making a play for two babes. So, I had not only ripped pants but also a guilty conscience.

A couple of days later we moved a short distance to the east to the village of Höztelroda (my diary and battalion reports call it Hotzelsroda). Censorship had not yet been relaxed enough to give our location in letters home. So on 16 May I wrote that there wasn't much to report on our activities. Mostly, we were guarding certain installations within a given area for an indefinite period and were charged with maintaining law and order in the area. We were living in nicely furnished houses with running water and electricity, and nearly everyone had a bed. Our mess hall was located in a schoolhouse. We were promised there would be a beer hall in the town auditorium soon. Our blankets were to be cleaned and there was to be some provision for having our laundry done. The weather was warm and clear days were numerous. "So you can see," I assured the folks at home, "life could be a helluva lot worse." It was in Höztelroda that I first learned of the common German name, Gisela. Mothers would stand on their front stoops and call loudly for their daughters, "Geese-a-la!"

Our guard duties consisted primarily of guarding a German trainer airplane, a granary, and a large farm. The purpose was to "protect" them from the Polish, Russian, and other displaced persons in the area. We also guarded a nearby Polish DP camp. It seemed a crazy world! At the DP camp guard post, I became acquainted with several young Poles, male and female. All in the camp had been forced

The author and a Polish friend from the Displaced Persons Camp near Eisenach on 27 May.

laborers in nearby factories. Originally there were 1,800 there, but some were being moved out each day to a larger camp at Eisenach for transportation to Poland. The Eisenach camp had a capacity of

Emery Bliesmer sitting in front of a granary guarded by the survey section at Berka, near Eisenach.

24,000 and was a sort of POE (port of embarkation) for every nationality. These Poles hated the Germans and the Russians with equal vehemence. One night, during my period of guard duty, a dance lasted from 8 p.m. until 5 a.m. It was a real celebration and the schnapps flowed like wine. I met a young Polish girl named Eva and we had a great time talking in a combination of Polish, German, French, and English. Little did any of us then know that she and all the others soon would be returning to a country behind an iron curtain.

Guard duty was on 24-hour-a-day schedules. At the granary and the Polish DP camp, we had four-hour shifts and pulled eight hours in a 24-hour period. At the farm there were morning, afternoon, and night shifts. The granary was in the town of Berka about seven miles from Höztelroda. It reportedly contained about 40,000 bushels of grain. The farm was a large estate. The alleged reason that we guarded it was to protect the Germans from the Polish and Russian workers there. The lady who ran the place spoke flawless English. She was a shrewd one, using all the subtle Nazi techniques plus a few of her own. We gathered that the only thing she held against Hitler was that the Deutschland lost the war.

The Polish DP camp was an interesting, but tragic, place. I wrote my parents, "You really have to see all this to realize how much displacement and confusion, not to mention tragedy, the Nazis created in their slave labor policy. These Poles worked in a nearby airplane factory, well camouflaged by trees. Apparently they had enough to eat, but the camp itself is filthy and I understand there are a lot of TB cases."

My fraternization attempts with girls in Höztelroda got even more hilarious. On 18 May I arranged a date with a blonde. When we arrived back at her house late one night, a watchdog cut loose with howls and yowls. The blonde's mama wouldn't let me come in. Four nights later, I decided to visit the blonde again. After sneaking like a panther over fences and behind trees up to the window of the house to outfox the dog, I looked in and discovered that two other GIs were there with her and another girl.

My mother wrote a long letter in response to my Mother's Day letter to her. She said she had never received anything that surprised or pleased her more. She couldn't believe I even knew when Mother's Day was, let alone that I would have a chance to write. She said the usual things like realizing she had made mistakes in rearing me and was far from a perfect mother. "I'm not belittling myself," she wrote, "for I doubt if I'd do any better if I had the opportunity to try again — but each generation must improve upon the last if there is to be any progress in this world. You have been raised in a home where love and mutual respect were its foundation, the mistakes that have been made in it were due to human weaknesses, not intentional disregard for one another." She closed by saying it was lovely to see the Capitol and the Washington Monument light up again and added, "How wonderful it must seem to the people in England to have lights on again." Then, motherlike, she praised my part in "making those lights shine once more."

That letter, filled with appreciation and admiration for me, was followed a few days later with one replete with motherly admonitions to keep me on the straight and narrow. "Now that the fighting part of the war is over," she began, "I do not know what you're doing or what your set up is. However it may be that you'll have temptations to do things that under normal conditions would not interest you at all." She advised me to let my conscience (which she knew was "keen as a razor's edge") guide me and "cut you loose from anything that is not manly, clean or morally straight.'' The bottom line was ''Don't do anything that you'd be ashamed to come home and tell us about.'' To that, she added, ''God is walking right by your side. . . . Don't go anywhere, do anything or say anything that would embarrass Him.'' Then, putting it all in the context of the here and now, she suggested that my exemplary behavior might ''help another buddy go straight.'' She covered all the bases. In my bewilderment over whether to chase girls or not, I turned to my diary and wrote: ''Read beautiful letter from Mother warning me against some of the things I have been doing. I make no excuses. Someday all this shall pass.''

Along with guard duty, our outfit had a training schedule of sorts. Except for road marches, some of them as long as eight miles, it didn't amount to much. There was no mention of the school program we heard about earlier, but strong rumors were going around that we'd be leaving for the States by the end of June. It was entirely speculation. My opinion was the VIII Corps would definitely go to the CBI (China-Burma-India) theater of operations. In a letter home, I wrote, ''I've always had the feeling that I'd come through the ETO O.K. but going to the CBI also is just tempting the law of averages too much, although in many ways I'd like to go.''

A point system determined the order in which GIs were returned to the States and released from the service. I, as did every other GI, kept a running tab on points. I had 58 as of 12 May: 27 for 27 months of service, 11 for 11 months overseas service, and 20 for four battle stars, including Northern France, the Ardennes, the Rhineland, and Central Europe. Additional points were awarded for recipients of medals, such as the Bronze Star and Silver Star, and to soldiers with children. I didn't have any of those, stars or children, to add to my total.

May was almost over before I got to visit Wartburg Castle. It was about five miles from where we were housed on the other side of Eisenach. The palace part of the castle was closed, but we saw the room where Martin Luther lived for 10 months while translating the Bible and where he reputedly threw a bottle of ink at a vision of the devil. The spot on the wall had long since been chipped away. We also saw the stable room with collections of armor, and the tower with a 72-foot dungeon. Guides were GIs who lived in what was formerly a resort hotel near the castle. The owner, the Duke of something or other, still lived on the place.

With McNamara atop a tower of Wartburg Castle near Eisenach in late May.

Shooting sprees from moving vans, using whatever firearms were available, became a sport of some GIs during this period. On 29 May I wrote, ''Got the scare of our lives when a GI came up the road firing a sub-MG from a weapons carrier at telephone pole insulators. He had hit a pole just a few feet from our vehicle before we could see who he was; it sounded like a berserk SSer on the loose.''

Guarding the farm turned out to be an interesting experience. Known as Mittelshof, it was an estate of some size owned by a couple I shall call von Burg. The wife was definitely in charge. There was an overseer, whom I referred to as Simon Legree. At first when I was assigned to guard the farm, I found it really dull. No attempt, by the DPs, Russians, or anyone else, was being made to seize the place. The Polish DPs, assigned as slave laborers during the war, were still on the farm, as were several German girls from Eisenach. The latter were supposed to be farm workers too, but the von Burgs used them as housemaids. Farm guard became more interesting on the night that Madame von Burg, her husband, and the overseer left for a wedding, leaving the three girls behind. Two other fellows on guard, Cassidy and West, and I had a good time singing German and American songs with the girls. A line in my diary said, ''They took off like three bats out of hell when they heard Madame von Burg and party returning.'' The favorite songs that night were ''Lili Marlene'' and ''You Are My Sunshine.'' The latter was a great favorite among Germans.

The close of the war in Europe ended the after action reports. The day-by-day report for June was designated a ''diary.'' At the beginning of June, this was the official report:

1 June 1945

On the opening day of the new month, the Battalion was engaged in the mission of Organization, Occupation and Government of a large area of Landkreis Eisenach north of the city limits. All targets of potential military or strategic value were being protected by unit personnel, and a security patrol was maintained thru all towns in the area to prevent disturbances or sabotage. Several Displaced Persons Camps were also being guarded but these were being emptied out as rapidly as possible.

Just before leaving for Frankenheim to the south of Eisenach, we GIs learned for the first time from German civilians that all of Thuringia would become part of the Russian Zone. The zones were to be established within weeks. Actually, the boundaries of occupation

A close-up of Wartburg Castle, above the city of Eisenach.

zones had been determined months before and confirmed by the Big Three at the Yalta Conference. Nevertheless, I was shocked to know the Russians would be moving so far west. For several days, I just couldn't believe it.

Back at the farm, one of the girls who joined us in the evening songfest on 30 May and I started hitting it off. She called herself Gyp. That was neither her real name nor her nickname. It was the name of the heroine of a John Galsworthy novel with whom she identified herself to me. I was so taken by her and she by me that we saw each other every day or evening until the Sixteenth moved to Frankenheim nine days later. On 31 May I took photos of Gyp and another girl, Lora. Lora then took a picture of Gyp and me. I noticed Gyp seemed uncomfortable when I put my arm around her for the picture. Here, indeed, was a different type of girl.

The following afternoon, I was assigned to farm guard and immediately sought out Gyp, who was washing windows in the farm office. Laying aside my carbine, I pitched in to help her. To do that, I knew I must really like her! Before, afterward, and to this day, I have done all possible to avoid "doing windows" of any size, shape, or description. Before Gyp and I finished the last window, Herr von Burg and "Simon Legree" entered the office. They appeared to be quite surprised. That afternoon was the first time Gyp and I were alone with each other. Her English was quite sufficient for good conversation. For several hours, she spoke to me on a great variety of subjects. Bursting with enthusiasm, she poured out her heart to me. It was as if she had been waiting for a long, long time to talk to someone. She told me her father, of whom she was obviously proud, was a professional violinist and her mother, a singer. At the age of 46, her father was a prisoner of war, as was her only brother, age 19. She talked about reading John Galsworthy and Oscar Wilde, authors with whom I was only vaguely familiar at that time. I was amazed. Here, in the heart of the Third Reich, was a girl interested in literature, music, dancing, all the fine arts. Her interest extended far beyond the traditional German feminine interests of Kinder, Kuche, and Kirche (children, cooking and church) which had become a part of the Nazi new social order.

We had our second songfest in the farm mansion the next evening with Gyp playing the piano. I could not read music but I could carry a tune and I sang out loudly. Gyp sang the same way she talked — with enthusiasm! By 3 June I was volunteering for farm guard. Without carbine or helmet liner, both of which were required when on duty, I took a walk with Gyp and the other two girls. The girls expressed their strong feelings about American soldiers "doing other things" with German girls and about German girls who chased GIs. In spite of myself, those girls, and especially Gyp, were bringing out the best in me. For the moment, I was following my mother's instructions.

The farm was placed off limits to GIs the next day but I was determined to see Gyp again. It was still quite light when I went to the farm around 9 p.m. I did some careful maneuvering to arrive at the pond on the farm without being seen by anyone in the battery or by Frau von Burg, who, I suspected, was probably responsible for the off-limits order. To my surprise, Gyp was there with Lora. I talked with Gyp for about half an hour after Lora left. It was all strictly platonic but I enjoyed the conversation and sensed that she did, too. We talked of girls wearing rouge and lipstick, of her mother and father, of cars and driving and a myriad of other things. Dave McNamara joined me in defying the order on the following evening. We waited under the trees near the farm for a long time before we managed to get someone to contact Gyp. She invited us inside, where she played the piano and a new girl showed us pictures. Frau von Burg was fairly hospitable, which could be explained because she was pumping us for information. We stayed late, until almost midnight.

The next day was the first anniversary of D-Day, an official holiday. It also was our last day in Landkreis Eisenach before moving to Frankenheim. I went to see Gyp that evening. We sat at the edge of the woods beyond the pond. The new girl was with her. My diary gave this account: "We talked of many things; all seems so futile in that neither of us knows what will happen from one day to the next. She had a 'story' to tell me — that when she comes to America she will see me and when I return to Germany I shall see her; of course that is all we can do. I believe that if it were ever possible to meet each other under halfway normal (what is normal?) circumstances the situation would be different. . . . I gave her my address and she gave me hers; perhaps in several months we will be able to write to each other."

Although our survey section moved to Frankenheim the next morning, through a stroke of luck I arranged to return to Höztelroda with Charlie Shelton to pick up our duffel bags. Thus I was able to see Gyp again and tell her goodbye (for the first time!) I spent an hour or so with Gyp, Lora, and the other girl. They had to be in before 11 p.m., because the night before they were locked out by Frau Simon

Legree and had to climb through the window of someone else's room to get to their room. I promised to send Gyp copies of the pictures I took whenever it was possible. She also asked me to write to her. The girls apologized because they couldn't show me a better time.

In Frankenheim I began at once to scheme to write to Gyp and to see her again. I worried about what would happen to her when the Russians occupied Thuringia. There was no mail system in operation between the army and German civilians, so letters were delivered by way of what I called the underground mail system. One would ask a fellow GI who happened to be going to the town in question to deliver the letter. Often the letter would pass through several hands before delivery. Frequently, it never was delivered.

My first letter was delivered by Don Gindele. It was left with Frau von Burg herself. Several days later I learned Gyp had been hospitalized and I fretted about that and prayed for her recovery. That worry soon passed with delivery of Gyp's letter to me, via Frau von Burg and Bill Gross. Gyp was out of the hospital and at her home in Eisenach. The big news was that she and her mother had word that her father was alive and well. "We are so lucky!" she exclaimed. Two days later, on 22 June, I arranged to return to Eisenach for the sole purpose of seeing Gyp. The attempt was frustrated because she had moved in the meantime and my ride had to return to Frankenheim before I could locate her. The following day I was successful in getting there, courtesy of what I thought of as the "underground people system."

It seemed each of the thousands of vehicles in the army in Germany was on the road every day. Often, legitimate business was combined with monkey business. My diary gave an account of my touring around on 23 June: Our vehicles let one fellow and his brother off in Eisenach, then drove through Stregda to Mihla and on through Höztelroda to Mittelshof, the farm. There I asked Frau von Burg for Gyp's address. The driver let me off in Eisenach early in the afternoon. Gyp seemed happy to see me. Her mother, a very pretty woman, and a friend, Mrs. Schneider, were there also. Gyp had a letter, in almost perfect English, which she was just getting ready to send me. Her father, she said, was giving concerts to American troops near Heidelberg. She and her mother had passes to go there but they were awaiting transportation. I took a letter from Frau Schneider to send to her brother in Connecticut, and I promised Gyp I would try to find out whether or not her brother was a prisoner of war. She gave me a new picture of herself and I gave her the ones I had taken. I stayed only an hour but had a very good time, my diary said. "All strictly platonic, of course," I wrote, "but I suppose it's best that way."

Three days later I caught a ride with the mail orderly, and was back in Eisenach. Arriving in midmorning, I nearly scared Gyp to death when she opened the door on her way out to go shopping. I stayed until noon, went to the enlisted men's transient mess for a nice plate lunch prepared by Italian cooks and served by young women from Holland. Then I returned to Gyp's and stayed for a couple of hours. "All in all, this has been a very nearly perfect day," I said in my diary. "Of course I'm much enthused about Gyp — I hope I can see her often through the years." The "very nearly perfect day" was the last time Gyp and I saw each other, but my thoughts of her continued throughout that summer. The next day I wrote, "Many thoughts of Gyp all day; I hope I can see her just once more. You've maneuvered yourself into a sentimental, heartbreaking situation again, Hope ole kid, but as long as you're you there's not much you can do about it. Perhaps it will all work out for the best."

I wrote Gyp again on 28 June and she replied the next day. "I think you will be very very lucky when you come back to America! And later, when the war with Japan is finished and you will come to Germany, to see many places, including Heidelberg, you could not see now, I would like to show you the imposing and nicest buildings and places of the romantic city of Heidelberg. And I want to come to America also — perhaps as a 'star' singing and dancing! And then, you can see me again. Is it very good? We should be very grateful to you, if we can hear something of my brother."

I replied in a long letter, which because of the vicissitudes of the underground mail system, was never delivered. Several times in the summer and through September I visited Gyp's aunt and uncle at their home in Heidelberg and also saw her father there after his release from POW camp. Each time I hoped I would find her there and worried and fretted when I didn't. By October I despaired of ever seeing her again and, fickle as always, I began thinking seriously of other girls. No one knows what attracts a girl and a boy to one another, especially in a platonic friendship, but I believe I know the bond which bound Gyp and me that summer. We were both dreamers

and romantics. Although our dreams were different — hers to be a
famous actress, singer, and dancer, a "star," and mine to be a
"famous statesman" — we shared them together. Both of us knew
we were dreamers and sensed, I believe, that the dreams probably
would not come true for either of us, as indeed they did not, except in
minor ways.

Through my friendship with Gyp that late spring and early summer, I learned that beneath all the depravity and evil of the Third
Reich there lay another Germany, one that was there long before
Adolph Hitler came to power and one which would rise again from
the death, chaos, and rubble created by him.

It brought me a little closer to growing up.

Chapter 11

Goodbye to the Sixteenth — and Summer Doldrums

By 12 June our battery was settled in Frankenheim in a former rest home, taken over by the army for our use. Our most recent surveying was for a firing range for VIII Corps. Since our battalion was officially in charge of the range, it followed that we would be the range guards. The rest home had beds or cots for everyone, and three or four of us shared a room. There were running water, toilets, and a large dining room. Hot water was promised. And there were girls to clean the place. Some of them, along with other girls and women from the area, began sharing bedrooms with some of the GIs. Those of us who pulled early morning guard shifts saw these females leaving together at daybreak, chattering and laughing among themselves.

"There's no sound to compare with the giggling of a bunch of well f---ed women," a battery philosopher observed.

Our outfit had expected to stay in Höztelroda as long as we were in Germany. I might have been in the minority in wishing we had. C'est la guerre, once again. "By all indications this is only a temporary setup and we should be moving back through the States to the CBI before the summer is over," I wrote in a nine-page letter home. "According to Kahner, who, as a T/5, is something of an assistant bn. commander, as soon as the definite no. of points required for discharge is announced, every ETO unit will be classified & if we're marked No. 2 (CBI) we should be home within two months from that date. This is only conjecture, of course, but it's all I know."

Many of my thoughts were turning homeward. I said I hoped I'd be back in time to get in on some of the victory garden vegetables. Because of my father's hobby of growing roses, I took particular

Privates Hand, Dean, and Sargent on KP at the Sophienhohe (rest home) at Frankenheim, Germany, in June.

notice of the roses growing in Germany. I saw quite a few and assumed there would be many more in peacetime. ''Nearly all German civilians seemed to have received orders through their burgomeisters to work on the farms,'' I wrote, ''but it's apparent that many, particularly girls from the cities, don't know a thing about it and consequently there is considerable 'goofing off' on the job.''

I heartily approved of my father's voting for the extension of the Reciprocal Trade Agreements, as I felt they were necessary to show other nations we were willing to meet them halfway. It seemed to me that the effect of the tariff upon employment had been greatly overemphasized. On another subject, I wrote, ''Increasingly in the last few weeks lots of guys here and myself have been having misgivings about the Russians. It's gone so far that we've been talking of having to come back to the ETO to fight them after we defeat Japan. I was all for them several months ago but since they've established virtual puppet governments in every country they've 'liberated' that enthusiasm has waned considerably. Several of our vehicles have been used to haul Russian DPs from Ohrdruf through the Russian lines at Chemnitz and all our drivers report that it's virtually impossible to get through the lines. They have to make a long detour to reach there and at least one time they almost had to shoot a Russian guard to get through, although we're doing this (hauling DPs) entirely for them. They have machine gun positions, etc., all along the border.''

It bothered me that the Russians were given such a large area of Germany that we had conquered. ''I say this out of no sympathy for the Germans, but it's evident that the more of Germany we give Stalin, the more resources he'll have. Not only that, but he'll either make good communists out of them or use them as forced labor. I'm all for working German PWs, but not for rebuilding a Russian war machine which could be turned against us. Of course, I know that it sounds like I'm falling for Nazi propaganda, but nevertheless I've been here long enough to realize that there are some 'good' Germans, or at least ones, particularly children, who could be 'salvaged' under our occupation if it were handled right.''

I was quick to admit this was a far cry from several months back, during the winter, when I had advocated eliminating Germany as a nation. ''I sincerely believe I was wrong then and am right now,'' I wrote. It was easy enough to spot former Nazis; they were very obvious about who they were. But most other Germans were simply either opportunists or had absolutely no interest in politics. A good number of these, under leadership of Germans formerly in concentration camps, could be salvaged, I believed. ''However, if we give Stalin over half of Germany, I don't see how this'll be possible,'' I said in the letter. ''I know that we'll prevent any Germans moving from Russian-occupied territory to our own but I believe this is definitely a mistake. Our CIC (Counter-intelligence Corps) so far has been very good in handling obvious Nazis. . . . I suppose all this sounds to you like I'm turning into a Germanophile, but I believe my opinions are based on common sense and the power politics which we'll have to use in dealing with Uncle Joe. Although some GIs hastily advocated giving all of Germany to the Russians, I believe that by this time most share my beliefs.'' I asked my father for his opinion on the subject.

Going on the assumption I wouldn't be wiped out in the Pacific, I was going forward with my postwar planning. I definitely wanted to study for some type of foreign service when I went back to college and couple it with either some sort of work with the Allied Control Commission or employment as a newspaper or magazine correspondent. "Don't know that I'd want to devote the rest of my life to this sort of stuff," I wrote, "but I'd definitely want to devote a few years to it. I feel that I could gain a helluva lot of experience this way which would be very helpful in whatever I might later decide to do."

My longtime yen for travel was intensified. I went so far as to call it incurable. "As I get older, I suppose it may be somewhat dampened but I'm sure it will never be extinguished. That may be unfortunate but that's the way it is. I would never want a job in business or anything of that nature. That's why I've always wanted to enter politics; because your scope is broad and you can never tell what the hell is going to happen next. Above all, I never want to get in a rut. I've seen too many examples of that all through life. Don't get the idea that I have in mind being a perpetual nomad, far from it. It's just that I want to do something constructive in a broad field. The overwhelming desire of most GIs is to go home and stay there, and so thinking exactly opposite I believe the field should be more 'wide open' than any other."

I asked my folks for their "detailed opinion" of my plans. Specifically, I asked my father to get information on the Allied Control Commission or any other special agencies we might have "over here." I asked him, too, what the possibilities in journalism might be. I left no doubt that I was eager to get into the postwar world as soon as possible. Apologizing for forgetting his birthday, I told Pop what I wrote him the previous year "still goes — double!" In Eisenach, I had 11 rolls of film developed. Out of 88 possible pictures, 33 came out. "They present a fairly good record from the last days of the Bulge to now," I wrote.

Only three days later, I was writing home again and almost apologizing for doing so so soon. "I believe this is the first time since I've been in the ETO that I've written you without having had a stack of your letters to answer," I said. The news I had to relate was that our battalion was put in the Seventh Army. In itself that didn't mean much. Howevder, according to Kahner, the outfit now was in Class 4 (surplus — subject to demobilization), although it hadn't been officially announced. "If this is true, the outfit could be broken up either here or in the States, but in any event we should be over here for several months yet."

Spurred on by this news, I wrote to the University of Kansas for information on correspondence courses in French and/or German. I didn't know how much I could get out of such a course but it seemed it would be easy to pick up a speaking knowledge of either language if I had some help with the grammar. I also talked to the battalion Information and Education officer about schooling in Europe. I wasn't even sure if it was possible, but I wanted to make my interest known. The Class 4 report concerning the Sixteenth was confirmed. Some high-point men were to be transferred into the Sixteenth and the lower-point men (most of us) would be transferred out.

It was a time of nostalgia and general good feeling in our outfit. The bitching and carping at one another had all but stopped. In addition to hastily compiling the informal battalion history, John Jarvis, Robert Adorjan, Bob Gray, and Ed Kahner edited a mimeographed battalion newspaper which ran for at least five issues. Notes and comments from others were solicited, so I wrote a sketch about McNamara (Bruno), commenting on his pungent remarks on various subjects and occasions. To encourage contributions, Colonel Lushene offered a bottle of wine for the article judged best each week. One week mine on Bruno tied with one submitted by Private Perry of A Battery. Kahner got me out of bed to inform me of the honor. The 22 June issue of *Eyes & Ears* gave this somewhat exaggerated report:

WHO GOT THE BOTTLE?

From among last week's bewildering number of contributions, Pvt. Perry of "A" Battery and Cpl. Hope of Hq Btry each relieved the Colonel of the necessity of carrying a bottle of wine. Hope was not too happy about it, convinced that his article on McNamara was responsible for his buddy's transfer. He was last seen sadly drinking toast after toast to his departed pal and his tears flowed like wine.

This referred to the transfer of McNamara, Lieutenant Tyler, Bob Mason, Giulio Anfuso, Emery Bliesmer, and seven others from Headquarters Battery to the 13th F.A. Observation Battalion. I wasn't crying but I was mighty sad. They had become like family to me, a part of my life. For the remainder of the month, transfers, including my own, came thick and fast.

Although I spent much of my time during June conniving to see Gyp, it was pleasant enough at Frankenheim. Our duties were light and, like growing boys of any day, I spent much time sleeping. As a corporal, I was pulling CQ (Charge of Quarters) duty for the first time. The CQ was a noncom in charge of the battery headquarters office for a given time period. For social life, some of us promenaded around the local swimming pool every evening possible, looking for girls to look at. Nothing much ever happened and for myself, then thinking of Gyp. I didn't much care.

On 24 June I wrote home for the fourth time within two weeks, expressing sadness at the breakup of the Sixteenth and, now that censorship had been lifted, telling all I knew about the work of an observation battalion. I said I'd been to Eisenach several times but I skipped saying a German girl prompted the trips. It didn't seem necessary to worry Mom. Something else I didn't tell was that I received the Good Conduct Medal. Enlisted men were eligible to receive it after only a year's service. I had been in for 28 months. Three days later, Johnny Piccolo, the battery clerk, told me that Jim (Dishface) O'Connell, Seymour Solomon, John H. Brown, and I were being transferred to the 13th FOB the next day. My immediate thoughts were noted in my diary: "While it should be a good deal, it foils my plans for seeing Gyp again. Once more, for perhaps the hundredth time, I am forced to say 'C'est la guerre.' Spent most of evening getting addresses, seeing Carus and Kahner and various other guys, and writing a letter to Gyp to be delivered by Garrison tomorrow."

After I finished packing on the morning of the 28th, I worked on draining two bottles of wine provided by Shelton. My mellowed condition lasted almost until I loaded into a GMC in midafternoon. Riding in the back with a bunch of enlisted men and Captains Carter, Hunter, and Rowland, we followed a route through Eisenach and Erfurt to Sangerhausen, a good-sized town. Solomon and I went to the headquarters battery with Rowland as battery commander. The system of survey seemed to be different here, and I didn't know or much care where I would fit into it. We were put up in houses with showers. The battery had a bar and liquor was plentiful. What I wanted most was to receive a letter from Gyp.

On our first morning in Sangerhausen, we stood reveille for the first time since 15 August at Lopscombe Corners in England. It wasn't as much effort getting out there as I thought it would be. There was little to do in the morning. In the afternoon, we went to the town theater to see *Hollywood Canteen* — again! I got a letter from Gyp and wrote about it in my diary: "A very nice letter, although of course it's still on a strictly 'friendly' basis and I suppose it always will be. But every day and night I pray God to bless her and watch over her." In the evening I was out strolling around again with Bruno and Solomon. We checked a bombed-out railroad station, a civilian cafe where we tried what we called "banana oil schnapps," and a Polish DP camp, and ended up in a room back in the survey house drinking "buzz bomb juice."

We left early on the morning of 2 July for the long drive, 225 to 250 miles, to Burstadt, which was near Worms and south of Frankfurt. As we went through Erfurt and from there on the Autobahn past Eisenach, I took a long, last, sentimental look at the city spread out down in the valley with Wartburg Castle towering on the hill above it. It was after dark when we went through Frankfurt. Main sections of the town were badly damaged, apparently mostly by fire bombs. Arriving after midnight, we bedded down for the night on the concrete floor of the bathhouse near a swimming pool at the edge of town. There were many outfits in the same area, since this was a concentration area for troops going back to the States. I was eager to move on soon.

On 7 June my parents received a letter in which I detailed our adventures from the Battle of the Bulge to V-E Day. Mom replied at once, saying she read and reread it "with a sort of dazed feeling." It was hard for her to realize I had experienced the things I wrote about. Her main emotion was gratitude that I came through unharmed. "I'm very glad, too, son that you never had to kill a German. It had to be done, I know, but I'm glad you escaped that experience." Two days later, Pop wrote. He also expressed his thankfulness. "There are so many sad stories of boys who have been killed or badly crippled. People write me about many of them, and I learn of them thru compensation and insurance cases that people ask me to take up." Although I might still have a lot ahead of me, he felt I had passed the crisis in the Ardennes. He wrote, "There are a good many people who think the Japs will quit before going through a battle of annihilation, but I don't see anything in their conduct thus far which would lend any support to that theory. So the chances are undoubtedly that you will go to the Pacific. There seem to be quite a few rumors here in Washington that the 9th Army will go to C.B.I. but nothing official that I know of. I'm told that's the rumor in India and China also.''

Because I mentioned a lot of places in my letter which they couldn't find on the maps they had, Pop said he was going to get a map from the War Department which ought to have all of them on it. They got out newspapers published during the Ardennes drive and from the maps in them were able to trace the general course of my outfit. "By the way," my father wrote, "this is my birthday and I'm now an old man of 52. I feel fine and certianly (*sic*) not my age."

On the weekend of 23 June Pop wrote twice. In the first letter, he described "the biggest events in the U.S. in the preceding week" — four receptions for General Eisenhower in Washington, New York, Kansas City, and Abilene (Kansas) plus a day at West Point. "I don't believe there has ever been anything quite like them. The people came out in the main to acclaim Eisenhower the general but they left acclaiming Eisenhower the man. He was so natural and modest about it all that he won everyone's heart. For all of his modesty, he wasn't the least bit embarrassed but took it all in his stride. His speeches in every case were statesmanlike and constructive. It is easy to see how he was able to wield the allied army into the great fighting force it was and to handle all the political and personal rivalries in such an effective way. He would be a great diplomat or rather is a great diplomat and statesman. Raymond Moley has suggested him for Secretary of State. He could have any office he wants. The Republicans would nominate him for President. But he doesn't want any office. Makes all of us Kansans proud to be from the same state."

The second letter responded to the nine-page letter I had written early in the month at Frankenheim. He said quite a few divisions had been listed in the newspapers as having been ordered to return home, while others were named as going direct to the Pacific by way of Marseilles. He asked me to let him know what divisions comprised the VIII Corps at the time to help him get information from the War Department. "You aren't the only ones who are worrying about the matter," he said in reference to what I wrote about how the men in my outfit felt about the Russians. "It's certianly (*sic*) a matter of grave concern. Of course, the occupation zones in Germany seem to have been agreed upon at Yalta, and I don't think there's a thing that can be done about the matter now. Apparently there's some differences of opinion between ourselves and Russia as to just what were some of the agreements at Yalta, but I haven't heard anyone raise any question as to the occupation zones."

As to my postwar plans, Pop felt there would be plenty of opportunities for foreign service after the war not only in the government but also in business and probably in journalism. "I'm simply basing that statement upon the fact that we're all over the world now and to a greater or lesser extent are going to have to stay there, whether we want to or not. But in the main I think we'll want to. Also with all the developments in aviation, there's going to be a tremendous amount of world travel. I don't think we even have any comprehension of it now."

He emphasized that the best opportunities would be open to those well trained along some definite line. With that pointed out, he made it clear I should "get at your schooling and finish it as soon as possible." He explained further, "The trouble with doing anything as soon as you get out of the Army or even while you're still going to school is that as yet you aren't trained to do anything. All you've ever done (except in the army) is to go to school and all you've had in school is very general and hasn't fitted you to do anything practical. If you had a language or two it would help. If you knew shorthand or bookkeeping or any one of a dozen other lines there might be immediate opportunities but they would be at the expense of schooling and preparation for something better."

If I was serious about my interest in foreign service of any kind, he said my best bet would be to specialize in languages — French and German, but more especially Spanish and Russian. And, perhaps, Chinese. In his usual candid manner he wrote, "I don't think you have any particular talent for picking up languages and it may be hard work, but you can do it all right." He suggested that I might think of taking trips to some countries in which I was interested during vacations from school after I got back. "I think this will be easy to do after the war and fairly cheap."

Pop made it perfectly clear that I needed to aim at something definite, be it foreign service, law, or something of that sort. He added that bottom line which has been a mainstay of parents for ages: "Learn something which you can use in making a living." His response to my mention of a career in journalism was that it wasn't something I could just jump into without some pretty thorough preparation. The men who are foreign correspondents, he said, worked up to it over a period of years through hard apprenticeships, starting as police court reporters, graduating from small town papers or taking long, demanding courses in journalism.

That said, he went on, "I think your main talents lie along the line of law or public service, including foreign service, if you want to devote enough time in preparation for it." He added, "There isn't any reason why you shouldn't make a success in some line of business if you were willing to apply yourself to it. I think that business management in the next few years is going to offer some great opportunities." While there might be things I would like better, he reminded me "the fellow who makes all the money which makes it possible for lawyers, diplomats, journalists, educators and scientists to carry on their work is the businessman who has the ability to bring capital and labor together for the production of goods. He's the arch which holds up our entire modern civilization. In the foreign field there are many business opportunities and will be more. Most of them involve salesmanship but not all. Some of them are along the lines of economics and diplomacy."

Education and preparation were the keys to limitless opportunities in many fields. That was his message. And behind it, as I later came to know all too well as a parent myself, was his fear that I might not choose to finish my education. "I know that you may feel that it's going to be pretty tedious to take several more years of school," he wrote, "but I don't think you'll find it so when you get started." It was too big a subject to discuss by mail, he wrote at the end of many pages. He hoped I'd have a furlough so we could spend time discussing "a lot of things together man to man."

Back in Burstadt, Germany, things were going to hell as far as I was concerned. I was shocked to be forced to live in a pup tent again and to have a training schedule of sorts. Presumably the tents were because there were so many troops in the area, but most of the houses in the town were still occupied by German civilians. "I can't figure it out," I wrote home bitterly. "Sometimes we all wonder who won the war. This is quite a comedown from the life we've been leading, although it won't be so bad if the heavy rains don't come." My folks had asked what some of the common GI gripes were at the time. Well, those pup tents primed me to respond. How much of the tent and training schedule stuff was due to higher headquarters and how much to the outfit itself, I didn't know. "I know that there's a bathhouse here which is being used to store equipment of the battalion and which could very easily house all of the men sleeping in pup tents. I don't honestly believe that there's any excuse for any American troops in Germany sleeping in pup tents.'' Using German civilians as KPs, however, was something I applauded.

The training schedule started, of all times, on the Fourth of July, supposedly a holiday. We were to have things like 30 minutes of close order drill daily, informal guard mount and lectures. The lecture on the day I wrote was "on field sanitation, etc., by a new lt. we have who didn't leave the States until after V-E day.'' It beat me what good his lecture, read from a field manual, could do for troops like us who had been in Europe for a year. I figured if we didn't know enough about that stuff by now, we never would. That was just an example, I reported, and I expected there'd be plenty more in the days ahead. "Just how does all this help beat the Japs?'' I asked.

Lightening my tone a little, I assured my parents that such things really didn't bother me the way they did when we were back in the States. The tragedy of it, as I saw it, was the amount of time and manpower wasted. "As far as I'm personally concerned, I could be ordered to pick dandelions 12 hours a day and it wouldn't bother me now. And believe me, I've done things that are a lot sillier than that.'' Returning to the pup tents, I explained that one bad aspect of them was that they were full of ants. None had bitten me so far, and as long as none did, I didn't mind their crawling around on me. The outfit picked up a number of dogs from various places. One night one of the the pups slept with me in my pup tent. That seemed appropriate and was all right with me. The training program, I feared, would keep us from getting to visit Heidelberg. I tossed that in as a final complaint.

OCS quotas for all branches for ETO veterans were supposed to be open, according to *Stars and Stripes*. I asked my father to see what information he could find for me. I knew I'd never be completely satisfied that I had done all I could in the army until I had at least tried for OCS. "Not,'' I wrote, "that it makes a damn bit of difference one way or the other though.'' But of course it did. Hadn't I observed over and over that an officer leads a helluva lot easier life than an enlisted man?

Passing through Eisenach on the Autobahn and seeing the Wartburg Castle really made me homesick because that was where I spent the first three weeks after the war and I enjoyed that time more than

The author in front of his pup tent at Burstadt, Germany, in early July.

any I had spent in Europe. I didn't mention in my letter home that my
real homesickness was for Gyp or that she was the reason for my great
interest in visiting Heidelberg. Gyp was much on my mind the very
next day as I made plans to go on a sightseeing tour of Heidelberg
with our battery on Sunday. I thought Gyp would be there, although I
wasn't at all sure I would be able to see her. At least, I thought, I
might manage to get a letter to her.

Sunday turned out to be a beautiful day filled with sunshine. I
didn't have guard duty, so Solomon, Bliesmer, and I set off for
Heidelberg with a bunch of other GIs by way of the Autobahn and
Mannheim. Except for a couple of bridges across the Neckar River,
which apparently were destroyed by Wehrmacht engineers, Heidelberg was undamaged. The Seventh Army and Sixth Army Group
Headquarters occupied a large number of the university buildings so
it wasn't possible to see most of them. We did take a tour of the
historic castle on the steep hillside above the town. A good portion of
it was destroyed by the French in 1693 (the German guide placed
emphasis upon the ''French''). We also saw the ''Gasthof zum Roten
Ochsen,'' a famous gathering place for the students at Heidelberg.
After lunch Solomon walked with me up the bank of the Neckar to
Wieblingen to find Gyp's aunt and uncle. They spoke some English.

Gyp wasn't there and they had had no recent word of her, but they were expecting her to return sometime soon, so I gave them a letter to give her. After a couple of shots of strawberry schnapps, we left, hitching a ride back in a weapons carrier full of Polish girls and one GI.

Despite my griping I was enjoying being a corporal during this period — commanding a platoon in close order drill for the first time since the ASTP days at Maryland and pulling corporal of the guard (rather than walking guard) for the first time ever. On 11 July I was guard at the courtmartial of a fellow accused of attempting to steal pork from the kitchen. It was the first time I'd ever heard courtmartial proceedings. I thought the guy got a raw deal. We had the opportunity to see quite a few movies, some of them new ones and many special service shows. One night we went to Mannheim to see the GI version of "Carmen" put on by the 253d Infantry of the 63d Division. Mannheim bore many scars of the war, damage everywhere, but the theater, an extremely modern one, was undamaged. The review of "Carmen" in my diary went, "very filthy but also very good, although certainly couldn't be appreciated by anyone not in Deutschland." I also recorded how I thought of Gyp all the way back from Mannheim. "I hope very much that she comes to Heidelberg soon and that I can see her there. Why do I think so much about such a difficult situation and about a girl who wants to be regarded as no more than a friend? But I can't forget her."

When I next wrote home, I reported that conditions had improved somewhat. We were now sleeping in old hospital tents, which, although crowded, were all right. The ants and mosquitoes were bad. We received candy rations every two weeks, but you had to eat the candy fast to keep the ants from getting it. My outfit was great on building things. In the short time we were there we had a mess hall, consisting of a roof with tables and benches beneath, and a bar. We also had about a dozen Germans working on a tennis court.

The mornings were still occupied by a halfhearted training schedule. Things like hauling gravel and filling holes in the roads took precedence over the training. In the afternoons and evenings there were athletics and movies. One day we went to Frankfurt to see an air show put on by the 508th Parachute Regiment of the 82d Airborne Division (the honor guard for SHAEF there). We watched a couple of planes drop 18 men each. Most of them landed in a wheat field, but one kid came down square on top of the tarpaulin on the back of a GMC truck. Frankfurt had been badly bombed and we walked around among the ruined buildings and rubble. The Red Cross Club had plenty of hot dogs — I guess in Frankfurt they were frankfurters — and cokes, plus a full liter of beer for five cents and a good German orchestra.

Another trip was arranged the following Sunday. Bliesmer and I went to church first, and by the time we got out our battery group had left without us. We arranged to go with a group from B battery by a different route. Once again I walked to the home of Gyp's aunt and uncle in Wieblingen. She wasn't there. Her uncle, who was very hospitable, thought she might possibly be in Bad Nauheim, north of Frankfurt, with her great uncle. The uncle said he planned to go there on Wednesday and, if Gyp was there, he'd bring her to Wieblingen. He obviously was doing all right repairing cameras for officers of the Sixth Army Group. He had a good supply of cigarettes and other scarce items. Everywhere in Heidelberg there were GIs walking with German girls. The nonfraternization rules were greatly relaxed. The day we moved from tents to houses, some of us celebrated with drinks at the battery bar and went for a walk, striking up a conversation with a couple of girls who were hanging out of a window reviewing whatever troops passed by. During the fraternizing ban, fraternizing was done indoors or out of sight in the woods. Now it was all right to be seen with Germans almost anywhere. Tired of seeing GIs 24 hours a day, I talked one of the ''babes in the window'' into letting me come into her home the next evening. I went to her home fairly often in our remaining weeks in Burstadt, but I am certain that she was as bored by me as I was by her. I took pains to note in my diary: ''Incidentally there's absolutely no comparison between Gyp and ____. She is strictly a passing fancy.'' She was fairly plump. I made note of that.

Toward the end of July the heat seemed terrific. The fact that we were still wearing our ODs (olive drab uniforms) added to our discomfort. There was an entire week without rain, a first in all the months I was in the ETO. The first basic training schedule relaxed some, just in time to be replaced by one that was worse. Reveille was a half-hour earlier, and a new order required ties after 5 p.m. Our battalion participated in a two-day shakedown of German civilians one weekend, going to the small village of Kirchhausen about 10 or 12 miles away on Friday night and coming back Monday morning.

We searched houses all day Saturday and also established roadblocks to check passes, both civilian and GI (the latter an attempt to pick up a few AWOLs). We didn't find anything of value. Of course, after the first few houses the effect of surprise was gone, to the point that most occupants had all their passes and a bottle of wine on the kitchen table to greet us. I was astounded at the collections of stuff in the houses in the farm village. I never had seen such conglomerations of old clothes, rags, nuts, bolts, and just plain junk. The people must never throw anything away, I decided. From the thick cobwebs, it appeared that the doors of some rooms weren't opened more than once a year. This was true only in the villages. Except for the bombing damage, I noticed little difference between the German cities and our own, in appearance.

I applied for the liberal arts course at the Army University Center, which opened 30 July at Shrivenham, England. The quota for VI Corps Artillery was only seven, or about one per thousand, so I knew I didn't stand a chance. Bliesmer and Lieutenant Tyler were chosen for education and engineering, however, and left for the eight-week courses. Another school was due to open at Biarritz in southern France about the middle of August and I planned to apply for it.

To answer my mother's questions about the food I was getting, I wrote that it must be similar to what they were eating. "Usually there's fried eggs, pancakes, or French Toast and hot or dry cereal in the morning and some sort of meat or stew and various vegetables and mixtures for lunch and supper. Canned fruit is usually for dessert, although we've had ice cream occasionally. Coffee, iced tea and lemonade provide the drinks. There's plenty of white bread. About 12 candy bars and a few packages of gum every two weeks come in our rations."

Truman and Eisenhower were in the area one day in late July, and some of the guys saw them drive, at about 10 miles an hour, through Bensheim, just on the other side of the Autobahn from Burstadt. I agreed with what my father had written about Eisenhower. To me he seemed the ideal commander for a great citizen army such as ours. I told Pop I also agreed that he was right about my getting further education. "Maybe," I wrote, "I'll agree with you someday about the businessman being the arch that holds up our civilization. It seems to me that our civilization consists of more than just dollars and gadgets and that the businessman has his reward in the money he makes, while the sincere and honest stateman's usual reward is only the knowledge of a job well done or attempted." I was able to report that I had been to church the last two Sundays and probably would be going again. Expressing my surprise at Churchill's defeat, I wrote, "I had expected to see him squeeze through, but I believe Britain will fare all right, because the British are very level-headed about their socialism, but I'm afraid the victory may lend encouragement to a lot of half-pint, would-be dictators here on the continent who are now trying to raise their heads."

On the last Sunday in July I went to Mannheim and then on to Heidelberg. For a third time, I made the walk to Wieblingen only to learn that Gyp was still not there. I gave her aunt and uncle the letter I received from the States verifying that her brother was a prisoner of war in the ETO. The aunt and uncle said they would send it to Gyp, along with my previous letter, with a friend who was supposed to be driving to Eisenach the next day. I surely hoped she would get it, answer it, and get to Heidelberg soon. Back at Burstadt, I had a long talk with Mason and also saw Lieutenant Johnson, who gave me some advice on going to OCS. I went to see the plump girl but her father said she was "tired and sick." After wandering around a while longer, I settled down with my diary and gave a thought to writing up some of my experiences in the ETO. I was really floundering around. An entry in my diary is proof:

"A re-reading of this day's activities would certainly lead one to the conclusion that I could be doing something more worthwhile to say the least. Unfortunately, I cannot say that I'm not enjoying this life, because I am to a certain extent, but I certainly must strive to do something more worthwhile. How I wish I could see Gyp every evening; she could provide just the spiritual and cultural uplift I need, and at the same time, suppress my 'animal' instinct. Keep her safe, God. Someday all this shall pass — a war-broken, chaotic world, with senseless, amoral human beings running rampant within its confusion."

On the last day of July I appeared before our battalion commander for an interview for OCS, for which I had applied on July first. I named Field Artillery, Corps of Military Police, and the Armored Forces as my three choices. My diary gave this report: "Mac, Gelwick, & Cook from A Btry. there. He approved Gelwick's & Cook's & disapproved Mac's and mine. Think I owe my failure to nervousness in appearing before him (as always) & also lack of conviction about really wanting to be an officer. The rejection itself does not mean much to me, because I think the other men's chances of going are slim — considering quotas, etc. but of course the thing that hurts is the fact that two were accepted while I was not.''

Although we were living in houses, eating well enough, and had army shower units available close by, we did not have laundry service or facilities, so I sought out a German laundress. She was older than I and had at least one child. Presumably her husband was a POW. In spite of my ''animal instincts,'' my upbringing was such that I never even thought of making a pass at a married woman. My memory of that German wife and mother is quite hazy, but I know I enjoyed visiting with her. My diary notes that on one occasion we had three shots of corn schnapps together. A few days after that, my diary mentions her for the last time: ''My laundress just received official word that her husband had been killed (presumably on the Russian front). A whole roomful of crying & sad-faced women, and before I realized what was happening, I was sitting down and not knowing what to say or how to say it in German if I did. I quickly left and offered to take the laundry elsewhere but her 11-year-old girl said to leave it there. Only one of the many peculiar and oftentimes heart breaking situations here all the time.''

Early in August I was beginning to see the chances of our outfit going to the CBI decreasing. Or, if we did go, I doubted we'd ever be in combat. At that time, of course, we didn't know an atomic bomb even existed, let alone that it had been tested. In two weeks it was to be loosed on Japan, ending the war. The month started with a trip to Heidelberg to see a Jack Benny show on the top of the Holy Mount in Morris Memorial Stadium. Martha Tilton, Ingrid Bergman, and Larry Adler were part of the star-studded cast. ''I was sitting so far from the stage that I couldn't tell Ingrid Bergman from Jack Benny,'' Seymour Solomon said to sum up the show for all of us.

Still dreaming of Gyp, I wrote in my diary on 2 August: ''Filled out new application for Army U center in morning; would really like to make it. My plan: Study German there; pull a 'snow' job & get in Army of Occupation, situated somewhere near Gyp. 'The best laid plans of mice and men gang aft agley.' '' That turned out to be a prophetic choice of quotations. Two days later I received a rude shock when my name appeared on the guard list for Saturday night and Sunday. It seemed to me that Sergeant Britton was applying the screws to me. The duty knocked out my plans for a trip to Heidelberg and another attempt to see Gyp. I ended a diary report on this revolting development with "C'est la guerre — how many times am I going to have to say that?"

For some weeks Pop had been writing about the possibility of his coming to Europe as a member of a House of Representatives Committee, and I had been reporting back to him the latest rumors on when our outfit might be leaving. Toward the end of July he wrote that plans were pretty well complete for the overseas trip. He would be traveling with the Postwar Committee. The State Department was setting up the itinerary and would send a foreign service officer along to manage the trip. The army would also send a man to take care of transportation, hotel, food arrangements, and army contacts, and also provide clerical services.

The committee was to leave in mid-August on the *Queen Elizabeth*, landing at Glasgow and proceeding to London, he wrote. The return trip would be from London by boat the first week of October. "Our schedule is definitely worked out except that we do not know and probably won't know at the time we start whether or not we will be able to get into Russia. The State Department is trying to get us in but it is very difficult. If we can't get into Russia, we'll take an alternative trip thru Austria, Yugoslavia and Greece. Other countries on the itinerary are France, Belgium, Holland, Denmark, Norway, Sweden, Germany, Italy, Egypt, Saudi Arabia and Iran. Of course, we can spend only one day in some of them. I don't know just where I'll contact you, but I'll try and get that worked out as soon as I get over."

There were eight members on the committee. Traveling with them would be Marion Folsom of Eastman Kodak, director of the committee, and Dr. Wm. Y. Elliott, who was resigning as director of civilian requirements for the War Production Board. Elliott, Pop wrote, was a Harvard professor in peacetime and a brilliant man. The group was to visit industrial, business, and political leaders in each country. "Going over on the boat we'll hold some sessions with Elliott and Folsom to get what preliminary information we can on the countries we are to visit and will meet with State Department officials here in Washington before we leave in order to get all the information they can give us," he explained. "I'm looking forward to seeing you more than anything else, but I can see I'm also going to get a wonderful lot of information.''

The committee was the Special House Committee on Postwar Economic Policy and Planning, chaired by Rep. William M. Colmer of Mississippi. It was commonly known as the Colmer Committee. A few changes came up in the details Pop outlined. Only seven members of the committee made the trip, and landing was in Southampton instead of Glasgow. At the time, I was in no hurry to get back to the States, but I eagerly looked forward to Pop's visit and hoped it would be possible to see him for several days.

On 7 August Sergeant Britton, whom I'd been bad-mouthing ever since we arrived in Burstadt, told me I was to have a furlough to England on 12 August. In arranging it, Britton remembered a chance remark I had made to him about having a cousin in London. My cousin, Wilmot Ragsdale, was a correspondent for *Time* magazine there. This good news threw me into a flurry of worries. Having accepted the furlough offer, I started counting the problems. One was solved by a letter from my father saying he should arrive on the 21st. It would take me six days to get to England, so the timing for meeting Pop there should be good, but other complications loomed. What if, by some long shot, I were accepted for Army University Center No. 2 at Biarritz? I talked to Lieutenant Ling about it and he advised me to take the furlough. Acceptance at the AUC would take precedence over the furlough in any event, he said. Also, I wanted to go on a speaking tour for the Seventh Army. Ling said I should wait until Friday or Saturday to submit my application for that, so that my furlough wouldn't be screwed up. Then there was the awful truth that if I left on furlough on the 12th, a Sunday, I'd miss going to Heidelberg to try again to see Gyp.

In my diary I sketched a solution: ''If nothing develops, I may go there (Heidelberg) later in the week on the pretext of seeing Winsor at Bensheim or if not, get Solomon or Mac to go there and find out what they can from her uncle.'' So preoccupied was I with my own small world, it was August eighth before I got around to commenting on the atomic bomb that was dropped on Hiroshima on the sixth. Even then, the event received only passing mention: ''Sorted out papers & miscellaneous items for furlough to England. I certainly long to see Gyp or at least find out about her before I go to England, but on the other hand, I don't want to take too much of a chance, because that

*Seymour Solomon in the courtyard of the
castle at Heidelberg, July.*

furlough will really mean plenty to me, for obvious reasons and also
because I'm certainly going to try to arrange a deal for the Army of
Occupation while on it. What with the atomic bomb & the terrific
beating the Japs are taking, I doubt if I could ever 'do any good' in the
CBI and hence believe I could best serve in the Army of Occupation,
taking into account, of course, that I'd like it better than any thing else
I could be doing in the Army.''

Two days later we received the first (although false) report that the
war was over. I really hung one on. I was at the Red Cross Club in
Bensheim when a fellow came in and announced that VI Corps said
the war was officially ended. I returned to Burstadt and started
drinking wine with some GIs (my diary listed Bynum, Meagher, and
Sanford). We sang, danced on table tops and got thoroughly drunk. I
awakened blearily the next morning, August eleventh, to learn the
war was still on.

After finding out that Winsor no longer was in Bensheim and
consulting with Solomon, I decided not to risk going to Heidelberg
(on the pretext of going to see Winsor) and being caught AWOL. I
didn't want to jeopardize the furlough in England and the possibility
of seeing Pop. In my diary, however, I wrote, "If I were sure Gyp
was in Heidelberg it'd be different, but she very likely isn't." The
next day I left on my furlough and a month of interesting adventures.

Chapter 12

With the Colmer Committee — A Fabulous Furlough

The month in which I would meet General Eisenhower, Prime Minister Attlee, ambassadors and other big brass, have a brief venture in the Berlin black market, and mingle with Paris hookers began inauspiciously enough. On 12 August, a Sunday, I wrote another letter to Gyp, which she would never receive, before catching a ride in a weapons carrier to Kassel, Germany, far to the northeast, to board a train for Paris which was almost directly west of Burstadt. The trip in a coach with straight-back seats took almost a day and a half, traveling through the Ruhr, Maastricht, and Belgium. In Munchen Gladbach I purchased two quarts of schnapps. That made for easier riding and guaranteed passed-out sleeping the second night on the train. I awoke, however, feeling "as if someone had been standing on my chest all night."

Arriving in Paris hungry and exhausted, I must have looked like a DP. I looked up my buddy from basic training, Al Buckberg, and his boss, Maj. Jim Putnam of Emporia, Kansas. Only a few weeks earlier I had bitched to myself about Buck when I learned he had received the Bronze Star while spending the war in Paris. Now, I forgot and forgave all that. After a scotch, shower and shave, and a ride in a civilian car with him and Putnam, I was a new man. Another all-night train ride brought me to Le Havre and then to Camp Pall Mall (cigarettes were popular in those days) at nearby Etretat. Back in a camp atmosphere, I complained away in my diary. It was 15 August 1945, and I spent most of it waiting in line — for chow, to get assigned to a group, and to get billeted. I was supposed to leave Le Havre the next night or sometime after that. Although I was tired, I walked around Etretat, a seashore fishing village, just to pass time. It was worth it: "Tall, white chalk cliffs with green moss-covered shore below. High wind, with many white caps in azure blue channel. Concrete pillboxes & fortifications built in cliffs (the famed Atlantic wall) and remains of barbed wire fortifications. Area not yet cleared of mines.'' It made an impression. I commented, ''What hell war is.''

In *Stars & Stripes* I read that Pop and the House committee were supposed to sail on the *Queen Elizabeth* the next day. I prayed I could manage to make the right connections; I wondered if the war was over; I thought about Gyp. The next day I did more hurrying up to wait. It should have been some kind of red-letter day because it was the day I finally learned the war was officially over. I read that in *Stars & Stripes*, too. My diary made small note of it. ''Everyone here seems aware of it, but there is no attempt to celebrate — just a great sense of relief. It's difficult to believe that it's really 'all over' and that no more do we have to sweat out the CBI.'' It turned out I was not to leave Le Havre for another two days. This made six days of one-way travel time for what was supposed to be a seven-day furlough. It was a good thing that travel time, regardless of how long, was in addition to the furlough. With thousands of GIs traveling hither and yon all over Europe at the time, being in transit for six days was not unusual. Once in London, I checked in at an American Red Cross facility before attempting to locate my cousin Wilmot. It turned out he had moved, and the *Time* office where he worked was closed, so I spent the evening prowling the streets and parks of downtown London. I was, according to my diary, ''propositioned on the street by a fellow who offered 3 bottles of pre-war Johnnie Walker, a gold watch & a camera for 4 pounds — sounded just a little too phony.''

The next day I reached Wilmot. From a call to the American Embassy, we learned that the Colmer Committee was to arrive at Waterloo Station that very evening. The two of us were there when it arrived. Greeting Pop when he stepped off the train was one of the big moments of my life. He was completely surprised. Photographers of the *Chronicle* and *Daily Sketch* had us do a repeat of our meeting. We checked into the Savoy Hotel and had a scotch before a magnificent dinner. I wrote in my diary that it seemed almost criminal to be living this way after what I'd just left behind.

Three days after we got together, my father wrote to Mom: ''Was I surprised when I stepped off of the train here in London and found him waiting for me. It was a mighty happy reunion and we've had a fine time since. He's right up here in the Hotel with me sleeping in my pajamas and on a soft bed once more. He seems to be able to accustom himself to it all right.'' His next letter to Mom was a classic. A perfect example of his blunt honesty, it contained a memorable line that I have quoted often: ''I don't think you need to worry about the war changing him,'' he wrote of me. ''I can't see that he's changed a bit either for better or worse.'' He went on, ''I think he could come home right now and within two or three days you'd forget he'd ever been away. We're having a fine time together and have had quite a little chance to talk things over about school and other things.''

I had prepared an agenda for our discussions headed ''The Meeting of the Big Two: Hope and Hope.'' My joy in being with Pop after a long absence did not keep me from thinking of other things. I confided guilt-ridden and confused thoughts to my diary, saying I had a strong desire for ''companionship with some babe'' here but I felt I should hold back because of being with Pop. ''Don't get me wrong,'' I wrote, ''I never intend to do anything that would jeopardize my chances to best serve my ultimate goal, world peace, but will 'take on' anything which will not interfere with it.'' I noted I had evolved a hard-bitten philosophy in the army which could hardly be considered Christian, but I clung to a steadfast hope that everything would be all right in the end. I still thought about Gyp now and then.

I wrote only one letter to Mom and Martha for the next several weeks, although I knew how absence of word from me added to Mom's stress. I penned my apologies, explaining that I was in a daze at my luck to be with Pop and was hoping it would last to allow me to go on with him to Paris, Frankfurt, Brussels, Stockholm, and Berlin. I wrote details about sightseeing and mentioned a 15-minute visit with Prime Minister Attlee. You'd think that would have made a lasting impression on me. The truth is I remember nothing of that visit now. Pop was able to make arrangements for me to travel as far as Berlin with the committee. Again I had guilty feelings, but they soon began to disappear and were gone completely by the time we reached Paris. I rationalized that I would not be gone from my outfit much longer than if I had had a seven-day furlough in England with 12 days travel time.

Impressions of the Colmer Committee members are recorded in my diary along with various notes I made at the time. In general, the members were studious and hard-working. Their objective was to study and make recommendations relative to U.S. policy toward Europe and the Middle East in the immediate postwar years. After Berlin, the committee traveled to Moscow, Teheran, Cairo, Athens, and Rome. The highlight of the trip was a private audience with Stalin in the Kremlin. The members with whom I became best acquainted were Jesse Wolcott of Michigan and Orville Zimmerman of Missouri. Both were genial, pleasant, and homespun. I always felt at ease with them. Other members of the committee, in addition to Chairman Colmer and my father, were Charles A. Wolverton of New Jersey, Jay Le Fevre of New York, and Sid Simpson of Illinois.

One member typified the public's impression of many representatives and senators today. He complained loud and long about the food and service at the Hotel Savoy, where because of the war powdered eggs and "sawdust" sausage were still being served. He commandeered a U.S. vehicle to drive him to his ancestral home in Britain. When in Rome, my father later told me, this guy bought a great number of rosaries for distribution to his Catholic constituents back home. He shoved the rosaries, heaped in a large box, under the nose of Pope Pius XII, requesting that they be blessed. The Pope, Pop reported, seemed taken aback but obliged the pushy politician.

Marion Folsom, who acted as secretary for the committee, was an official of Eastman Kodak company; and Professor William Y. Elliot of Harvard, who had been a vice-chairman of the War Production Board, was a committee adviser. Having spent the past two and a half years in a somewhat different level of society, I felt privileged to associate with those gentlemen.

Considering how lucky I was to be able to make the trip with the committee as far as Berlin, I knew it was ungracious of me even to think about the differences in accommodations and mess facilities provided for the committee members and staff and those for the enlisted men in the group, which included me, T/4 Ray Malaspina, who served as secretary and typist, and the enlisted crew of the C-47 airplane assigned to the committee. But you can bet I did complain. My diary heard all about it. After London we were assigned to smaller rooms on lower floors of hotels. At the Hotel Raphael in Paris, we ate in the basement. At a lunch stop on the drive from Paris to Frankfurt, we ate at the same long table as the committee but at a lower level. On the other hand, on evenings when the committee did not have an official dinner, I was able to eat with Pop and other members. The highlight of my official social life was in Paris where I was invited to two cocktail parties, one at the American Embassy. I told my diary, "Served drinks & sandwiches by a full colonel — what a life!" I met Ambassador Jefferson Caffery and "a Polish Prince from their army in Scotland."

Although I was having a fabulous time, I did not forget I was a GI on his first trip to Paris. There were things to be done here. My pent-up desires burst forth. After midnight for three nights running, I walked to the Champs Elysées. Street-walking hookers sauntered along its broad sidewalks. For the most part, these women appeared about my age. I preferred to call them hookers rather than whores, a word which to me had a more evil connotation as it seemed to describe longtime professionals in the business. Of course I was in a quandary as to what I should do. On the one hand, I thought of that professor's no-nonsense advice about the best way to avoid VD. That, for sure, would square with my mother's admonitions and with my upbringing in the middleclass morality of the 1930s. Specifically, I knew one of the first questions Mom would ask when I returned: "Clifford, did you do anything with girls in Europe?" (Indeed, that *was* one of her first questions.) I knew I would have to tell her the truth, whatever it might be. On the other hand, I had all the normal desires of a frustrated 21-year-old far from home. Or, for that matter, at home. Actually, I believe it was more a matter of curiosity and status for me than lust. How could I explain I had been to Paris but had not spent a few hours with a hooker? With all my faults, I never was able to fabricate stories of sexual adventures. Although I knew she was right, I resented Mom's moral and religious lectures about wholesome girls. I blamed her for my indecision and inaction.

The first night, after staying in Le Lido nightclub until closing time, I wandered to the Champs Elysées, where according to my diary I had "several interesting conversations with street walkers, but no acceptance, shaking hands with one before she took off." My memory of that girl is quite clear. She was slender, sleek, and pretty with the perfect French look. One of the reasons, perhaps the only one, we didn't make a deal was because that night I had only U.S. dollars with me. She was not interested in currency exchange. When I shook hands with her, I didn't think about the cartoon in which Sad Sack, the quintessential inept soldier, went to a dance after seeing the

With his father, Representative Clifford R. Hope, at Bovington Airport before flying to Paris with the Colmer Committee on 26 August 1945.

army VD film with its graphic portrayal of the ravages of venereal disease. When a buddy introduced him to his girl, Sad Sack whipped out a rubber glove and put it on his right hand before shaking hands with her. I might have thought about it afterward. I do know that for a long time I fantasized about what it would have been like to have been with that Parisian girl for a few hours. The next night my diary recorded me "sneaking out for tour along Champs Elysées for several hours, but finally deciding against my inclinations & going back."

The third night was our last in Paris. It was then or never, I told myself. Most of the girls were young and healthy-looking. I noted one, pretty but plump. She looked straight off the farm. She had a large, oval face which reminded me of a farm relative on my Mother's side of the family. She asked me my name. I blurted out, "Bill." It was as if the FBI were recording the conversation! When I looked at that girl's happy face, I felt more comfortable and safe being with her than I had in merely talking and shaking hands with the sleek hooker of two nights before. Although I felt safe enough with that apple-cheeked girl, the night turned out to be a depressing experience. It cured me of any further desire to mess around with hookers. Whatever would become of that girl and the others like her was never part of the talk among the GIs I knew. Surely, I would never give voice to such speculation; but I thought about it a lot after that night.

Ironically, by the time I returned to my outfit, no one even asked me if I had been to Paris, let alone what I had done or hadn't done there. My respect for my father was such that I did not mention those nights in Paris, nor did he ever inquire about them. He never gave me unsolicited advice about anything. When I did ask for it, however, I got it. It was always thoughtful, comprehensive and to the point.

And so Corporal Hope left Paris with the Colmer Committee and its staff on a leisurely two-day drive to Frankfurt in four army staff cars. I had to pinch myself to believe my fabulous furlough was continuing. At Reims we visited the cathedral, a huge salvage depot which employed thousands of POWs and French women, and the room in which the German armistice had been signed on 7 May. On our way to Luxembourg City that afternoon, we drove within 14 km. of Arlon (Belgium). I felt a great desire to go there, as I recalled pleasant times at the VIII Corps Rest Camp just prior to the beginning of the Battle of the Bulge.

At the hotel in Luxembourg I had a "very nice room although, of course, we EMs ate in the basement again." I never spared my diary any of the details regarding such "rank" discrimination. In the morning, Professor Elliott, a master raconteur, delighted in showing us the Platz (square) in front of the city hall where he personally, he said, broke up a revolution at the end of World War I. The drive through eastern Luxembourg was a nostalgic journey. It had been less than a year since our survey trips there and the deaths of Priebe and Michael on the ill-fated "secret mission." I thought again of how lucky I was and had been and I wondered why. For several days the committee was billeted in the Victory Guest House (for VIPs) at Königstein, northwest of Frankfurt. There, the diary noted, we were "permitted to eat in a small room next to the kitchen." Another important detail recorded was that on our first night there, Ray Malaspina and I downed a half bottle of Irish whiskey which Pop had procured for us.

When the committee visited General Eisenhower in his Frankfurt headquarters, I tagged along. Everyone, including me, was greatly impressed with Ike. There he was with a bunch of professional politicians, completely in command. Here again, my diary entry was painfully subjective. It told of my discomfiture at "committing great faux pas and breach of military etiquette by sitting while a Lt. Col. and Major were standing at parade rest." I remember yet how I fidgeted in my chair and straightened my tie several times. No one, least of all General Ike, gave any evidence of noticing me at all. A French lieutenant whom we called "Louie" was attached to the committee at the time. He was said to be the oldest lieutenant in the French army. He let it be known he had led a dashing, exciting life. Perhaps that's why he looked so old. At any rate he, too, sat in Ike's presence with total aplomb.

The following afternoon, I hitched a ride to Heidelberg. I had postwar business of my own — finding Gyp. As fate would have it, she was not there, nor had her relatives had any word of her. Her father was there, having arrived only three days previously, apparently from a German prisoner of war camp. He did not look at all like a picture Gyp had given me of him. He was worn and haggard. He wore ill-fitting clothes, probably those of his brother-in-law. It was a tragic sight to see him and to realize how often these circumstances were repeated throughout Europe. Gyp's aunt and uncle said they had given my letter to their friend who was going to Eisenach, who would in turn give it to a friend to deliver to Gyp. There was no way of knowing if she received it or not.

The Colmer Committee meets with a relaxed General Eisenhower in his office at Frankfurt on 1 September 1945. Left to right: General Ike, "Louie" (who claimed to be the oldest lieutenant in the French Army), Chairman William Colmer, Rep. Orville Zimmerman, a very nervous Corporal Hope, James J. Farriss of the State Department, and Rep. Clifford R. Hope.

On 3 September the committee, flying low in General Crawford's plane, surveyed Koblenz, Remagen and the Ludendorff Bridge, Bonn, Koln (Cologne), and Hamburg. Landing in Hamburg, we toured the port, where we saw extensive damage to oil refineries, the huge submarine pens, and the fire-gutted "Strength Through Joy" liner, *Robert Ley*. At noon, at an RAF airfield, we had a good meal and Ray and I actually got to eat in the same room with the Congressmen and officers. Segregation was back when we arrived in Brussels that evening. The committee and officers billeted in the British officers' hotel, and Ray and I were in a smaller one across the square. We finagled a good meal: "U.S. mess closed & having no francs, got Pop to try to get us some Belgium francs and in so doing British mess officer gave us chow on mezzanine floor, although it was a 'bit irregular.' "

The next day as Ray and I were taking an early morning walk, we were accosted in front of a cafe by the proprietor, who looked a lot like Sidney Greenstreet. Speaking in a livelier voice than Sidney's, he invited, "Black market breakfast, boys. Come on in!" We followed him inside and were treated to two large fried fresh eggs and thick slices of bread and jam. Because of the fresh eggs, it was tastier than any breakfast I had had since leaving the States. It was worth the price of 100 Belgian francs (about $2.20), an enormous sum at the time. I spent most of that day waiting at the Swedish Consulate to obtain a visa to enter Sweden. It was handed to me by a white-gloved gentleman who spoke in extremely formal English. Entering the other countries on the tour was no problem because the U.S. had military bases in them.

On 5 September we were off to an overnight stay in Norway with a lunch stop at the Copenhagen airport. There I drank my first glass of milk since living in the schoolhouse at Aldringen, Belgium, the previous autumn. The airport was 60 kilometers north of Oslo. Since the city had no facilities for GIs, we stayed behind while the committee went to an Oslo hotel and dinner. The next morning the members observed the treason trial of Vidkun Quisling, the infamous Norwegian traitor. Back at the airbase, operated jointly by the RAF and the U.S. Air Transport Command, the flight crew — Ray, Hank, and Bob — and I were royally treated by the boys on the base: "getting exceedingly drunk on English beer and French cognac at their bar, then going to open-air dance one and a half miles away. Talking to Norwegian soldier & promising babe a pair of silk stockings, although I have very hazy recollection of the whole affair. Stumbling down highway to barracks and being enabled to reach there only through the 'sixth sense' of Hank."

Although I had been more drunk that night than at any time in my life, I was raring to go to Stockholm the next day. Ray and I were put up in what was apparently a converted ballroom at the Grand Hotel, Stockholm's finest. Since Sweden had escaped involvement in World War II, Stockholm was a shopper's paradise. Taking a tip from the mess sergeant at the Oslo airbase, Ray and I bought cheap watches for the purpose of selling them to the Russians in Berlin. We ran into Hank and Bob on the streets, the only other GIs we saw. What a glorious experience. We made plans to meet them at the Cafe Blanch for drinks and dinner.

At the cafe I observed a portly black man, immaculately dressed, seated by himself at the end of the bar.

"What's that nigger doing here?" an American officer seated

Flight engineer and radio operator with the Colmer Committee airplane at a Norwegian airbase on 6 September.

nearby asked.

A Swedish patron who overheard the remark explained quietly, "He is the owner of this cafe."

After dinner Hank and I wandered about half a block down to the Salle de Paris. We were looking for girls, of course. To our dismay, we learned that no liquor was served there, but we did find many unescorted girls. After several minutes we spotted a couple of blondes who were looking through an English grammar and went over to offer our help. "The yellow blonde spoke English fairly well, but the other, mine, hardly had anything to say at all, being very shy and bashful," said an entry in my diary. Their names were Ingrid and Bridget, and we persuaded them to go to Cafe Blanch with us. Later I took Bridget, the quiet one, to a train for Rotebro, the suburb where she lived. Hank took Ingrid to her bus.

The next day I shopped again. In addition to buying another watch, I picked up gifts for my family and for Dorothy Ford, my friend from Iowa. I made a note that this was "a long standing obligation" since she had sent me a box of candy on my birthday at Matton, France, during the Bulge. It was some kind of special day all right. I had the only formal date I ever had in my 18 months in Europe. Hank and I

In the driver's seat of Herman Goering's car in Berlin in September.

went with Ingrid and Bridget to the Skansen, ''sort of a large, quaint
park entered by the longest escalator I've ever seen,'' I said in my
diary. Later, I learned the Skansen was the world's oldest open-air
museum. My diary got a complete account of the night's activities.
We ate in a quaint, two-story tavern, where the waitresses wore
seventeenth-century-type costumes, and topped the meal with
schnapps, beer, and cognac. Bridget called her boss to say she
wouldn't be at work that night. After we took pictures, we went to the
Cafe Blanch for bourbon and soda, on to the Cafe du Boulevard for
vermouth, grog, and dancing, back to the Blanch and then on to Salle
de Paris, where we had soda pop out of a large bottle and danced
while a Danish girl sang American songs in English. We split up,
with me taking Bridget home to Rotebro in a taxi. ''It must have been
about halfway to Oslo.'' It was very dark when I said goodbye to her
at what must have been a farmhouse. Anyway, I took the taxi back to
the Grand Hotel: ''22.50 Kroner fare, but what the hell. All in all, the
best and nicest night I've had in the ETO.'' Needless to say, I had
temporarily forgotten Gyp, Irene, and all the other girls I pined for. In
spite of everything I had a good feeling about having had a wonderful
date with a nice Swedish girl when some of the guys got to boasting of
their sexual adventures in Stockholm.

The next day we were off to Berlin. The committee stayed at
Harnack House, another VIP place, while Ray and I were assigned to
the 82d Airborne Division area. The following night, however, a

The remains of Hitler's office in the Reichschancery in Berlin, from which members of the Colmer Committee carried off souvenirs.

Ruins of the Reichstag in Berlin, September.

Lieutenant Wills, who was in charge of the committee's Berlin visit, put us up at his quarters ''after buying us a couple of drinks . . . a damn nice fellow all the way around.'' After a Sunday morning appointment with General Lucius Clay, the U.S. commander, the committee members visited the ruins of the Reichschancellery and I went along. That's when I learned Congressmen were as good as, if not better than, GIs at souvenir collecting and looting. Each of them got a large splinter from Hitler's desk. (I did, too.) We had no positive proof that it was Hitler's very own desk, but we all convinced ourselves it was as we ripped it apart. I learned later that Hitler's desk was marble-topped. Chairman Colmer also picked up a large metal hoop which apparently had been around a globe, and Sid Simpson latched on to part of a large light fixture. I wonder what they ever did with those prizes.

Later that day I met Donald Heath, a Kansan and career foreign service officer who was then counselor to Ambassador Robert Murphy. When he learned that I was interested in the Foreign Service, Heath asked if I'd like to be transferred to Berlin to serve in military government for my remaining time in Germany. I was excited at the prospect and told him so. I realized, of course, that the paperwork for such a transfer would take some time.

With four watches and four packs of cigarettes, I headed for the black market area at the Alexander Platz the next day. Two burly Russian soldiers with whom I was striking a deal insisted that I ride, seated between them, in their beat-up truck to find their "officier" before they could complete the transaction. We drove for what seemed like miles into the Russian Zone. Finally the "officier" was found, and I unloaded the four Swedish watches, which cost me a total of 70 dollars, for $1,060. For the cigarettes I got 40 bucks. My Russian customers did not offer to drive me back, so I began a long walk of four or five miles up, or down, the Unter den Linden, losing my way and finally being picked up by a kindly AMG (American Military Government) captain.

Percentage-wise, that little black market deal was the most profitable of my life, before or since. It appeared that every soldier who had the opportunity, officer and GI alike, was profiting in the black market. Although I had ranted and raved against wartime profiteering in the States, my brief flirtation in the field didn't bother me at all. I invested the money and put it to good use for family expenses after I was married in 1948.

My diary makes no reference to the utter devastation, mile upon mile of it, in Berlin. By that time, I was so inured to destruction that I didn't think it worth mentioning. Not so my father. In a long letter to my mother he described the overall situation in Berlin in detail. It was a great contrast to Stockholm, he told her. The destruction might not have been worse than in other places, but the bombed area was much larger. There were miles and miles in the center of the city where practically every building was destroyed. Some walls or parts of walls still stood. There were supposed to be almost three million people in the city, but where they all lived was a mystery — anywhere they could find shelter. The people looked bad, worse than in Frankfurt or anywhere in the American zone. Berlin was in a state of siege for several months before it was captured, and food was scarce even before that time. The children showed effects of malnutrition. There was not much to look forward to in the winter ahead because there would be no coal and far less than adequate supplies of food. ''In a large part of the area, it looks like a dead city, especially in the Russian Zone,'' Pop wrote. But he cited some improvement in conditions. Water was available in most parts of the city, although the lights were still off in most places. The streetcars were running and the subway was open in some areas. The city still smelled of dead bodies on warm days. Bones would be dug out of the rubble for years to come. Misery and destitution were everywhere.

You didn't see any begging because the military were everywhere, but if someone threw away a cigarette butt there were half a dozen people ready to pounce on it. There was nothing much to buy, but the Russian soldiers who got pretty good pay and who weren't paid for three or four years before the end of the war gave fantastic prices for the things they wanted. The main reason was that the Russian government would allow them to take only a very small amount of money home. In other words, they had to spend practically all of it in Germany. It was the Russians' way of completing the looting of Germany. The soldiers were paid in German marks that the future German government would have to redeem. Meanwhile the Russians were buying up everything the Germans had to sell. The thing they most wanted was wrist watches. In the early days of the occupation, U.S. soldiers sold their wrist watches for four or five hundred dollars each. The Russians didn't care what kind of watches they were, just so they had black dials and ticked. Now, they were a little more discriminating. They found out some watches had jewels, so prices for cheap watches went down some. The Russians were fond of sweep second hands and ornaments on the watch faces. A Mickey Mouse watch reportedly brought a thousand dollars. The current price for an ordinary watch ranged from two to three hundred dollars.

Brandenburger Tor (Brandenburg Gate) in Berlin, September.

The standard black market price for American cigarettes was 10 dollars a pack and a Hershey bar sold for five dollars. A lot of American soldiers have grown rich, my father wrote home. "The boy who drove our car in Berlin has $8,000 in marks. Some have even more. All of them have considerable. The thing that is worrying them is how to get this money home."

There was no regulation, that anyone knew of, against a GI changing his money for dollars when he went home and taking the dollars with him. However, the army ruled he could not send home an amount in excess of his monthly pay, plus 10 percent, each month. Some GIs were afraid that by the time they left they would be restricted in what they could cash in. The only way they had to get dollars, of course, was through the army finance offices. The whole Berlin situation was unbelievable. Some people were starving and freezing while cigarettes were selling for 10 dollars a package. Cigarettes were legal tender for anything. Unfortunately, my father never wrote a book or otherwise documented his experiences, but his letters home, saved by my mother, gave fairly comprehensive, on-the-spot reports.

The committee left for Moscow on 11 September. I went to the airport to see them off on General Eisenhower's plane (Sunflower II). Their regular plane was to get Russian clearance later. I was pretty sure that I could have gone with them if we had started working on it earlier or if Pop had pushed it. However, as I wrote in my diary, "I'm very glad he's like he is, and who am I to complain with such a wonderful trip behind me." And then I added, "Maybe I'm prejudiced, but Pop appears to me about the finest, fairest member of the committee &, God knows, that's what counts in the final analysis." I caught a plane ride to Frankfurt on 12 September and a jeep ride from there to Markgroningen, northwest of Stuttgart, the new headquarters of the Thirteenth. My fabulous furlough was over. It was back to army routine while waiting to go home, with the possibility of a transfer to Berlin in the meantime.

Chapter 13

Gefangen Lager 71 and the Village

My last three and a half months in the army, although often frustrating, were filled with new and good experiences. Working in the office of a POW camp for political prisoners was, in fact, the most interesting job I had in my army service. And, of course, there was yet another girl. Although a part of me wanted to go home to resume college and civilian life, another part wanted to continue the carefree life I was leading. Aware of my nature, I knew that once I returned to the States and my own agenda it would be rush, rush, rush.

On my first evening back with the Thirteenth, because of rumors that specific orders might soon be issued restricting the amount of cash each GI might take home, I located three buddies and distributed three thousand marks ($300) plus a 10 percent "service charge" to each, with the understanding that each would mail $300 to my home address after their arrival home. They were trustworthy, and in due course I did indeed get my $900. I am certain that others used more complicated schemes for returning much greater amounts of black market profits or card game winnings.

At long last I began to understand that army life could be made easier by going with the system rather than bitching from the sidelines. A small detachment from the Thirteenth, commanded by Lieutenant Ling, was assigned to run the office of Prisoner Camp (Gefangen Lager) 71, and the very next day that good lieutenant got me assigned to his charge. The camp, originally built and used by the Germans, was located between Ludwigsburg and the village of Aldingen, which was on the banks of the Neckar River. It was a nice set-up mainly in that "there's no one to bother us here," my diary noted.

Prison Camp 71 (Gefangen Lager 71), a camp for Nazi political prisoners, near Ludwigsburg, Germany, September 1945.

There were about two and a half thousand war criminals in the camp. Most of them were ''ortsgruppenleiters'' (German for what, in our country, we would call ''ward heelers'') of the Nazi Party. Many Gestapo agents were among them. Soon we were to open another camp for about a thousand spies brought back from North and South America. I wrote to my father, still on the Colmer Committee tour, ''They really have these guys on the ball; they snap to attention whenever we pass, and they operate showers, a barber shop, tailor shop, and film-developing establishment, in addition to bringing us coffee or tea every morning and afternoon if we want it. The job probably will get monotonous after awhile, but it's certainly one of the best in the battery now.''

We were assisted in the camp administration by an inmate, whom I shall call Herr Schmidt, and a staff of seven or so prisoners he recruited to help him. He was a clerk who had been doing the same sort of work for the Nazis. Each morning he walked from his barracks wearing his business suit and carrying his briefcase just as if he were going to a regular job. He and his helpers were in a small room adjacent to our office. When one of us GIs entered their room,

Schmidt would shout "Achtung!" and all would rise and click their heels, usually knocking over their straight-back chairs in the process. "I wonder what Schmidt would do if I told him to place an order for five hundred coffins," Lieutenant Ling once mused, grinning slyly. "He'd dutifully carry out the order, hoping that one of the coffins was not for him but ready to jump in one and close the lid over himself if so directed," someone in the office suggested. There was no doubt among us that Schmidt would do just that.

The camp barber was a former SS trooper. In addition to haircuts, he gave shaves with a straight razor. Having survived almost three years of the war thus far, I decided it best not to tempt fate. I continued shaving myself. Later I learned that Fritz Kuhn, leader of the German-American Bund, was prisoner No. 1 in the other camp our outfit was running; that the stage manager of the Oberammergau Passion Play was an inmate of Camp 71; and that those who portrayed Jesus, Mary, and St. John in the Passion Play were inmates in other prisons. On the evening of 15 September I was at the administration office with O'Connell during the interrogation of Fritz Reinhardt, former state secretary in the ministry of finance in Berlin. Foster Adams of G-5, Finance, at Frankfurt, conducted the questioning and obtained a signed statement from Reinhardt, who was visibly shaken.

Typing detention reports soon grew boring, so I volunteered to deliver our prisoners to other points whenever possible. On 17 September I went to Heidelberg with four prisoners for the Seventh Army Interrogation Center at Seckenheim. The group consisted of a lieutenant colonel of the Yugoslav army, a professor of physics at the University of Vienna, an official of the Benz works in Berlin, and a Waffen SS corporal. I hadn't forgotten Gyp. I stopped at Wieblingen to give her father a letter for her. He said he would be going to Eisenach the next day. In my diary, I noted, "I still pray for her every day."

Things happened fast in the postwar days. With typical army logic, men with 70 to 80 points left one day. Those with more points, 80 and above, left a few days later. Only 27 men in the original battalion remained. Most of them were guys like me who came from the Sixteenth. The replacements for those who left had from seven to 75 points, so it looked as if the outfit would be at the camp for some time. With 66 points I was one of the high-point men left, but since so many were leaving at one time, I figured I would be stuck for a while.

A letter from my old friend Houston Smith informed me that Irene
was engaged to someone at Notre Dame. I hadn't heard from her for
about five months so I had suspected something of the sort. I wrote
my mother and sister, "In any event, I guess that's another one I can
mark off the list." I went on to tell more of my pursuit of women
across Europe than I had in previous letters but only in the most
general way. "You know I'm a rather fickle guy," I began. "(I had)
feminine acquaintances in England, France, Belgium, Luxembourg,
Germany and Poland in the last 15 months and on the trip with Pop I
met one of the nicest yet in Stockholm, Sweden. So you can see how
it is." I added, parenthetically, "Don't get the wrong idea, or I
wouldn't be telling you this."

The saga of Irene did not end officially until I wrote her in January
1946 soon after my return home. She responded immediately to tell
me she became engaged on 19 May to a boy from Notre Dame and
Washington, D.C. "Cliff," she wrote, "I started several letters at
various times to tell you all of this but I never knew whether you
would rather hear about it or not hear from me at all. I, of course,
couldn't write to you and not tell you about it. That wouldn't have
been fair to anyone concerned. I decided it would be better not to
write at all. I didn't know how much it would mean to you either way.
I still don't know whether I did the right thing or not, but I'm glad I
have the opportunity to tell you now. From the *Telegram*, I thought
you all were coming here for Christmas. Mother and I wanted to have
you and the family over some time because they had been so nice to us
the Thanksgiving we were in Washington. I know now why you
didn't make it for Christmas. It's a shame you had to be just one day
late getting in. Cliff, try to get out here with your Dad. I would really
like very much to see you again and talk with you. And, please know
that I still have great faith in whatever you plan to do for the future."
In a postscript, she said, "Keep the St. Christopher medal with you.
It's always good to have one handy."

All in all, I thought this was a nice ending to a romance which
never really had gotten off the ground. Irene died in 1962 at the age of
37.

Meanwhile, back in Germany, I experienced more of the sordid
aftermath of war. While returning on a Saturday night from taking
more prisoners to the Seckenheim Interrogation Center, I was persuaded by my jeep driver to stop in a village so he could spend the

night with his girlfriend. He was, according to my diary, "strictly a jerk — what characters one meets in the Army!" We went to a house crowded with refugees. Among them was a girl who was staying there with her sister. Her parents and five other sisters had been killed in a single raid on Dortmund. According to the people in the house, she was made pregnant by a GI who took off. In her determination to get to America, the girl tried to pin the paternity on another soldier. She ended up having an abortion. "To me," I wrote in my diary, "this sums up all the tragedy of human degradation and misery left in the wake of war — things which do not disappear with the coming of peace, but rather whose terrible influence lasts for years."

When I arrived back at Camp No. 71, I learned I'd been promoted to buck sergeant. Had I known that was coming up, I probably would have been more careful the day before, I admitted in my diary, elucidating, ". . . things such as picking a babe up in the jeep and taking her for thirteen or fifteen miles in broad daylight." The next weekend, after delivering prisoners, I was with another jerk driver, but for some reason I was driving. I think it might have been that he was too drunk. As I was driving at a mad rate over an unknown road back to Ludwigsburg, this character was throwing apples at the civilians we passed along the way. "And then some people wonder why we should be brought home," I commented in writing about the incident in my diary.

In the same entry, which covered a nine-day period, I told about a prisoner who worked in the prisoners' personal property office. He was a staff sergeant in the 1st SS Panzer (Adolph Hitler) Division and helped chase us out of Belgium in 1944. He was very well informed but typically Prussian in his line (or lack) of reasoning. I judged him, from all appearances, to be an "incurable" and felt he would have to be held under some sort of restrictions for the rest of his life. He was another example of tragedy wrought by war on the human character. On the subject of human character, I addressed a few lines to myself: "Incidentally, Hope ole kid, don't think that because you write these philosophical 'odes' that you're any 'angel' yourself, because you're not and you have a helluva lot of room for improvement. . . . I still love to 'tear' around and think it's a good thing up to a certain point."

My promotion to sergeant was reported in a letter home on 24 September. With exaggerated self-effacement, I wrote "Surprisingly enough, they've decided to fill up the T.O. (Table of Organization) to the definite advantage of us 'old men' in the outfit. Anfuso made S/Sgt., McNamara Cpl., and O'Connell T/5, and I made Buck Sgt., so you can see that they'll give anybody a rating these days. If I hang around a few more weeks, I might make S/Sgt.'' Also in that letter, I wrote about meeting an eight-year-old girl in the next village whose father was in a POW in a camp in Kansas. She was the first German I had come across who had ever even heard of Kansas. Her father had evidently been a member of the Afrika Korps.

I saved only a few letters that I received in September 1945. Among them, however, was a letter from my sister, Punkie, which I treasured. She wrote, ''In looking through *Life* I noticed that physicists are turning their talents to such inventions as machines that remember and reason logically. That's all very wonderful, but it seems to me that we should begin to turn our thoughts from mechanical devices that perform the functions we're meant to perform to some of the things that are really important and always will be important. Surely the purpose of humans on earth is not to find how we can get the most work done with the least effort. I wonder what it is in the makeup of the American people that makes them want the security of material possessions above everything else. I could go on but I guess I sound like too much of a philosopher already. I think you and I can have some really good discussions when you get home. In the past year I've learned to think more.''

Pop wrote from Rome in late September. He thought I had already been transferred to Berlin and expressed the hope I would be home soon. He guessed I would be leaving Europe in November. Mom was making big plans for a trip to Garden City for Christmas, he said. ''If you get home when you should, you can probably start in school for the second semester or at least sometime earlier than next fall.'' He said nice things about our time together in Europe, adding that the other fellows on the committee were interested in me. ''The trip and the fellowship we had together makes me all the more anxious for you to get home as soon as possible. You'll be leaving home for good before too many years and every day of association we can have together is precious to me.''

Mom was back to full-scale preaching and she admitted it in a letter she wrote toward the end of September. The gist of it was twofold — the importance of my getting back in school, and girls. She hit the latter head-on. ''Now some advice about girls. I too think Irene might have written you of her engagement. Barbara never calls so she's probably interested in some one else which is probably O.K. with you. I'm not at all distressed about you having a girl in every country. In fact, just now the more *nice* girls you have the better. I've always preached to you about having girl *friends* — not just *girls*. You need the companionship, friendship & comradeship of girls just as much as you do men — and if you don't have it you've missed something very fine in life. I'm going to be critical, if you don't mind — I think your trouble is falling too hard for a girl or maybe I should say you let the girl fall too hard for you. You develop a 'case' or a 'crush' or what ever your term for it is. Then when you recover from the infatuation there is nothing left to base a lasting friendship on. It doesn't distress me to see you have a lot of girls, but it does make me feel badly for you to drop them. If a girl doesn't have the qualities that are worthy of friendship then she isn't worth your time at all. You'll be far better qualified to pick out a wife having had a lot of girls, whether they remain friends or not than in only knowing a few. But try to go a little easier, Son, & don't go off the deep end every time you meet a nice girl. And I'm implying that the girls you do get interested in are nice girls. Don't waste your time on any other kind, Son. You'll regret it all the days of your life if you do.''

She closed on a joking note, acknowledging it had been a long time since she'd given me such a ''talking-up'' but complimenting me for always being ''swell about letting your Mom advise you. My counsel is free,'' she said, ''anything else you want to know just ask for it.''

My Mom's advice was nothing if not timely. Almost every night since I had been at Camp 71, except when I was off on some wild-assed trip, I went to Aldingen and had a few beers in a gasthaus, a village gathering place similar to an English pub. By October I was patronizing the same gasthaus every night because I had become deeply infatuated with Hilda (not her real name), a village girl who had worked in the local burgomeister's office since 1941. She and her friends at the gasthaus became a sort of security blanket for me in my longing to continue my present way of life and not face up to going home to college and whatever else might be expected of me. The early days of October were very happy ones, according to my diary accounts. Hilda was the main reason. Work at the camp was interesting, too, as we transferred and received several hundred prisoners. Among them were numerous SS and German ''Com Z'' officers.

Between 2 and 12 October I saw Hilda at the tavern in Aldingen eight times, and one Saturday night I visited her at her home. It was fun at the tavern, playing German folk games, dancing and listening to Hilda play the piano. I became acquainted with a number of interesting people — a woman and her daughter, a shrewd old lady, the mandolin player and his wife, and many other civilians. All of them had war tales to tell. I lost a lot of sleep, returning to camp from one to three every morning. "It was worth it seeing Hilda," a diary note affirmed.

Then, on 12 October I was transferred to Service Battery of the 131st F.A. Battalion in the 36th Division, the first step in the long process of getting home. The Thirty-Sixth was then stationed in the area of Schwabisch Gmund, east of Stuttgart. Service Battery was in the nearby village of Strassdorf. In my diary I philosophized and fantasized: "Probably half my overseas diary has been filled with 'writeups' of various girls and what I've thought of them and I suppose that in rereading them each would sound about the same. All of which proves you're a very fickle guy I suppose, Cliff old kid. Someday, though, you're going to fall, and reversing the opinion you've held before about getting a helluva lot of experience, perhaps it's better not to 'experiment' too long for fear that you lose all sense of ever 'settling down.' . . . And in regard to Hilda, in view of what you've said about your fickleness — wait until you've been home six months or a year — if then you're still thinking of her as you are now, then it's the real thing, kid, and you can set about to figure out what to do about it."

I believe I realized at the time but would not admit it that I was more enamored of Hilda than she of me. She was good and kind to me in a motherly way and perhaps that was what I really needed at the time. As things turned out I would not have to be concerned about what to do about Hilda in six months or a year. The day I poured it all out in my diary, I also wrote home. I thanked my mother for her advice on girls even as I was ignoring it. I went so far as to say I looked forward to discussing "all that kind of stuff" with her in person. While I hoped I was in the last step on the way home, I was frank about hating to leave the internee camp. "Think I had the best time there that I've had anyplace overseas, with the exception, of course, of the time I spent with you, Pop." I explained about the interesting work there with no one bothering us and about the nightly walks with O'Connell to Aldingen. We were more or less taken in as members of the family at a tavern where I also met "a very nice girl," I reported.

At Service Battery about the only duties were guard. I had not been sergeant of the guard before, so I had a new experience to look forward to. The first sergeant (Goodfellow) seemed as good as his name and entirely different from the typical old army "first nub" from North or South Carolina. The first shipping information sounded good. The division was supposed to leave on 28 October, boarding a boat at Le Havre on 2 November. I understood the British had taken the *Queen Elizabeth* and the *Aquitania* away from us as troopships and it occurred to me that might delay departure some. At any rate, I thought I could be home for Thanksgiving and most certainly for Christmas. I wrote my folks that it would be great if we could go to Garden City and have a family reunion over the holidays. I told them not to write me any more, realizing I might regret saying that. It seemed logical at the time.

My transfer to Berlin to serve in military government came through on 4 October, but in view of what I thought would be our imminent departure for home, I did not accept it. I wrote Mr. Heath in Berlin to explain why I wasn't coming. He agreed with my parents that I should resume college as soon as possible. In the meantime, my letter announcing my promotion to sergeant reached my parents. Mom said she saw the "Sgt." on the envelope before she opened it. She wrote the expected glowing, flowery congratulations. Embarrassing as it was, I liked the sound of it: "Your explanation that 'they'll give anybody a rating these days' is quite satisfactory. I cannot help but think how lucky it is you just happen to be around when the Army decides to hand out a few ratings. We're still very proud of you, sweet boy, and not only because of your new rating but the modest way in which you make mention of it. . . . I want you to always be proud of your accomplishments but *never* to be conceited about it. Your modesty is a very commendable and redeeming asset. . . . That was the quality about Eisenhower that struck me so forceably. He was so humble, unassuming & unpretentious yet so strong and sure of himself."

During the latter part of October, along with conflicting emotions of looking forward to going home as soon as possible and wishing to stay in Germany in a kind of limbo, great thoughts still churned in my mind. At the time, my thoughts centered on the future of Germany as a nation. I wrote a paper which I called "The Control of Germany." In it I pointed out that the four allied powers charged with the occupation and administration of Germany had not given evidence of either a uniform occupation policy or a program to carry out such policy whenever it might be adopted. I outlined two broad alternative policies.

The first would be along the lines of revenge — stern justice for everyone who had made the slightest contribution to the Nazi war effort. This would amount to an indictment of the vast majority of the German people. Perhaps such a policy would be justice, but it would intensify the terrible hatreds already caused by World War II and pave the way to another war. Furthermore, I pointed out, such a policy could be carried out only by a virtual reign of terror. There was already an example of this in the forced migration, within the period of a few months, of Germans from western Poland and Silesia, when such migrations could easily have been made in an orderly manner within a period of several years. "It has been my naive belief," I wrote, "that one of the things we were fighting for was to end such things."

The aim of the alternative policy would be the prevention of another war through a serious, sincere attempt to remake Germany as a democratic nation with a standard of living equal to that of the rest of Europe. My reason for setting a standard of equality was that a perpetually lower standard would give the Germans no incentive to work or hope for the future. Also it would cause the most suffering among small children who were in no way responsible for the war. The standard, I explained, would be based upon a peace economy. There should be no German war industry or armed forces.

I outlined a specific program to carry out the objectives I listed, dividing the program into periods of 1945-1950, 1950-1960, and post-1960. I did not foresee the Cold War, or at least not the extent of it, or the creation of an East and West Germany. Reading those recommendations so many years later made me want to smile and cry at the same time.

Ever eager to share my great thoughts with others, I sent a copy of my plans for Germany to *Time* magazine. Much to my surprise, I received a nice thank you. No doubt it was from a woman assigned to reply to writers of sincere but unsolicited papers such as mine. That paper represented coming full circle in my thinking about the "control of Germany." Long before I advocated the obliteration of Germany and Germans as an aftermath of our Ardennes retreat, I had written a paper as a high-school senior in June 1941. Entitled "In Defense of Germans," it suggested reorienting the direction of German energies. The building of a truly democratic Germany would be the goal once Nazism was destroyed. Friendship would be the first step to bringing freedom to the new Germany. We could, I envisioned, organize a Europe of economic equality in which Germany would have a part. Germany could be kept disarmed if all the rest of the world also disarmed and invested sole police powers in a new federation of all nations. German scientific knowledge, which destroyed our old world, could aid in the reconstruction of a new one. Through free, democratic education, Germany could bring forth new Albert Einsteins, new Thomas Manns, I expounded. "If we are tolerant, forgiving, and helpful, in the world of the future, the Germany of Goethe and Schiller shall live again."

On our first Sunday in Strassdorf, I went to church in Gmund. A diary note on the occasion said, "For the first time since July — not a record to be proud of." We had few formal duties apart from guard and miscellaneous assignments as we waited to sail for home. The correspondence course in German I had enrolled in through the University of Kansas began arriving in mid-October. In addition to working on those lessons, I tried my hand, for the first and only time while in the army, at writing fiction based on fact. Perhaps this was the forerunner of what some later called the nonfiction novel. An excerpt recalling the happy days and nights at Camp 71 went:

"He turned off the narrow ribbon of asphalt and walked slowly down the trail, deeply-rutted for decades by all manner of oxcarts and wagons and more recently by bouncing jeeps. It had become a familiar road for him — many nights in the last three weeks he had left the Gefangen Lager after chow and gone down to the village. Yes, the Gefangen Lager with its acres of flimsy barracks now housing the pride of the Herrenvolk — a thousand underlings and lackeys — SS men — they with the perfect bodies and the warped minds — a sprinkling of quislings — and hundreds of Ortsgruppenleiter — the community leaders who were the low men of the Nazi Party totem pole. But he was not thinking of the Lager now — of his job in the administration office of the camp (a soft touch it was —

no formations — no guard — prisoners to wait on you hand and foot), of his buddies back there who night after night played poker in the barracks, or went to the city to see an old movie in the patched-up Opera House, or went out fraternizing, or got roaring drunk on some of the local 'buzz bomb juice,' or perhaps just lay back on their bunks and bitched. No, his mind was elsewhere — everywhere and nowhere at the same time.

"Yes, the last three weeks had been about the best he could ever remember having in the army. But that wasn't the best part — now he was going home — yes home. He didn't know when — you never know exactly when anything's going to happen in the army — but it should be sometime within the next few weeks."

That page was the end of that literary effort. In other writing, especially in the letters home, I returned to bitching. On Saturday, 20 October, I gave the navy a bad time. Our sailing date from Le Havre was postponed from November 10th to the 15th. If it got postponed again, I predicted, there'd be a lot of guys blowing their brains out. I gave a typical GI opinion by citing how much resentment there was against dock strikers "or whoever is responsible for the strike." I agreed that it was understandable that the British took the *Queen Elizabeth* and the *Aquitania* back. What was not so understandable, I ranted, was "why in hell the Navy has to have such gigantic, stupid Navy day celebrations in all the home ports when those ships could be used to much better advantage bringing guys home from here and the Pacific." I was expecting my parents to gather information on good foreign service schools, and I let them know I would like to have it available by the time I got home. Tuition costs, I mentioned, preferably should be within the $500 limit of the G.I. Bill of Rights.

That weekend, I caught a jeep ride back to Camp 71 with a guy who was going on to Markgroningen. My reason was to see Hilda and her friends in Aldingen, not my buddies at the camp — which was just as well, for when I arrived most of the personnel were at a 36th-100th Division football game at Ulm, and O'Connell had gone to Paris. After eating supper with Gelwick, I did the old familiar three-kilometer walk to Aldingen. Everyone in the family seemed glad to see me. Hilda came over in a little while and everything was going fine until a GI, who had previously given us schnapps, thought I was responsible for making his girl cry. She said everyone was laughing at her and him for smooching. "It's all your fault, sergeant," the GI said as he swung at me, landing a fast punch in the middle of my face. My nose spurted blood all over me and Hilda. She and another girl, Anna, rushed me out of the room and upstairs, blood dripping all the way. Later, when I indicated I wanted to go back downstairs, Hilda pleaded, "If you love me, do not go back." I decided the place would get wrecked if I did. Eventually practically everyone came up to see me, including Wallace. He said one of the "motorcycle boys" had drawn a pistol on him after I left. So I spent the night in Anna's room. She was not in it with me, incidentally. When I woke late the next morning, Hilda and Anna came in to look me over. My left eye was deep purple by this time. They took good care of me, bringing hot packs along with breakfast in bed — coffee and bread with preserves. When Hilda and I were alone at last, she called me her "little boy," adding other endearing terms. I had dinner at the gasthaus. I didn't want to, because of the food situation, but my German friends insisted and, under the circumstances, it was a great meal — cauliflower soup, boiled potatoes, some sort of meat and noodles, and lettuce with potatoes in it, followed by pie and coffee later in the afternoon. Hilda, Anna and two friends from Munchen Gladbach walked up to Camp 71 with me in the afternoon. It was late in the day when my ride called to say he'd be a little late. Much later, I woke up the lieutenant to tell him my ride hadn't appeared yet. He told me to stay over until morning.

In the morning I wrote a letter to the battery commander explaining why I was AWOL. Lieutenant Gold signed it. After a haircut and shower at the camp, I took off for Gmund in Gold's jeep. Lieutenant Ling and the boys in the administration office got a big kick out of my shiner. When I arrived at Strassdorf at noon, everything apparently was OK, but I had a lot of explaining to do about the black eye. The guy I was supposed to have ridden with offered some lame excuse for not picking me up. Apparently he was at the camp that night. I never did know why he didn't come in.

That was the first and last time I got a black eye and was AWOL in the same weekend. My bruised eye got more than the normal amount of attention for that sort of thing because I had no reputation as a fighter. In fact, I hadn't been in a fight since I pounced on Phil Hand for calling me a dog robber back in England in the summer of 1944. Not unexpectedly, I was grounded by the battery commander the next weekend. Thanks to that, my family was blessed with a long letter from me in which I reported the latest on the point situation, outlined my plans for returning to college, and expressed some worries.

We found out during the week that the 16th FOB was to get a battle star for Normandy. We weren't in France during the Normandy campaign and didn't really deserve it, I said in my letter home, but every point counted. It made 71 for me. When I went back to college, I wanted it to be someplace with a beautiful campus and all the other things generally associated with college life. I didn't care how silly or sentimental that notion might seem, I wrote. I didn't know of any college around Washington that offered that. Also, I went on, whenever I lived at home I was inclined to get in a rut — read too many newspapers, take too many naps. It happened when I was going to high school and to George Washington University. Therefore, I was looking for a place which would meet the foreign service requirements and my own requirements as well. My present plans were to specialize in German and Russian because my interests definitely were in that part of the world as far as foreign service was concerned. I indicated I wanted to start school in February.

An article I sent from the 36th Division newspaper hit the nail on the head in many particulars, I told my parents. I said I would share my observations when I got home, but until then I felt "it all boils down to the fact that virtually no American here gives a damn about his occupation job and unless something drastic is done to remedy the situation, it'll end in catastrophe. It wouldn't be so important, if so much of our relations with the Russians didn't hang upon it — and friendly relations between Russia and us is certainly the all-important factor in keeping the peace." I told my sister I was planning to do lots of things with her when I got home. She was one of the good things in life that I had missed out on so far, I wrote. "A lot of things that used to seem important (and still are to some people) seem absolutely worthless now and vice versa."

The army routine of calisthenics, close order drill, motor stables, and separation center lectures were getting to me. I couldn't see the necessity of it all. Repeated complaints about all the "C.S." showed up in my diary. (C.S. was the abbreviation for "chicken shit.") I carried on about that, not using that choice term, of course, in another letter home. To help my parents get the picture I gave a few examples of why so many men were leaving the army so bitter against everything military. It hadn't been bad until the past week, I said, but then it turned into basic training all over again. Some of the officers were particularly arrogant, "seemingly bent upon having a last fling at screaming and making themselves generally obnoxious before they become civilians again and are forced to accept former enlisted men as equals," I wrote.

I cited this, for instance: Two men in the battery with 88 and 90 points were supposed to leave for an outfit going home right away. The day before they were to leave, they were investigated by the Inspector General's department because they had sent an undue amount of money home in July. Consequently, they missed the shipment out. I was sure many men would go out of the army hating their officers more than they ever hated the Germans or Japs. As I had before, I told my folks not to worry about me. I insisted that nothing really bothered me much any more and it took very little to make me happy. That said, I went on to tell them I favored peacetime conscription only to the extent necessary to occupy Germany and Japan and our strategic bases, "unless a drastic change can be made in the system of training and the Army caste system." All I knew about actual "soldiering" could easily be learned in three months; if there was universal conscription it should be for that period only, coupled with traveling time to Germany and Japan, where I thought the basic training should be given.

No longer grounded, I was free to go to Aldingen the first weekend of November. That Sunday afternoon, Hilda confessed to me that she was no longer working in the burgomeister's office where she had been since April 1941. From May 1942 to November 1944, she was a youth leader of 30 girls, aged 10 to 14 years, at the "request" of the local Ortsgruppenleiter. She instructed the girls only in athletics and never attended a leader's school, but she had to be discharged from the burgomeister's office, by order of the Military Government in Ludwigsburg, because of that. That prompted a speech from me about democracy and freedom in the USA, and she agreed with me. At that time, U.S. Military Government (MG) was quite zealous in rooting out anyone who had held any position, however insignificant, under the Nazis. The other occupying powers were much more pragmatic in their approach.

Previously, I had written Hilda a well-intentioned but sanctimonious letter saying just because I liked her didn't mean I liked everyone or everything in Germany. American soldiers, I said, would never have come to Germany if it hadn't been for Hitler and the Nazi Party and the people who supported them. "I know that for years you could not know the truth because of Goebbels' propaganda but in America, although there is much propaganda, anyone can say or write what he pleases and in that way we learn the truth," I pontificated. I told her I hated the Nazis and all they stood for — war, persecution, and concentration camps. Germany could never become a great nation again until all these ideas were cast aside. While there were many things wrong with America, it became a great nation because of a belief in freedom of speech and religion and the right of any man to do what he wants provided it did not hurt others. People of all races, religions, and nations, including Germany, made America great, but they did it only by forgetting their differences and becoming good Americans.

"I know that we destroyed German cities and caused much suffering, but we did this only because we were forced to and only after Hitler and his supporters had caused destruction in most of Europe," I continued. "I know because I have seen it. Germany's only hope is to forget the past and try to become a democratic nation. Although many American soldiers will always hate Germans just as many Germans will always hate us, there are many others, including me, who want to help Germany provided the past is forgotten. This is one very important reason why I want to become a diplomat — in order to create better understanding between nations and thus prevent terrible wars."

Time dragged on. Our departure date for Marseilles and passage home was postponed several times. I managed to arrange weekend trips to Camp 71 and Aldingen on the next two weekends. My excuse for one weekend was an appointment for plastic contact lenses at an optical establishment located in the bombed-out ruins of Stuttgart. My own stupidity ruined that weekend. The enlisted men of Camp 71 threw a party for their officers in Ludwigsburg. German girls, including Hilda and her friends, were invited. My diary told the story: "I made the very stupid mistake of getting very drunk very fast." I spent Sunday morning apologizing to Hilda, then returned to Gmund and Strassdorf, to moan and groan in my diary.

The following day, sober again, I wrote less nonsense, noting that after I studied my German lesson, I talked to an 11-year-old girl, Lisa, who lived next door. I learned that her family once lived in

Bessarabia, then moved to a camp at Lublin in Poland with the coming of Hitler's armies. Then they came to Strassdorf when Stalin's army overran Poland. It was another example of how the population of Europe was scattered, even more after the war than before.

"Polski nicht gut," she said.

"How did you expect the Poles to act when the Germans overran their country?" I asked.

"Ja, Polski nicht gut, Deutsche nicht gut, Americans prima!" she replied.

When I asked her about school and tried to see some of her schoolbooks, she said she had none. It seemed each child went to school only three or four hours a week, presumably due to the shortage of teachers. "We shall certainly have to do something to improve this situation," I wrote in my diary.

A week of packing and crating desks and other items to be returned to the States made us sure we'd be leaving soon, although we still did not know the exact date. After debating with myself about the wisdom of going to see Hilda one last time, I decided to take my chances and do it. I knew the risks involved. The outfit might leave for Marseilles and I might have more packing and crating to do Sunday morning. As it was, we worked until midafternoon Saturday but I was lucky in catching rides and arrived at Camp 71 before 7 p.m. I went first to Hilda's house, then to the home of the gasthaus owner, and then back to Hilda's. We talked of many things, all the things I intended to say the last weekend. She gave me a plywood figure of an angel and a candle she had made and painted. In my diary I wrote, "That sort of 'got' me. Maybe I'm too sentimental — I don't know. In any event, there's no point in elaborating on all this here — we'll just have to wait and see what develops."

As destiny would have it, nothing further developed between Hilda and me. I thought about her until the following spring. In my mind she represented a time forever gone but one to which I tried to cling. Soon after our last visit, she wrote telling me of her German boy-friend, a POW who she learned would be returning to her soon. She gave the letter to a GI buddy of mine, still at Camp 71, to mail to me. (Mail service between German civilians and the States was not restored until the spring of 1946.) My buddy, a happy-go-lucky fellow, never mailed the letter, so I did not learn what Hilda wrote me until late in the spring. In June she married her German boyfriend.

As for Gyp, my thoughts of her were in a kind of limbo, where they remained until 1947, when we resumed corresponding again for about a year. It was not until many years later that I learned that she married an Austrian music conductor in 1949 and moved to Austria the following year.

Thus, as 1945 and my army service came to an end, I had no serious girlfriends anywhere. Considering my emotional state, this was a good thing for me. And it pleased my mother very much.

Chapter 14

Afterword

"It's hard to believe we're finally going home," I wrote in my diary on 19 November. That was the last entry written in Germany. I was sergeant of the guard that night. Then began a dismal, four-day ride in truck convoy to the Calas Staging Area near Marseilles. The stops were few and far between. We left Strassdorf at 8 a.m., on time for a change, following C Battery through Goppingen to the Autobahn to Karlsruhe, and then on Highway 10 through Homburg and Saarbrucken to Metz. The sun was shining when we left, but fog soon set in and stayed for most of the journey. We arrived at our destination late and everyone was cold. I believe we were billeted in a former German OCS barracks.

The next day we didn't travel as far but it was just as miserable — cold and foggy. "Tortured by kidney trouble," was a recurring note in my diary. After arriving at Dijon Garrison Area in early evening, I got to take an almost-warm shower and spent an hour or two in the good library there. Day three brought cold and fog again. Before noon we stopped at GI Joe's, an old airfield, and got to the St. Rambert bivouac area around dark. After a turkey dinner in the mess hall, we bedded down in a winterized tent without lights. The next morning we had fresh fried eggs for breakfast. Cold and fog hung on until afternoon. In late afternoon we arrived at the Calas Staging Area, a desolate-looking place. Once again, we were in unlighted, winterized tents.

Keeping in character, I spent my last days in Europe bitching. The 13 days we spent waiting to board ship provided ample reason. Much of it was the usual stuff — hurry-up-and-wait, long lines and ridiculous chores. For instance, Service Battery was ordered to nail waterproof paper on the urinal troughs in the latrine. We shouted, "48-49-50 Some Shit!" in the presence of the battalion commander and other officers. That chant was commonplace at the time. It was neither the first nor the last time high-ranking officers would hear it. "Right now most of the men in the outfit are ready to either hang themselves or shoot the post commander," I wrote in my last letter home on December third.

The point system didn't seem to mean a damn thing. We were scheduled to sail that afternoon on the *Admiral Cappes*, a transport which would make the trip to Hampton Roads in eight days. However, someone miscalculated the capacity of the ship by five hundred. Consequently our battalion was thrown off in spite of the fact that there were many 65- to 69-pointers who stayed on. (McNamara was one of them.) My battalion was all 70-pointers or above, ranging up to 90; the fellow who sat across the table from me had 85. Also, there were over-age men in our group. Considerable transferring within the division was done while we were still in Germany to prevent this very thing. You had to believe you simply can't win in the army. "As far as I'm concerned, the incompetence and stupidity of whoever is responsible is inexcusable," I wrote home, adding, "And then some people wonder why some G.I.s are bitter."

A tentative plan had us sailing the next day on the *John Jay*. We didn't know whether it was a Liberty or a Victory ship or where it would land, but the word was the trip would be a rough one and last from 10 to 15 days. Another report had it that we'd get 30-day furloughs instead of discharges upon returning. I hoped that would be the case, since it was the only chance I had of being home for Christmas at this point. I figured I might possibly be home by the 18th or 20th.

As it happened, we didn't board ship until three days later. Getting up at 5 a.m., we loaded into huge trailer trucks to go to the port of Marseilles on 6 December. Some four hours later we started to board the *John Jay*, a Liberty ship. It was a difficult climb up the steep gangplank with our loaded duffel bags. A high wind was blowing. A number of dogs were sneaked aboard, including the one in Sergeant Hall's duffel bag just ahead of me. On board, warm quarters and good food awaited us. I settled in and read some of *Report from Red China*, and visited with Solomon and Bliesmer a number of times during the day and evening. They were the only other GIs on board from our old Sixteenth survey section. The *John Jay* was one of 2,751 Liberty ships of identical design built between 1941 and 1945 by 18 U.S.

shipyards. These ships played a large part in making Allied victory possible. They carried cargo of every description as well as troops. The *John Jay* had transported wheat in her hold, I soon learned.

We sailed on 7 December, the fourth anniversary of Pearl Harbor Day, about midmorning. The weather was rough and so was the sea. Many GIs were heaving and I wasn't sure how long it'd be before I joined them. I was glad a staff sergeant took over being section leader instead of me. The library cases and books in front of my bunk were strewn all over the floor, and wheat from previous cargoes cascaded down from cracks in the ceiling hatch every time we hit a rough spot. My bunk was on the level next to the floor of the hold and near the latrine, which, as the voyage progressed, became the site of all-night poker parties and crap games. By forcing myself to eat something at each meal, I controlled my seasickness and made the whole trip without heaving. I was thankful for that. I read incessantly, in part to take my mind off my stomach. Being right next to the library bookcases, I got some exercise picking books off the floor as the rough sea spilled them out frequently.

I began keeping my diary entries in two- and then four-day segments. It took the *John Jay*, with a maximum speed of 11 knots, three days to get out of the Mediterranean, I recorded. If anyone had told me when we boarded that, in the year 1945, it would take 20 days for a steamship to sail from Marseilles to Newport News, I would have thought him crazy. The second two days were calm, and except for the monotony, the trip became pleasant. I finished reading the book on China and turned to *What to Do with Germany*, by Louis Nizer, and *The Making of Modern China* by Owen and Eleanor Lattimore. We saw some of the Balearic Isles, the coast of Spain, and then lights from Gibraltar and Tangier. Solomon and Bliesmer had recovered from seasickness, although Solomon was still a bit woozy. He looked like a corpse during much of the trip. Years later, I learned that he chronicled the voyage in his diary in these few words: "Sailed at 10 a.m., heaved at noon, two and four."

The boredom of the voyage sent great thoughts whirling through my head again. In my diary I laid out all of my ambitions and reached the rather terrifying conclusion that it was lucky I hadn't been born in Germany. "Under the influence of a Nazi regime, with my natural inclinations, I'd undoubtedly be a Geopolitik, etc., fanatic." Bliesmer, Solomon, and I agreed that many GIs, given the proper training, would make good SS men. Recording that discussion in my diary, I commented, "This only seems to reinforce my two basic contentions: 1) War is hell & eventually drags all participants down to the same level and 2) People must be judged as individuals and not as groups; there are 'good' and 'bad' people everywhere." This contributed to a thought I had for working out a plan of action for the promotion of democratic ideals (American version) throughout the world, mainly through the UNO, but with due consideration for power politics.

It occurred to me that I might be reading and thinking too much amidst the poker and crap games. A diary entry on 11 December noted, "Have been reading (my eyes hurt) & thinking seriously too much, but there's so little else to do & it is important." I also mentioned that our compartment had failed to pass inspection the past two days, and "Major Sapp (his real name) is on the rampage." Although the weather was clear and fair at the time, my absorption in reading and thinking continued for two more days — struggling with Henry Adams, discovering Thomas Wolfe, thinking of conquering the world, and longing to return to Germany. After a good try, I decided to quit reading "*The Education of Henry Adams*" because, in addition to striking me as obscure, it was becoming dull. I read his chapters on "A Dynamic Theory of History" and "A Form of Acceleration" but failed to get much out of them. Reading Thomas Wolfe's "*You Can't Go Home Again*" suited me better.

After I saw the movie *The Keys of the Kingdom,* I wove its theme into my thinking. I found it a very stirring film which "certainly confirms the belief that the highest purpose of life on earth is direct service to mankind," I wrote. There followed a dissertation on my increasing obsession with thoughts of my old desire to "conquer the world." I admitted it was strange that after all I'd seen of the horror of war and its aftermath I'd make such a statement. But the increasing world anarchy and general aimlessness of nations (particularly the U.S.), reflected also in most individuals, prompted the recurrence of these old thoughts. If the world could be conquered, that is if it could be forcibly united without bloodshed or with only a minimum amount of it and if it could be done before the conquerors became corrupted, I would favor the attempt. Surveying what I knew of the history of the world, however, I admitted I could see no way these conditions could be met. I reminded myself that all would-be world conquerors should consider what state the world would be in if their attempts to conquer failed. It didn't seem likely that someone out to conquer the world would take the time to make such a consideration, I allowed. Undaunted, however, I wrote on, "If I knew that the world could be permanently united, democratically, by the sacrifice of a million lives, I would be the first to sacrifice mine. I don't mean this vain-gloriously; I say it quite humbly." All of this heavy thinking put me in a somber mood. I closed the long writing, "With a feeling of melancholy I looked back across the water (standing on deck last night) toward the northeast. It's certainly true that I'm 'leaving part of my heart in Germany.' How long this feeling will last I don't know — only time will tell."

Rough seas on 14 and 15 December apparently jarred me back to the here and now. My high-blown thoughts gave way to basic bitching. The bad weather slowed our speed. In a 24-hour period we traveled only 216 miles. After serving as sergeant of the guard, I noted that the guard on a liberty ship consisted of four sergeants, four corporals, 32 privates, plus supernumeraries. "What stupidity," I exclaimed in a diary note. I still had hopes of being in Hampton Roads by the twenty-second. The chances of being home for Christmas were remote. The first anniversary of the beginning of the Battle of the Bulge on the 16th made me thankful to be on a ship going home in spite of continued rough seas. There were 888 miles to go. "Not much chance of 'making it' before sometime Tuesday, Christmas Day. C'est la guerre!" Two more anniversaries followed in close succession. On the nineteeth, I thought back to a year before at the hill at Champlon. My birthday, on the 21st, was a "slightly happier occasion," I wrote in my diary, than the previous one at Matton, France.

Excitement overcame my melancholy feelings as the *John Jay* approached the States. My diary entries became shorter and shorter. For the period between 22 and 25 December I reported: "Continued rough seas, with the exception of one night, until Christmas day, which dawned clear, with a smooth sea, and very beautiful." I also made note that I finished reading *Forever Amber* (not all of my reading was serious). It was a hot novel at the time; today, it would be considered quite tame. I had to wait for a number of days to get my turn at a well-worn copy from the ship's library. I also read *The Willows*, by Algernon Blackwood, and *The Kreutzer Sonata*, by

Tolstoy, and browsed through many other books. "Numerous drunks on Christmas eve," my diary documented. "First time I ever heard 'Silent Night' sung with curses between verses." Early on Christmas morning, I took a shower with fresh water, put on clean ODs, and attended Christmas services and a talk by Colonel Orrick. It looked as if we'd dock on the day after Christmas.

My last week in the army is only a blur in my mind. The diary entry for the time is not much help. "Docking at Newport News at 1500 Dec. 26th, to Camp Patrick Henry (and steak dinner) until Dec. 30th (bidding farewell to Bliesmer, Solomon, and J.D. Thompson). Arrived at Fort Meade, Md. on Dec. 30th (by train). Home with George Reid (still in the army at Fort Meade) on night of Dec. 31st (seeing Mom & Martha — a very happy night for us all — Pop being in Kansas), driving car back to Ft. Meade, obtaining discharge on morning of Jan. 2nd."

As I was issued a new uniform at Ft. Meade, I remember being told that it really didn't matter that the trousers were three inches too long. "You can tuck them inside your combat boots." The army had not changed.

Pop had waited as long as he could for my arrival, but he had speaking engagements in Kansas to keep. In a letter he left behind for me, he gave me his usual practical advice before launching into a review of the college information he had gathered for me. Telling me to use the car all I wanted, he cautioned me to be as careful as possible of the four-and-a-half-year-old tires and to avoid going out if the streets were icy. He advised having the oil checked every time I bought gas, and if the weather got down around ten or below I should have the antifreeze checked, too.

One last event on the *John Jay* was not recorded in my diary. The 26th of December dawned clear and beautiful. Out on the sun-drenched deck, for the first time during that long voyage I saw Tech. Sgt. Virgil Craig, a young banker from Garden City. It was, I believe, the first time I'd seen a GI from Garden City since my first stay at Fort Bragg in 1943. That brief meeting seemed symbolic. I knew then I was home again.

The great historian-diplomat George F. Kennan wrote of the difficulty in determining a beginning and an ending for historical tales, observing that history itself lacks tidy beginnings and endings. And so it is, I believed, with a tale as simple as this memoir. The war was over. I was discharged from the army and home with my family. I was one of the lucky ones. For reasons known only to God, I had survived, with no physical or lasting psychological injuries. For a brief period in 1946 I suffered from depression, which I attempted to explain in a diary entry in January of that year. I recorded being "extremely depressed" and having cried several times, usually in the course of long talks with my mother, whom I came to know better than ever before. The awful tragedy of the entire world, emphasized by all I had seen in Europe, seemed suddenly to come down on me.

A few reminders of the war lingered on for a longer period. For a number of winters, cold caused my toes to tingle and my feet to hurt. A habit of sleeping with my head under the covers, acquired during the Battle of the Bulge, persisted, winter and summer, for several years. Most serious, however, was my acquired habit of cursing, a thing heretofore unknown in my family. I made strenuous efforts to cease, especially around my parents. But to this day, when something goes wrong, I often unthinkingly blurt out "son of a bitch!" — sometimes even in church.

In my diary and in other writings I discoursed ad nauseam about what I had learned concerning human nature and the effect of suffering and death upon all involved in World War II. Also I had learned, as had millions of others, that one can endure the lack of material comforts for months on end. I came to appreciate what people working and sacrificing together in a global common cause can accomplish. What else did I learn? Probably it was true, as my father observed, that I was no better and no worse than I had been three years before. I had made some progress in growing up, but I still had a way to go. I remained a romantic and a dreamer. However, my dreams, fanciful as some were, never kept me from doing my assigned tasks and a full day's work. Although I continued to worry and bitch about small things, I had learned to live with and to accept whatever disappointments came my way. To accept what comes, I believe, was the greatest personal lesson I learned in those three years.

What did I do to realize my dream of becoming a "famous statesman," working diligently for world peace? Somewhat to my surprise, I was admitted to Harvard College as a junior in February 1946. I decided to major in government with emphasis on international relations and with the goal of entering the U.S. Foreign

Service. By the following fall my ambitions had shifted back to my longtime dream of entering the political arena. I thought I could work more effectively for world peace and other worthy causes as an elected official. My father encouraged me to enter law school, pointing out what I already knew in my more practical moments — I would need some way to make a living while attempting to climb the political ladder. Also, Pop had his own dream of retiring from Congress in a few years so that we could practice law together. Hence, I graduated from his alma mater, Washburn Law School, in Topeka in 1950 and commenced practice with his old law firm in Garden City.

Aware that one cannot be assured of a career in elective politics and that there always are more losers than winners in elections, I filed for a seat in the state senate in 1956 and was elected handily. In 1958 my big chance came. Or so I thought. I ran for Congress against a popular incumbent. That year turned out to be the worst year in this century for Kansas Republicans, and I went down to defeat with many others. Growing family responsibilities precluded my running for Congress again. So, I settled back to become a country lawyer, a somewhat romantic appellation. I continued to be involved in politics and civic causes and became an amateur historian.

And what of girls? During the immediate postwar period, I was looking, with an all-absorbing intensity which became frantic on occasion, for a nice girl to marry. My failure to find such a girl until the summer of 1948 greatly interfered with my studies and my attempts to decide upon a career. That summer, on a blind date, I met Dolores Sulzman, a journalist born in northwest Kansas. She was of German-Catholic ancestry. Meeting Dolores that summer and marrying her at year's end in large measure brought stability to my turbulent life and the beginnings of true religious faith. It was the most fortunate event of my life. The main bond between us has been the sharing of common ideals. From her I have learned that one does not need to be rich or famous to strive for the true, the good, and the beautiful — and for world peace.

As the years after 1945 slipped by, most of my memories of the war faded. I would never have been able to write this book without the written records: my diary and writings, letters, and the official reports in the National Archives. Without them, I would have had only a miscellany of recollections, many of them inaccurate.

But the passing years did not dim the feelings and emotions from that far-off time. I still become misty-eyed when I hear "Lili Marlene," the universal song of the war. I am haunted by the melody of the "Horst Wessel Lied" when I hear it played and sung in film clips or movies. It is then, in my memory, that I hear again the horrible sound of the marching Nazi troopers in their hobnailed boots.

I cannot adequately describe what World War II has meant to my life. This is an attempt: I had the most thrilling and unique experience of my life in those few years — feelings of exhilaration and despair, ambition and frustration, hatred and love. All of them meshed together. For the opportunity to have been an observer, a minor participant, and a survivor of the greatest war in history, I am humbly thankful.

Appendix 1

Indoctrination for Return to the U.S.

HEADQUARTERS — U.S. ARMY
APO OOL U.S. ARMY

AG 4110.99 (DERGA)
October 1944
Subject: Indoctrination for return to U.S.
To: All Units.

1. In compliance with current policies for rotation of armed forces overseas, it is directed that in order to maintain the high standard of character of the American soldier and to prevent any dishonor to reflect on the uniform, all individuals eligible for return to the U.S. under current directives will undergo an indoctrination course of demilitarization prior to approval of his application for return.

2. The following points will be emphasized in the subject indoctrination course:

a. In America there is a remarkable number of beautiful girls. These young girls *have not* been liberated and many are gainfully employed as stenographers, sales girls and beauty operators, or welders. Contrary to current practices, they should not be approached with "How much?" A proper greeting is "Isn't it a lovely day?" or "Have you ever been in Chicago?" Then say, "How much?".

b. A guest in a private home is usually awakened in the morning by a light tapping on his door and an invitation to join his host at breakfast. It is proper to say, "I'll be there shortly". Do NOT say, "Blow it out your ____!"

c. A typical American breakfast consists of such strange foods as cantaloupes, fresh eggs, milk, ham, etc. These are highly palatable and, though strange in appearance, are extremely tasty. Butter, made from cream, is often served. If you wish some butter, you turn to the person nearest it, and say quietly, "Please pass the butter." You DO NOT say, "Throw me the goddam grease."

d. Very natural urges are apt to occur when in a crowd. If it is found necessary to defecate, one does not grab a shovel in one hand and paper in the other and run for the garden. At least 90% of American homes have one room called the "Bathroom," i.e. a room that, in most cases, contains a bathtub, wash basin, medicine cabinet, and a toilet. It is the latter that you will use in this case. Instructors should make sure that all personnel understand the operation of a toilet, particularly the lever or button arrangement that serves to prepare the device for re-use.

e. In the event the helmet is retained by the individual, he will refrain from using it as a chair, wash bowl, foot-bath or bath tub. All these devices are furnished in the average American home. It is not considered good practice to squat Indian fashion in a corner in the event all chairs are occupied. The host will usually provide suitable seats.

f. Belching or passing wind in company is strictly frowned upon. If you should forget about it, however, and belch in the presence of others, a proper remark is "Excuse me." DO NOT say, "It must be that lousy chow we've been eating."

g. American dinners, in most cases, consist of several items, each served in a separate dish. The common practice of mixing various items, such as corned-beef and pudding, or lima beans and peaches, to make it more palatable will be refrained from. In time, the "separate dish" system will become enjoyable.

h. Americans have a strange taste for stimulants. The drinks in common usage on the European continent, such as under-ripe wine, alcohol and grapefruit juice or gasoline bitters and water (commonly known by the French term "Cognac") are not ordinarily acceptable in civilian circles. These drinks should be served only to those who are definitely not within the inner circle of friends. A suitable use for such drinks is for serving to one's landlord in order to break an undesirable lease.

i. The returning soldier is often apt to find his opinions differ from those of his civilian associates. One should call upon his reserve of etiquette and correct his acquaintance with such remarks as, "I believe you have made a mistake" or "I am afraid you are in error on that." DO NOT say, "Brother, you're really f----d up." This is considered impolite.

j. Upon leaving a friend's home after a visit, one may find his hat misplaced. Frequently, it has been placed in a closet. One should turn to one's host and say, "I don't seem to have my hat; could you help me find it?" DO NOT say, "Don't anybody leave this room, some S.O.B. has stolen my hat!"

k. In travelling in the U.S., particularly in a strange city, it is often necessary to spend the night. Hotels are provided for this purpose and one can get direction to the nearest hotel from anyone. Here, for a small sum, one can register and be shown to a room where he can sleep for the night. The present practice of entering the nearest house, throwing the occupants into the yard, and taking over the premises will cease.

l. Whiskey, a common American drink, may be offered to the soldier on social occasions. It is considered a reflection on the uniform to snatch the bottle from the hostess and drain it, cork and all. All individuals are cautioned to exercise extreme control in these circumstances.

m. In motion picture theaters, seats are provided. Helmets are not required. It is not considered good form to whistle every time a female over 8 and under 80 crosses the screen. If vision is impaired by the person in the seat in front, there are usually plenty of other seats which can be occupied. DO NOT hit him across the back of the head and say, "Move your head, Jerk; I can't see a damned thing."

n. It is not proper to go around hitting every one of draft age in civilian clothes. He might have been released from the service for medical reasons; ask for his credentials, and if he can't show any, THEN go ahead and slug him.

o. Upon retiring, one will often find a pair of pajamas laid out on the bed. (Pajamas, it should be explained, are two-piece garments which are donned after all clothing has been removed). The soldier, confronted by these garments, should assume an air of familiarity and act as though he were used to them. A casual remark such as "My, what a delicate shade of blue," will usually suffice. Under no circumstances say, "How in the hell do you expect me to sleep in a get-up like this?"

p. Natural functions will continue. It may be necessary frequently to urinate. DO NOT walk behind the nearest tree or automobile you find to accomplish this. Toilets ("d" above) are provided in all public buildings for this purpose. Signs on some doors will read "Ladies," which, literally interpreted, means "OFF LIMITS TO ALL TROOPS."

q. Beer is sometimes served in bottles. A cap remover is usually available, and it is not good form to open the bottle by the use of one's teeth.

r. Air raids and enemy patrols are not encountered in America. Therefore, it is not necessary to wear the helmet in church or at social gatherings or to hold the weapon at ready, loaded and cocked, when talking to civilians on the street.

s. Every American home and all hotels are equipped with bathing facilities. When desiring to take a bath, it is not considered good form to find the nearest pool or stream, strip down, and indulge in a bath. This is particularly true in heavily populated areas.

t. All individuals returning to the U.S. will make every effort to conform to the customs and habits of the regions visited, and to make themselves as inconspicuous as possible. Any actions which reflect upon the honor of the uniform will be promptly dealt with.

For the Commanding General:

J. E. BLANK
Colonel, A.G.D.
Adjutant General

DISTRIBUTION: X

Reproduced Hq, ___Corps
Distribution: XX

Reproduced Hq, ___Bn
Distribution: XXX

Appendix 2

Bob Van Houten's Prisoner of War Experience

19 December 1944 to April 1945

by Bob Van Houten

(Bob Van Houten was one of nine members of A Battery of the 16th Field Artillery Observation Battalion who were taken prisoner in the Schnee Eifel area on the Belgian-German border on 19 December 1944, together with several thousand other surrounded American soldiers. I did not know Bob at that time and did not become acquainted with him until I joined the newly organized Veterans of the Battle of the Bulge organization several years ago. Bob was then the vice president working on membership, and he contacted me after my membership was sent in.

As I wrote the chapter on the Battle of the Bulge, I thought it would not be complete without a report, if possible, from someone from the Sixteenth who had been captured by the Germans. I asked Bob, therefore, if he could write me a summary of his experiences, and he very kindly consented to make a tape-recording of his experiences as best he could remember them over 40 years later. The following is a transcript of that tape recording.)

* * *

Several days before the breakthrough, I was sitting in a very large bunker built by the 2d Division. The bunkers were about chest high, with the one that I was in extending about 20x20 feet. It had a log roof and dirt over the logs to protect from highbursts, and I could just look out over the edge of it. I realize after looking at some old maps that I must have been in Germany because A Battery CP was in Auw, Germany. The concrete bunker we slept in must have been on the Siegfried Line: we slept in a concrete bunker and then moved out to a dirt bunker during the day to our observation work. We were only there a couple of days when the Second moved out and the 106th moved in. It was evident they were pretty green. I can't remember whether they were there or the Second was still there, but I know at night there was a lot of activity down the hill from us. When I say "down the hill" it was so steep that we could stand in the doorway of the bunker with the Germans looking and firing at us but the only thing they could hit was the steel beam above us. The Germans were in a concrete bunker below us, and at night, several days before the Bulge, I could see all sorts of truck lights — it seemed like hundreds of them. We could also hear mess kits rattling, fellows talking, and movement of various vehicles. I reported this back to our CP, who I assume passed it on to the VIII Corps. A couple of days later, I was told Corps said we were just hearing a P.A. system out there.

"P.A., hell," I said. "I'm sitting here looking at them."

This really made me mad because one of the things they always said about FOs (Forward Observers) and anyone else on the front lines was "pass any information back so G-2 can verify it." In this case they apparently didn't really pay much attention to it.

On 15 December I decided that instead of my men taking a break, I would go back to the CP for a full night's rest. A fellow from the flash section was sent out to take my place for the night, to return when I came back.

Around 5 o'clock on the morning of the sixteenth, the fellows came upstairs and said, "You better get out of here because the Germans are shelling us."

Having been up front for so long, I could recognize the shells and since they didn't seem very close, I said, "Aw, forget it, I'm going back to sleep," which I did until about 7 o'clock.

I woke up and walked downstairs, and the fellows said, "Your OP telephone lines are all out."

We had two lines, one alternate and one direct. I said, "Well, you'd better take me back." They did, but in leaving I forgot the mail, which included a Christmas package from my mother, a part of a fruitcake and a can of peaches. I wasn't too concerned, for I thought, "I'll be back."

When I got to the OP, I sent my second in command, Buck Buchanan, back, keeping the flash fellow with me.

I looked down the hill and I got all excited, because the Germans had several rockets on truck chassis, firing like mad. They were shooting those things off left and right, really blasting away at us.

By then, the wire section had one line fixed, so I said, "Let's get things fixed up so we can talk, because I want to send you some information."

I don't think it was 15 or 20 minutes before they said, "We're getting out of here. We are surrounded on three sides and we think we have one way out and we're going to leave."

"What do you want us to do?" I asked.

"We don't know," they said.

Since we were with the 106th I said, "Well, I guess there's safety in a Division," feeling sure we were safer with a division than with a battalion.

"Goodbye," I said, "see you in the good old USA." Little did I realize how true that might be.

The fellow who was with me and I walked back to see if we could find somewhere we could be of some use. After all, we couldn't just sit around there. The first fellow we saw was a chaplain, and I never will forget him. I told him our plight and that we were trying to hitch a ride.

He said, "What kind of a gun do you have?"

"A carbine."

"Sorry, fellows. I want somebody with a rifle."

"You so and so," I thought.

The next fellow I saw was a captain in the artillery. He still wore his bars, tie and everything else a well-dressed officer wore. So I told him our plight.

"Well," he said, "what do you want to get into?"

"We want to get in artillery. Hell, we're trained in artillery. Who wants to get in a hand-to-hand fighting business?"

I sure didn't want anything to do with that. The fellow who was with me agreed.

"I'm going into the CP to meet with the Colonel and I'll come out and talk to you," the captain said.

I don't think he was gone 30 seconds when he came back out and said, "The Colonel wants to talk to you."

So we went into the bunker and here they had this great big sandbox, probably about 8 foot long and 4 foot wide, or maybe 8x8. It showed the front lines with various vehicles, along with the hills of the terrain.

The Colonel said, "I understand you've been here a long while."

"Yes, Sir."

"Show me on this board where we are."

So I did and he said, "Yep, that's right. I understand you want to work with us."

"Yes, if we can do something worthwhile, why not? I'm not used to just sitting around doing nothing."

"Would you do some FO work for us?"

"Well, that's more or less what I was trained for, observation or forward observation work."

"Okay, I'll have a driver take you out."

So the driver and I jumped in his jeep and he took me out to a field where there was just about one wall left of a concrete bunker. I could stand behind it and observe all across the field. You know, I didn't even need any glasses, for as I looked out, I never in my life had seen so many Germans walking across the field. There must have been 10,000 of them. I'm really not trying to exaggerate, because they were all over; left, right and as far as the eye could see. They were probably about a mile away, but it was flat, so I could see that far.

I got on the radio and said, "Colonel, I don't think you've got enough ammunition to shoot everything coming across that field."

"Get the hell out of there," was all he said.

The driver took me back and all I can remember from there on is we'd hop in trucks and move from one place to another, almost in circles. I never saw an officer or enlisted man fire a gun. Finally, we ended up one night in a house next door to the house where our old CP had been. Realizing this, I ran inside and found my can of peaches and fruitcake. The fellow with me and I ate them, not realizing it would be the last solid food we'd have for probably four and a half months.

It was 16 December when we broke up, but on the nineteenth we were still wandering around. We ended up in a valley and I woke up in the back of a 6 by 6 truck which was so packed with supplies that we could just barely crawl in the top. It was just starting to get daylight and I looked out and they had their 105 guns set up with the powder bags sitting out beside them. We were probably not more than 75 to 100 feet away from them, when all of a sudden the Jerrys started lobbing in a few mortars, hitting the powder bags. Well, you never saw so many fellows pile out of a truck so fast in your life. We ran up the hill with the mortars following us all the way. I could never understand how they could see us unless there was somebody up on the hill looking. We ended up on the opposite hill from the mortars, just sitting there, wondering what to do. I finally looked over to the right of me and there was a G.I. walking along a road on the hill about a quarter of a mile away with no one bothering him.

"We ought to go over there," I said to the fellow with me.

But just when we were going to walk over there, I heard somebody yell across the valley, "Throw down your guns."

I looked down over there and saw a white flag waving and I thought, "Gee! Have the Germans given up?"

I just couldn't visualize the Americans giving up, especially the whole 422d Regiment. They convinced us that it was us that were giving up. So I took the old carbine I had and smashed it against a tree, dumping the ammunition out on the ground, and walked out through the valley. Even then we didn't see many Germans, only an occasional one on the side of the hill, sort of guiding us down. But I did see, as we were walking down, that there was a firetower; that was apparently where they had their OP so they could see us and everything we were doing.

They marched us for three days. During that time, if the guards wanted anything we had, overcoats, shoes, anything, they just took it. If we tried to resist them, they would hit us with their gun butts. So while we were up on one of the mountains looking over a valley, we all ditched our overcoats and boots, all at the same time, throwing them all over the valley so they couldn't have them. All we had left were our field jackets. That didn't help our constitution any when we were marching.

On the march were a lot of fellows who had been wounded. I know one particular guy who, I think, had his leg shot off. Four other men had him in a blanket and were lugging him along, with the blood dripping out. I don't know what ever happened to him.

Going up and down those hills was so miserable; the nights were wet, rainy and snowy and we'd pass German tanks and all kinds of equipment. Those German tanks were so quiet that we didn't even know they were coming until they were practically on top of us. No wonder they could overrun American positions. Our tanks could be heard for practically 10 miles.

Finally we were marched into a town; ending up in the railway station. It had started to rain and, along with the cold, it was a thoroughly miserable night. The railway station was glass-roofed, at least partly, and I thought, "Oh, boy, at least we are going to get in out of the rain."

But, shoot, we weren't there 10 minutes when they said, "Everybody out."

So they marched us all out. At this time, I judge there were probably 500 to 1,000 of us, whom they put into a courtyard. But when we walked into the courtyard, which was all fenced in by a 12-foot-high fence, we saw they had four machine guns on a wall. They literally pushed us behind it.

"Oh, oh," I thought, "this is it. They aren't taking any prisoners."

Well, fortunately, the officer announced that they weren't going to use any machine guns unless somebody tried to escape during the night. I'll tell you, no one even moved a foot to stretch.

We were squatted down in the rain with only a raincoat to throw over our heads. We huddled together in twos and threes, bunched under the rain-coats. Believe it or not, we even slept to some extent, squatting.

The next day they started to march us again. Because we hadn't had any food the whole time, some of us were getting mighty hungry.

We kept asking them about it and all they would say was, "At the next town."

We must have marched for three days up and down through the mountains. It got colder and more miserable and snowed, and the only thing we had for our stomachs was snow, never any food. We never got any food on the whole march.

Finally we came to a town where they piled us into boxcars and locked them. German boxcars are called 40 and eights, since they hold 40 men or eight horses. But we must have had 120 men in each, because they really jammed us in, to the point where we could hardly move. It was very cold and the cars had open air vents on the top so high up we couldn't see out of them unless we were standing on somebody's shoulders. But we didn't give a damn anyway because we were getting so hungry that we were starting to feel very weak. We stayed in those boxcars for another three days because they never got very far before our allied planes came over and started to strafe us. Every time they did that, they'd stop the train, disconnect the engine and run it to the nearest tunnel. But our planes did strafe our boxcars and the bullets went through our car; fortunately no one got hit. I understand some fellows in other cars were hit by the strafings. It was really harrowing, being trapped in there, unable to get out.

It was so cold that our breath would freeze on the walls. I think it must have been about an inch thick when we finally got where we were going. I remember that one of the fellows couldn't even walk when he got out, because it was so crowded we couldn't lie down or sit. Just stand.

Finally, we ended up in Bad Orb, Stalag 9-B, which is in Germany, a little valley town. We got out of the train at the station and saw nothing but hills around us. They marched us up a long hill to the camp. When we got there, they decided that before they would let us in the barracks, they wanted some information from all of us. The officers were separated from us, so there were only noncoms and privates in this bunch. They wanted us to give our name, rank, serial number, father's name, mother's name, sister's name, brother's name, where we lived, and everything else. We told them to go jump. We'd give them name, rank, and serial number and that's all. Finally, after standing outside for about eight hours, we were all shoved into the barracks, but they still didn't feed us. It was now the twenty-fifth, Christmas. At last they came around with some food, which was nothing but shaved carrots. At this point, we really weren't hungry any more. But the minute we took one bite of that stuff, we were ravenous.

They had wanted to separate the Jews from the Gentiles. We said that we didn't know who the Jews were and if the Jews wanted to be separated, they'd have to do so voluntarily; we weren't going to tell them who were Jews. We also insisted that if Jews did agree to segregate themselves, they were not to be sent out of the camp. The Germans finally agreed to put them in the barracks right next to us. Some Jews went and some didn't. I don't know how they were treated because we were only in this camp about a month when they separated noncoms from privates and shipped the noncoms to another camp.

This camp was called Ziegenhain, which was Stalag 9-A. It was here I sweated the war out. It was the middle of January, and there was nothing to do in this camp.

I weighed 185 when I was captured and around 115 when released. Our daily menu consisted of what we called sassafras tea for breakfast, which was only sugar water, and at lunchtime they might come around with some sort of soup, as they called it. It might be sliced carrots or potato peelings and one day we had what looked like pine needles with cooked worms in it. But that was meat, so we ate it. We got to the point where we would eat anything. There was nothing like plates to hold our food. We used whatever we could find. Some fellows ate out of their helmets, some out of tin cans they'd picked up along the way. They did manage to give us a combination fork and spoon, but that was all. At night the meal consisted of what we called black Jerry bread. They gave us one loaf of bread for five men. It was about five inches long and maybe two and a half inches square. We cut it in five pieces. As time went on, we ended up with more arguments and fights over who got the biggest piece. Some fellows tried to save it to eat in the morning with their sugar water, but at night invariably somebody would steal it.

The bunks were wooden, three tiers high. No mattresses. There were just boards on them, and if you were lucky you at least might keep three — one for your head, one for your feet and one for your rear end. They gave us no blankets, so two of us slept in a bunk to keep warm. There was one very small stove, and each evening they would give us a small bundle of twigs. Those lasted about 10 minutes. With the barracks being so big, warmth was psychological rather than real. There were probably 250 of us in each barracks and the stove was about two feet square. That's why we burned our bunk boards except for the crucial three.

We did have a washroom in the barracks, but that was all. There was an outdoor privy. Soon you found yourself out there about every two minutes. You had to urinate every time you turned around, things were getting so bad. We did have Allied planes flying over our camp. It seems our bombers would congregate over Germany, coming from all directions, and we'd stand outside and cheer and clap. The German guards got so disgusted with us at this, every time our planes came over they would herd us back in the barracks so we couldn't cheer. One day one of our planes machine-gunned our barracks. I was sitting in the window watching when it happened, and I could see it move just like a zipper through the barracks beside us. The barracks were made out of yellow tile block. Fortunately it only went through our washroom, but I heard that one or two men were hurt in the other barracks. They had fences separating us, so we could talk to the (other) Americans through the fence. There were just two barracks full of Americans. The rest, I think, had some French, English, and Russians.

About once a month they would take you out and give you a nice cold shower, if you so desired. Naturally, all of us did, just to get out of the barracks. If you got sick, that was tough. If you had bad teeth, that was also tough. We just sort of existed, wandering back and forth and talking mostly about food.

The guard we had was good. He'd call roll every morning. We had with us an old master sergeant who sort of headed the deal, and he'd stand up there and cuss out the guard. This guard never would blink an eye, but I always was suspicious that he could speak English. The barracks next door had a rough guard. I heard he hit a few fellows with his gun or abused fellows in other ways. At least the fellows kept telling us that. We weren't really mistreated or forced to work. One day Allied bombers hit the nearby town of Ziegenhain. Our camp, situated on a hill, overlooked the town. It was about a couple of miles away, so we could see some of the action. We learned that the town was the central hub for all the railroad tracks carrying supplies to the various fronts in all directions. So hitting the tracks created quite a bad situation for them. This was the one time we were forced to go out and work, mainly to repair the railroad tracks. They forced us to work by threatening not to feed anyone if we didn't send some work crews out. So each barracks agreed to send some of their men out. I happened to be one who volunteered, but we were so weak that we couldn't do a heck of a lot. It took 60-80 men to lift one railroad track. But the funny part was that once we were there, they still didn't feed us.

"Oh, we'll feed you once you get back to the barracks," they said.

So we spent the whole day working without anything to eat. I'd learned enough German in one of my OPs where we'd stayed with a German family to converse just a little bit. We had an elderly guard that was from the German Wehrmacht. I'm not even sure they had bullets in their guns. I started talking to him while he was eating his lunch.

"Hey, can't you spare a little?" I asked him.

At first he said, "No, because if I get caught, it would be bad for me."

Finally he did break down and give us a little of his sandwich. I split it between three or four other fellows, although I don't really remember how many. At least we did have a little bit of something to eat.

One of the fellows saw a house not far from us with some chickens out in the yard. As we were being marched back, he grabbed a chicken and stuck it under his shirt. However, as he was holding it firmly to keep it quiet, the stupid thing began to squawk, and when he tried to choke it off it layed an egg right in his hand. I don't know what they ever did with the chicken or the egg, but they must have eaten them raw because there certainly wasn't anyplace in the barracks to cook.

When we did get back, they did give us a little heavier soup — barley. So it made up somewhat for waiting for it. But that was the last time we ever saw any heavy nourishment.

The bunks were so full of bedbugs and lice that they'd drop on us and we'd take off our clothes each night to clean them out. It was terrible. We'd get them in our mouths and eyes at night, falling from above. I understood then why we got all those shots. They were well worth it. I don't know what we would have come down with if we hadn't had them.

The anxiety and the frustration and not knowing what was going to happen to us was inconceivable. As I told one of our ministers here, who has a better understanding of it because he worked in a coal mine in England, people can do all the reading they want to about prison camps, but unless you've been there — and this is no reflection on their reading or on the writers — there's no way anyone can possibly conceive the anxiety, frustration, and fear about just what is going to happen.

We sat around camp and talked about food or wondered about people back home. Some fellows who were your friends prior to this camp experience ended up being your enemy. We found we couldn't trust anyone: when we got hungry, we were all for ourselves. Don't let anybody kid you.

Anyone who says, "Well, I'd share it with this one or that one," well, forget it, because you get to the point where life is very precious, and the more you starve, the more precious it becomes.

Fellows were trading watches, as I did mine, for the Germans to get you five packs of cigarettes. If you didn't smoke, you could trade them to others for their share of bread. One of the fellows convinced me to trade my watch for cigarettes, but after we got them and traded for bread, I never did see him again. It was a real cut-throat method of living.

We asked the guards about Red Cross packages through our interpreter, who was a Frenchman captured with us. He was told by the Germans that they had a barn full of them. He went with them to see and found that, while they had them, he felt they were eating them themselves, as they had no food. They did agree to give one box for every five of us. There really wasn't much in them, but it did add a little variety to our meager diet. As I recall, this happened only twice during our captivity.

About two days prior to being liberated, we knew something was happening because we could hear the guns coming closer and closer to the town of Ziegenhain. We could see puffs of smoke from our camp on the hill overlooking the city. It was at this point that the Germans finally decided to march us out of camp. So they ordered us into the courtyard, both barracks of Americans. We wanted to leave somebody behind to let the American troops know we had gone, because all we could think was that they were going to march us to the Eastern Front. Why they wanted to take prisoners with them, we didn't know. I was one of about five fellows who pulled up the floor boards and hid in the crawl space. We could see out vent holes under the barracks and watch the fellows outside. Most of us were so terribly weak by then that we didn't even want to march, or couldn't. The fellows outside had some tricks in mind, too. As the guards counted row by row and got about three rows back, the front row would go to the back. Others faked faints and were falling out or falling down. This must have happened for about 30 or 45 minutes, and every time the guards turned around, they only had one row behind them. This became so hilarious to them that we could almost see them starting to laugh. Finally, they sent everyone back into the barracks. One group they did move out were the English, who were prepared with homemade knives or anything else they could use as a weapon. They informed us they didn't intend to go very far, which they didn't before our troops brought them back.

I remember a jeep coming in. I think it was just a lieutenant, but as far as we were concerned, he was a hero. We had felt sure we were about to be released by our own troops, because the night before the gates were unlocked and very old German soldiers, in their seventies, were put on guard at them, marching back and forth. They carried guns but showed us they weren't loaded. Not only did our troops catch the English and bring them back, but also our original barracks' guards were taken prisoner. The Germans were put in the courtyard behind us, and the one guard from the other barracks was caught by some of their men and literally beaten to a pulp. Word had it that he died in the clinic.

But, as I said, it's hard to describe how we felt because no one knew where we were. They could have shot us at any time. In fact, the night before we were finally liberated, one fellow who was in our barracks decided he was going to escape, and since we had a feeling we were going to be freed about three or four days before we actually were liberated we told him, "No, no, no, don't try it." Well, the poor fellow tried to escape over two rows of fencing; if you did get over one, you still had another one to go over. He got over the first one and they shot him, just letting him hang there as an example to anyone else who might try to escape.

So those were the things that we ran into. I guess one of our biggest fears was that after we were finally liberated, and if the war was still going on in Japan, we would be sent over there. You know, our nerves were shot. We were so weak and what not, that if a car backfired or a gun was fired, we would jump a mile. It was just frustrating. We couldn't get our bearings. The U.S. Army didn't even give us new clothes when they shipped us back to Camp Lucky Strike.

The first food we had was creamed chicken, and that stayed down about as long as it took us to walk over to the makeshift tents they had for us before it all came up again. But everybody was so hungry that they'd keep going back after more until some stayed down.

Then we came back on a Liberty ship, and I remember they told us that we were the first batch of ex-P.O.W.s being repatriated back to the States. Just about every one of us wanted to work in K.P. Heck, that's where you get lots to eat. The Navy really fed us well. I don't know how it got started, but at 10 o'clock at night, we'd go down in the hold where all the food was being stored. An ensign would just open up the gate and say, "Fellows, you're going to get fed. It may cost another $10,000 for this thing before we get back, but you guys are going to eat."

Ten thousand dollars was a lot of money then.

They always made fresh bread. They just couldn't believe the amount of bread that we'd eat. And we'd finish up a meal and two or three of us would take whatever bread that was left and a bowl of sugar and butter and go out on the deck and just eat sugar, bread, and butter. By the time I got home, I remember my mother telling me that I looked like a butterball. And we all did. We really filled out fast. It took us two weeks to cross to the States, so we really had time to eat a lot. But one of the funny things was, as I said, we wanted to get on KP. I happened to make friends with an officer, so I talked him into working KP. in the officers mess. We worked on KP one day, reveling in all the pies and cakes the officers got. Then the captain found out we were all ex-P.O.W.s and took us all off duty and made the Air Corps people, captains and majors and everyone else, dump garbage over the side of the ship. Oh boy, were they mad.

"We'll do it," we said.

But they wouldn't let us do anything.

In a nutshell, that's pretty much my experience. I probably oversimplified the whole thing. It's one of those million dollar experiences, but believe me, I'd never go through it again even for a million dollars. I might not get out next time. I do understand that the privates we had left at the first camp suffered many deaths from malnutrition, pneumonia, and other health problems. I heard that they really took them out and had them working in mines and other places. They were allowed to work privates, but the noncoms and officers weren't supposed to work. But it is all over now and I hope I, nor anyone else, ever has to go through it again.

Index

Sonie Liebler

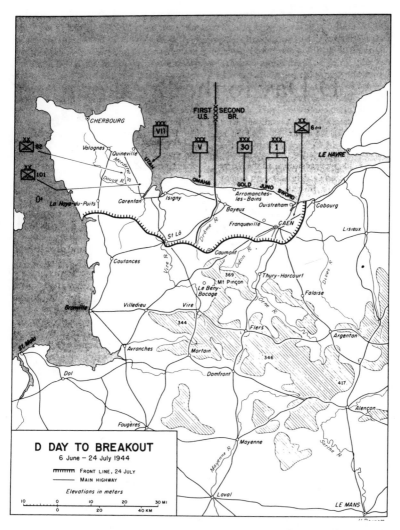

*D-Day to Breakout. (From **U.S. Army in World War II: The Supreme Command**, 1954.)*

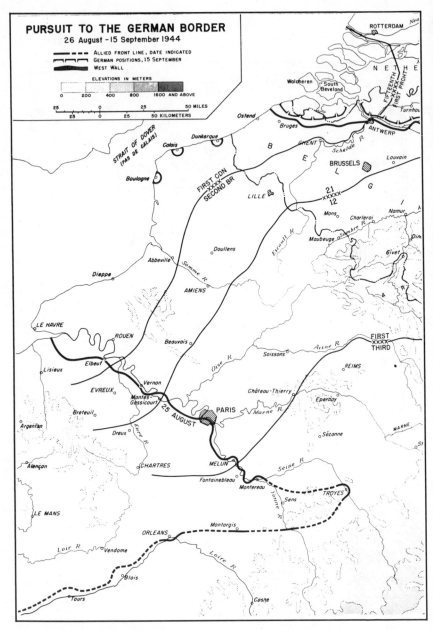

Pursuit to the German Border. (From *U.S. Army in World War II: The Supreme Command,* 1954.)